THE HEART OF
HAWTHORNE'S JOURNALS

Nathaniel Hawthorne.

THE HEART OF
HAWTHORNE'S JOURNALS

EDITED BY
NEWTON ARVIN

BARNES & NOBLE, Inc.
NEW YORK
PUBLISHERS & BOOKSELLERS SINCE 1873

PREFACE

In 1868, four years after Hawthorne's death, Mrs. Hawthorne, in response to the importunities of many readers for a biography of her husband, published a selection from his early journals under the title, 'Passages from Hawthorne's American Notebooks.' In 1870 appeared a volume of 'Passages from the English Notebooks,' and in the following year a volume of selections from the French and Italian journals. Hawthorne had expressed a wish not to be made the subject of a biography; and, in a prefatory note to the English journals, Mrs. Hawthorne explained that, in deference at once to this desire and to the legitimate demand of Hawthorne's admirers for information about his life, she was giving to the world, as a substitute, as much of his personal record as could properly be exposed to his contemporaries. A further incentive, as Mrs. Hawthorne herself pointed out, was the desire of his family to correct the general impression that Hawthorne was 'gloomy and morbid.'

As an editor, Mrs. Hawthorne was far less liberal with the scissors than a twentieth-century reader might be excused for expecting. Many passages in the foreign journals, later incorporated with few changes or none in 'Our Old Home' and 'The Marble Faun,' she wisely omitted; and many of her suppressions of trifling diaristic detail are grounds for the gratitude of every reader. More than enough was retained to give an adequate picture, deepened by a just perspective and with the light and

shade duly distributed, of Hawthorne's personality.
A later generation, none the less, can hardly be reproached
for regarding a few suppressions here and there as no
longer inevitable; and indeed, in the life of his father published in 1885, Mr. Julian Hawthorne included some of
these — such as the full description of Tennyson at the
Manchester Arts Exhibition and the passage on Margaret
Fuller in the Italian journal — which even at that time
might well have been generally accessible. An examina-
tion of the manuscript journals now in the possession of
the Morgan Library brings to light a few further passages that seem no less interesting than many that Mrs.
Hawthorne used, and particularly a large number of
phrases and sentences which, in the passages she did use,
Mrs. Hawthorne omitted or even altered.[1] As many of
these as are of real importance have been restored, and
the present editor has therefore to record his gratitude
to the trustees of the Morgan Library for permission to
make use of them.

How early Hawthorne began to make entries in his
journal we have now no way of knowing. There is record
that the habit of journalizing was first formed in him during his boyhood years in Maine, when he was given a
blank notebook on his birthday by an uncle, and urged to
use it daily for writing out his thoughts, 'on any and all

---

[1] The manuscript journals preserved begin with the entry for July 5,
1837; for the preceding entries, we are dependent on Mrs. Hawthorne's
version. Two volumes of the Italian journals — covering the periods
between March 11 and April 22, and between May 30 and July 2, 1858
(both inclusive) — are also missing: to the former, in all probability, belongs the passage on Margaret Fuller. Single pages and parts of pages
elsewhere throughout the journals have been deleted — not, proportion-
ately, in any great number.

subjects,' with an eye to the development of a sound prose style. Many years after Hawthorne's death a manuscript of this boyish diary, which appeared to be authentic, was discovered and published ('Hawthorne's First Diary': S. T. Pickard), and, though its genuineness has never been admitted by Mr. Julian Hawthorne, it was accepted by Hawthorne's son-in-law, G. P. Lathrop, and by many other persons whose judgment must be respected. The circumstances of its discovery, however, were, to say the least, ambiguous; and it has been thought best not to include passages from it in this volume.

At all events, no further record of Hawthorne's activity as a diarist is preserved, until abruptly, in the summer of 1835, toward the end of his long period of self-immurement in Salem, appears an entry in which Hawthorne describes a walk — one, no doubt, of a thousand such — down to Juniper Point on Salem Neck. From then on until the second year before his death the journal thus so quietly initiated (if that entry is indeed the first) continues with very uneven fullness and regularity. As a general rule, Hawthorne appears to have journalized most assiduously in the intervals between periods of active professional writing: it was as if the energy so liberated could find only partial outlet in un-literary pursuits — as if only his tireless pen could conduct its ultimate units. Thus the entries in his journal during such periods as the visit to Bridge in Maine in the summer of 1837 and the weeks at North Adams in 1838 are abundant and regular; and during the long years in England and Italy, when (until he began 'The Marble Faun') Hawthorne was on a protracted literary vacation, the

blank notebooks were enriched practically day by day,
with an industry which neither Hawthorne's arduous
duties as consul nor the inconveniences of nineteenth-
century travel could discourage or interrupt. On the
other hand, and quite predictably, there are stretches of
emptiness or brief and fitful record during such months as
those in Salem when he was at work on 'The Scarlet Letter,' or at Lenox when 'The House of the Seven Gables'
was in hand. And at one period, during practically the
whole of his Custom House experience in Boston and the
early months at Brook Farm, after Hawthorne had become engaged to Sophia Peabody, he appears to have
diverted into his letters to her the energy that would otherwise have gone into his journal. Extracts from these
letters Mrs. Hawthorne herself reproduced in her edition
of the journals, and, following in her footsteps, the present
selection includes some of the more notable passages.
For permission to correct the reading of these passages
by reference to the privately printed 'Love Letters of
Nathaniel Hawthorne,' the editor is under obligation to
Mr. W. K. Bixby, of St. Louis, the holder of the copy-
right.

Scarcely a page of the sixteen manuscript volumes of
Hawthorne's journals is quite without interest for the
special student, if only because, being relatively dull, it is
dull in a Hawthornesque fashion; yet for all but the special student there are hundreds of pages — pages on
which, for example, the conscientious tourist rather than
the poet is at work — that can easily be spared. What remains is, if not always pure gold, some metal with a value
of its own; and no one can hope to understand Hawthorne

at all fully who does not study it. We must not look in
Hawthorne's journals, it is true, for qualities that they do
not possess: fresh from Emerson's or Thoreau's, we must
not look for epigram and aphorism; fresh from Amiel's or
Marie Bashkirtseff's, we must not look for studious introspection and self-revelation. Not that there is neither
epigram nor introspection in these of Hawthorne's: more
than a few detached sentences have a saline smack not
unworthy of Emerson, and several precious passages of
'confession' throw a light far into the recesses of Hawthorne's nature. Yet these things are not the staples of
his work as a diarist: it is elsewhere that its charm and its
value must be sought.

The difference, after all, between Hawthorne and any
of those other writers of journals is the only too manifest
difference between a philosopher or an essayist and a
teller of tales. Not general ideas for their own sake, or
personal experience on its own level, but dramatic conceptions, the fruit of imaginative revery, or observations
of the external world, men and women no less than in-
animate nature — these are the central substance of
Hawthorne's journals. Much, no doubt, might be made
of them taken merely by themselves; their real interest
yields itself only to the reader who keeps in mind the
figure of the prose romancer behind them. Here one can
observe, almost without obstacle, the restless play of
Hawthorne's imagination over the strange data of the
moral world, entertaining one possibility after another,
returning again and again to characteristic conceptions,
and betraying always the special temper of his mind.
Here in the journals, not always easily recognizable, are

the original statements of the organizing ideas in tale after tale as we are now familiar with them in 'Twice-Told Tales' or the 'Mosses' or the 'Snow Image'; here is that extraordinary series of notes, beginning as early as 1836, in which the complicated unity of 'The Scarlet Letter' gradually asserts itself; here is the leading dramatic note of 'The Blithedale Romance,' stated some sixteen years before the book was undertaken; here are the first suggestions for 'The Marble Faun.' Such notes as thus bore fruit have a significance not to be missed: but the journals would be less revealing than they are if it were not for the dozens of entries that came to no similar consummation, entries that proclaim the wind's direction no less dependably.

Nor was it only as a storehouse for such 'ideas' that Hawthorne's journal proved of service to him. If he had been a mere allegorist he might have been content with these fanciful conceptions: he was also — perhaps (fundamentally) rather — an untiring observer of the world about him; and into his journal went, usually with the utmost clarity of statement and refinement of expression, the record of his observations. Hawthorne is not commonly spoken of, in the same breath with Thoreau or Burroughs, as a student of nature; and indeed he had little or nothing of Thoreau's passionate devotion to the details of plant and animal life for their own sake. Yet he was too good a child of the nineteenth century not to be susceptible to natural beauty, and in his own vein — that of a poet or impressionist landscape-painter rather than of a scientist — he wrote much and delicately about the Massachusetts coast, the Berkshire

hills, the scenery about Concord, and the English coun-
tryside. Especially in the transition from season to
season did the changing aspects of nature arrest his
scrutiny. And it is always curious to observe the interest Hawthorne took in birds and animals — an interest,
if one may say so, not less 'dramatic' than his interest
in human beings, as the swine at the Salem almshouse,
the hens at Lenox, and the monkeys in the London zoo,
are there to witness.

By men and women themselves, however, his attention
was far more steadily engaged; in them his interest was
not, except at rare intervals, to be satiated. In the earliest
continuous passages of his journal — those written during
his stay in Augusta in 1837 — we find him studying, with
unmistakable zest, the personalities of his host and of the
little French tutor, M. Schaeffer, and recording his impressions of Nancy the servant-girl, and the Irish laborers
on the mill-dam. Similar 'hints for characters' and 'remarkables' recur for many years. No individuals were
sufficiently humble to merit his indifference or sufficiently commonplace to escape his analysis. If he had a
predilection here, it was for men and women on the edge
of things, outcasts, 'wrecks,' people who had somehow
failed to swing into the general march of life, or had somehow fallen out of it. At North Adams, it was a traveling
surgeon-dentist and a one-armed soap-maker who had
seen better days; in Salem, it was the old apple-dealer in
the railway-station ('Mosses from an Old Manse'); in
Boston, the elderly ragamuffin in front of Parker's grog-
shop, who later appears as Old Moodie in 'The Blithedale
Romance'; in Liverpool, the bedraggled inhabitants of

the slums. Even when the objects of his curiosity seem
scarcely to belong in this class, it is, more often than not,
some note of waywardness, some hint of exile, that really
preoccupies him. It was an element of his interest in his
own children, of his interest in Una at all events, as her
transformation into little Pearl in 'The Scarlet Letter'
suggests; and observe what happened to the beautiful
Jewess at the Lord Mayor's dinner in London, when she
turned up as Miriam in 'The Marble Faun.'

In such passages it is still Hawthorne the writer who
has to be kept in mind: for many readers, the same thing
would not have to be said of those passages, memorable
surely on their own account as well, in which he recorded
his impressions and, frequently, his judgments of eminent or notable contemporaries. It is easy and natural
to think of Hawthorne as a solitary and a recluse, and in
fact he of course saw far less of society than most men of
his distinction. Yet he knew familiarly, if not intimately,
some of the greatest American writers of his time, and
wrote of them in his journals with a freedom and a cool
insight that bring them almost in three dimensions before
our eyes. So long as men retain their interest in Emerson
and Thoreau, in Margaret Fuller, in Bryant and Melville,
Hawthorne's account of these personages will have a
quite peculiar value. In England, if he failed through
want of effort to meet some of the very great (Thackeray,
Dickens, Tennyson, George Eliot, Carlyle), he became
acquainted, almost by chance, with the Brownings, with
Macaulay, with Leigh Hunt, with Coventry Patmore,
and with a number of lesser notables — Harriet Martineau, Douglas Jerrold, Monckton Milnes, Philip James

Bailey, Tom Taylor, Barry Cornwall — who have not yet been wholly forgotten. In Italy, where he saw still more of the Brownings and their circle, he was mainly attracted by a number of his own countrymen, artists for the most part, of whom Hiram Powers and W. W. Story interested him most keenly. In writing of these people, Hawthorne's kindliness may now and then have deserted him; his powers of characterization, never. On the basis of these passages, one might contend that, if he had not been one of the great romancers, Hawthorne would have been one of the great memorialists of his time.

Late in his life, and doubtless in response partly to external pressure, Hawthorne developed a certain fitful and uneasy interest in the plastic arts. First awakened at the exhibition in Manchester in 1857, this interest grew with amazing rapidity during the months of his stay in Italy in the following year, and the Italian journals are very largely occupied with comments on pictures and statues. It would be idle to argue that he ever learned to enjoy such things quite naturally or to appreciate them with real discrimination. Nevertheless, Hawthorne could not have written about art as fully as he did without making many shrewd or at all events piquant observations; and, if only on account of the emblematic figure of Praxiteles' faun, these passages in his journals will always repay reading.

The editor of 'The Heart of Thoreau's Journals' has justly pointed out how richly American was the personality of Henry Thoreau, and how truly his adventures, physical and philosophical, are a portion of our general experience. If a selection from his journals did nothing else, it should demonstrate that Nathaniel Hawthorne too, solitary that he was, lived through one whole chapter of our career and was a true participator in it. His mind, with all its idiosyncrasies, was none the less, in Emerson's sense, a 'representative' one; and the pages of his journal, in consequence, have a color and a fragrance that are not only Hawthornesque but also American. This is not their only significance, but it is for this reason that they will exercise their most lasting sway.

NEWTON ARVIN

NORTHAMPTON
August, 1928

CHRONOLOGICAL TABLE

1804. Hawthorne born in Salem, July 4.

1816–20. At Raymond, Maine.

1821–25. At Bowdoin College, Brunswick, Maine.

1825–37. 'The chamber under the eaves.'   Herbert Street, Salem.

1837. 'Twice-Told Tales.'

1838. Spent seven summer weeks in North Adams.

1839–41. At the Boston Custom House.

1841. At Brook Farm, May to November.

1842. Married Sophia Peabody, July 9.

1842–45. Living at the Manse in Concord.

1845–50. At Salem. Three years in the Custom House.

1846. 'Mosses from an Old Manse.'

1850. 'The Scarlet Letter.'

1850–51. At Lenox, Massachusetts.

1851. 'The House of the Seven Gables.'

1852–53. At the Wayside in Concord.

1852. 'The Blithedale Romance.'

1853–57. American Consul at Liverpool.

1858–59. Residence in Rome and Florence.

1859–60. In England again.

1860. 'The Marble Faun.'

1860–64. At the Wayside in Concord.

1863. 'Our Old Home.'

1864. Died at Plymouth, New Hampshire, May 19.

THE HEART OF
HAWTHORNE'S JOURNALS

1835–1838

[THE earliest entries preserved by Mrs. Hawthorne belong
to the years 1835 and 1836 — years when Hawthorne, a
decade out of college, was still maintaining his virtual
reclusion in his 'chamber under the eaves' at the house
on Herbert Street, Salem. His journal for these years, of
which hardly more than thirty pages remain, consists
largely of those brief notes, embodying ideas for future
tales, which were to be for some years a recurrent feature
of his journal, and never to be wholly abandoned. In
these earliest notes the germs of several of the latest-
written 'Twice-Told Tales' can be discovered.

In the spring of 1837 the first series of 'Twice-Told
Tales' was published, and the manuscript journals at the
Morgan Library begin on July 5th, when Hawthorne had
just reached Augusta, Maine, for a visit of a few weeks
with his college friend, Horatio Bridge. This month in
Maine was virtually Hawthorne's first resumption of
something like normal relations with his fellows, and it
was followed, the ensuing summer, by a longer stay at an
inn in North Adams, in the western part of Massachusetts. On both these trips Hawthorne journalized with
great fullness, assiduously noting 'hints for characters'

and 'remarkables' of all kinds, as if he could not store his memory too richly with tough and tangible realities.

Late in 1837, Hawthorne met and fell in love with Sophia Peabody, and the two were probably engaged to each other by the end of the following year. This change in his prospects, along with a growing incapacity to be content with writing as an exclusive occupation, led Hawthorne to seek official employment; late in 1838, as a result, he was appointed a Measurer at the Boston Custom House.]

Salem, June 15, 1835 [first entry preserved]

A walk down to the Juniper [on Salem Neck]. The shore of the coves strewn with bunches of sea-weed, driven in by recent winds. Eel-grass, rolled and bundled up, and entangled with it — large marine vegetables, of an olive-color, with round, slender, snake-like stalks, four or five feet long, and nearly two feet broad: these are the herbage of the deep sea. Shoals of fishes, at a little distance from the shore, discernible by their fins out of water. Among the heaps of sea-weed there were sometimes small pieces of painted wood, bark, and other driftage. On the shore, with pebbles of granite, there were round or oval pieces of brick, which the waves had rolled about till they resembled a natural mineral. Huge stones tossed about, in every variety of confusion, some shagged all over with sea-weed, others only partly covered, others bare. The old ten-gun battery, at the outer angle of the Juniper, very verdant, and besprinkled with white-weed, clover, and buttercups. The juniper-trees are very aged and decayed and moss-grown. The grass about the hospital is rank, being trodden, probably, by nobody but myself. There is a representation of a vessel under sail, cut with a penknife, on the corner of the house.

Returning by the almshouse, I stopped a good while to look at the pigs — a great herd — who seemed to be just finishing their suppers. They certainly are types of unmitigated sensuality — some standing in the trough, in the midst of their own and others' victuals — some thrusting their noses deep into the food — some rubbing their backs against a post — some huddled together between sleeping and waking, breathing hard — all wallowing about; a great boar swaggering round, and a big sow waddling along with her huge paunch. Notwithstanding the unspeakable defilement with which these strange sensualists spice all their food, they seem to have a quick and delicate sense of smell. What ridiculous-looking animals! Swift himself could not have imagined anything nastier than what they practise by the mere impulse of natural genius. Yet the Shakers keep their pigs very clean, and with great advantage. The legion of devils in the herd of swine — what a scene it must have been!

Sunday evening, going by the jail, the setting sun kindled up the windows most cheerfully; as if there were a bright, comfortable light within its darksome stone wall.

Undated

A sketch to be given of a modern reformer — a type of the extreme doctrines on the subject of slaves, cold water, and other such topics. He goes about the streets haranguing most eloquently, and is on the point of making many converts, when his labors are suddenly interrupted by the appearance of the keeper of a mad-house, whence he has escaped. Much may be made of this idea.[1]

A change from a gay young girl to an old woman; the melancholy events, the effects of which have clustered around her character, and gradually imbued it with their influence, till she becomes a lover of sick-chambers, taking pleasure in receiving dying breaths and in laying out the dead; also having her mind full of funeral reminiscences, and possessing more acquaintances beneath the burial turf than above it.[2]

A well-concerted train of events to be thrown into confusion by some misplaced circumstance, unsuspected till the catastrophe, yet exerting its influence from beginning to end.

The world is so sad and solemn, that things meant in jest are liable, by an overpowering influence, to become dreadful earnest — gayly dressed fantasies turning to ghostly and black-clad images of themselves.

A story, the hero of which is to be represented as naturally capable of deep and strong passion, and looking forward to the time when he shall feel passionate love, which is to be the great event of his existence. But it so chances that he never falls in love, and although he gives up the expectation of so doing, and marries calmly, yet it is somewhat sadly, with sentiments merely of esteem for his bride. The lady might be one who had loved him early in life, but whom then, in his expectation of passionate love, he had scorned.

[1] 'The Blithedale Romance.'   [2] 'Edward Fane's Rosebud.'

The scene of a story or sketch to be laid within the light of a street-lantern; the time, when the lamp is near going out; and the catastrophe to be simultaneous with the last flickering gleam.

The peculiar weariness and depression of spirits which is felt after a day wasted in turning over a magazine or other light miscellany, different from the state of the mind after severe study; because there has been no excitement, no difficulties to be overcome, but the spirits have evaporated insensibly.

To represent the process by which sober truth gradually strips off all the beautiful draperies with which imagination has enveloped a beloved object, till from an angel she turns out to be a merely ordinary woman. This to be done without caricature, perhaps with a quiet humor interfused, but the prevailing impression to be a sad one. The story might consist of the various alterations in the feelings of the absent lover, caused by successive events that display the true character of his mistress; and the catastrophe should take place at their meeting, when he finds himself equally disappointed in her person; or the whole spirit of the thing may here be reproduced.

Two persons might be bitter enemies through life, and mutually cause the ruin of one another, and of all that were dear to them. Finally, meeting at the funeral of a grandchild, the offspring of a son and daughter married without their consent — and who, as well as the child, had been the victims of their hatred — they might discover that the supposed ground of the quarrel was altogether a mistake, and then be wofully reconciled.

Two persons, by mutual agreement, to make their wills in each other's favor, then to wait impatiently for one another's death, and both to be informed of the desired event at the same time. Both, in most joyous sorrow, hasten to be present at the funeral, meet, and find themselves both hoaxed.

The story of a man, cold and hard-hearted, and acknowledging no brotherhood with mankind. At his death they might try to dig him a grave, but, at a little space beneath the ground, strike upon a rock, as if the earth refused to receive the unnatural son into her bosom. Then they would put him into an old sepulchre, where the coffins and corpses were all turned to dust, and so he would be alone. Then the body would petrify; and he having died in some characteristic act and expression, he would seem, through endless ages of death, to repel society as in life, and no one would be buried in that tomb forever.[1]

A person, even before middle age, may become musty and faded among the people with whom he has grown up from childhood; but, by migrating to a new place, he appears fresh with the effect of youth, which may be communicated from the impressions of others to his own feelings.

[1] 'The Man of Adamant.'

In an old house, a mysterious knocking might be heard on the wall, where had formerly been a doorway, now bricked up.

A young man to win the love of a girl, without any serious intentions, and to find that in that love, which might have been the greatest blessing of his life, he had conjured up a spirit of mischief which pursued him throughout his whole career — and this without any revengeful purposes on the part of the deserted girl.

Two lovers, or other persons, on the most private business, to appoint a meeting in what they supposed to be a place of the utmost solitude, and to find it thronged with people.

October 17

Some of the oaks are now a deep brown red; others are changed to a light green, which, at a little distance, especially in the sunshine, looks like the green of early spring. In some trees, different masses of the foliage show each of these hues. Some of the walnut-trees have a yet more delicate green. Others are of a bright sunny yellow.

To make one's own reflection in a mirror the subject of a story.[1]

In a dream to wander to some place where may be heard the complaints of all the miserable on earth.

[1] 'Monsieur du Miroir.'

Some common quality or circumstance that should bring together people the most unlike in all other respects, and make a brotherhood and sisterhood of them — the rich and the proud finding themselves in the same category with the mean and the despised.[1]

A person to consider himself as the prime mover of certain remarkable events, but to discover that his actions have not contributed in the least thereto. Another person to be the cause, without suspecting it.

October 25

A person or family long desires some particular good. At last it comes in such profusion as to be the great pest of their lives.

A man, perhaps with a persuasion that he shall make his fortune by some singular means, and with an eager longing so to do, while digging or boring for water, to strike upon a salt-spring.

A person to be writing a tale, and to find that it shapes itself against his intentions; that the characters act otherwise than he thought; that unforeseen events occur; and a catastrophe comes which he strives in vain to avert. It might shadow forth his own fate — he having made himself one of the personages.

It is a singular thing, that, at the distance, say, of five feet, the work of the greatest dunce looks just as well

[1] 'The Procession of Life.'

as that of the greatest genius — that little space being all the distance between genius and stupidity.

Four precepts: To break off customs; to shake off spirits ill-disposed; to meditate on youth; to do nothing against one's genius.

September, 1836

To picture the predicament of worldly people, if admitted to paradise.

'Though we speak nonsense, God will pick out the meaning of it' — an extempore prayer by a New England divine.

October 25

In this dismal chamber FAME was won. [Salem, Herbert Street.]

A council of the passengers in a street: called by somebody to decide upon some points important to him.

Every individual has a place to fill in the world, and is important in some respects, whether he chooses to be so or not.

A Thanksgiving dinner. All the miserable on earth are to be invited — as the drunkard, the bereaved parent, the ruined merchant, the broken-hearted lover, the poor widow, the old man and woman who have outlived their generation, the disappointed author, the wounded, sick, and broken soldier, the diseased person, the infidel, the

man with an evil conscience, little orphan children or
children of neglectful parents, shall be admitted to the
table, and many others. The giver of the feast goes out to
deliver his invitations. Some of the guests he meets in
the streets, some he knocks for at the doors of their
houses. The description must be rapid. But who must
be the giver of the feast, and what his claims to preside?
A man who has never found out what he is fit for, who
has unsettled aims or objects in life, and whose mind
gnaws him, making him the sufferer of many kinds of
misery. He should meet some pious, old, sorrowful
person, with more outward calamities than any other,
and invite him, with a reflection that piety would make
all that miserable company truly thankful.[1]

We sometimes congratulate ourselves at the moment
of waking from a troubled dream: it may be so the moment after death.

The race of mankind to be swept away, leaving all
their cities and works. Then another human pair to be
placed in the world, with native intelligence like Adam
and Eve, but knowing nothing of their predecessors or
of their own nature and destiny. They, perhaps, to be
described as working out this knowledge by their
sympathy with what they saw, and by their own feelings.[2]

A singular fact, that, when man is a brute, he is the
most sensual and loathsome of all brutes.

[1] 'The Christmas Banquet.'   [2] 'The New Adam and Eve.'

A snake, taken into a man's stomach and nourished there from fifteen years to thirty-five, tormenting him most horribly. A type of envy or some other evil passion.[1]

A sketch illustrating the imperfect compensations which time makes for its devastations on the person — giving a wreath of laurel while it causes baldness, honors for infirmities, wealth for a broken constitution — and at last, when a man has everything that seems desirable, death seizes him. To contrast the man who has thus reached the summit of ambition with the ambitious youth.

A Fancy Ball, in which the prominent American writers should appear, dressed in character.

A lament for life's wasted sunshine.

A new classification of society to be instituted. Instead of rich and poor, high and low, they are to be classed — First, by their sorrows: for instance, whenever there are any, whether in fair mansion or hovel, who are mourning the loss of relations and friends, and who wear black, whether the cloth be coarse or superfine, they are to make one class. Secondly, all who have the same maladies, whether they lie under damask canopies or on straw pallets or in the wards of hospitals, they are to form one class. Thirdly, all who are guilty of the same sins, whether the world knows them or not; whether they

[1] 'Egotism; or, The Bosom Serpent.'

languish in prison, looking forward to the gallows, or walk honored among men, they also form a class. Then proceed to generalize and classify the whole world together, as none can claim utter exemption from either sorrow, sin, or disease; and if they could, yet Death, like a great parent, comes and sweeps them all through one darksome portal — all his children.[1]

Fortune to come like a pedlar with his goods — as wreaths of laurel, diamonds, crowns; selling them, but asking for them the sacrifice of health, of integrity, perhaps of life in the battle-field, and of the real pleasures of existence. Who would buy, if the price were to be paid down?

The dying exclamation of the Emperor Augustus, 'Has it not been well acted?' An essay on the misery of being always under a mask. A veil may be needful, but never a mask. Instances of people who wear masks in all classes of society, and never take them off even in the most familiar moments, though sometimes they may chance to slip aside.

The various guises under which Ruin makes his approaches to his victims: to the merchant, in the guise of a merchant offering speculations; to the young heir, a jolly companion; to the maiden, a sighing, sentimentalist lover.

What were the contents of the burden of Christian in

[1] 'The Procession of Life.'

the 'Pilgrim's Progress'? He must have been taken for a pedlar travelling with his pack.

To think, as the sun goes down, what events have happened in the course of the day — events of ordinary occurrence: as, the clocks have struck, the dead have been buried.

Curious to imagine what murmurings and discontent would be excited, if any of the great so-called calamities of human beings were to be abolished — as, for instance, death.

Trifles to one are matters of life and death to another. As, for instance, a farmer desires a brisk breeze to winnow his grain; and mariners, to blow them out of the reach of pirates.

A recluse, like myself, or a prisoner, to measure time by the progress of sunshine through his chamber.

Would it not be wiser for people to rejoice at all that they now sorrow for, and *vice versa?* To put on bridal garments at funerals, and mourning at weddings? For their friends to condole with them when they attained riches and honor, as only so much care added?

If in a village it were a custom to hang a funeral garland or other token of death on a house where some one had died, and there to let it remain till a death occurred elsewhere, and then to hang that same garland over the other house, it would have, methinks, a strong effect.

No fountain so small but that Heaven may be imaged in its bosom.

Fame! Some very humble persons in a town may be said to possess it — as, the penny-post, the town-crier, the constable — and they are known to everybody; while many richer, more intellectual, worthier persons are unknown by the majority of their fellow-citizens. Something analogous in the world at large.

The ideas of people in general are not raised higher than the roofs of the houses. All their interests extend over the earth's surface in a layer of that thickness. The meeting-house steeple reaches out of their sphere.

Nobody will use other people's experience, nor has any of his own till it is too late to use it.

Two lovers to plan the building of a pleasure-house on a certain spot of ground, but various seeming accidents prevent it. Once they find a group of miserable children there; once it is the scene where crime is plotted; at last the dead body of one of the lovers or of a dear friend is found there; and, instead of a pleasure-house, they build a marble tomb. The moral — that there is no place on earth fit for the site of a pleasure-house, because there is no spot that may not have been saddened by human grief, stained by crime, or hallowed by death. It might be three friends who plan it, instead of two lovers; and the dearest one dies.[1]

Comfort for childless people. A married couple with ten children have been the means of bringing about ten funerals.

A blind man on a dark night carried a torch, in order that people might see him, and not run against him, and direct him how to avoid dangers.

To picture a child's (one of four or five years old) reminiscences at sunset of a long summer's day — his first awakening, his studies, his sports, his little fits of passion, perhaps a whipping, etc.

To picture a virtuous family, the different members examples of virtuous dispositions in their way; then introduce a vicious person, and trace out the relations that arise between him and them, and the manner in which all are affected.

A man to flatter himself with the idea that he would not be guilty of some certain wickedness — as, for instance, to yield to the personal temptations of the Devil — yet to find, ultimately, that he was at that very time committing that same wickedness.

What would a man do, if he were compelled to live always in the sultry heat of society, and could never bathe himself in cool solitude?

[1] 'The Lily's Quest.'

A girl's lover to be slain and buried in her flower-garden, and the earth levelled over him. That particular spot, which she happens to plant with some peculiar variety of flowers, produces them of admirable splendor, beauty, and perfume; and she delights, with an indescribable impulse, to wear them in her bosom, and scent her chamber with them. Thus the classic fantasy would be realized, of dead people transformed to flowers.

Objects seen by a magic-lantern reversed. A street, or other location, might be presented, where there would be opportunity to bring forward all objects of worldly interest, and thus much pleasant satire might be the result.

To show the effect of gratified revenge. As an instance, merely, suppose a woman sues her lover for breach of promise, and gets the money by instalments, through a long series of years. At last, when the miserable victim were utterly trodden down, the triumpher would have become a very devil of evil passions — they having overgrown his whole nature; so that a far greater evil would have come upon himself than on his victim.[1]

A town clerk arranges the publishments that are given in, according to his own judgment.

To make a story from Robert Raikes seeing dirty children at play, in the streets of London, and inquiring of a woman about them. She tells him that on Sundays, when

[1] 'The Scarlet Letter.'

they were not employed, they were a great deal worse, making the streets like hell; playing at church, etc. He was therefore induced to employ women at a shilling to teach them on Sundays, and thus Sunday-schools were established.

To describe a boyish combat with snowballs, and the victorious leader to have a statue of snow erected to him. A satire on ambition and fame to be made out of this idea. It might be a child's story.

Our body to be possessed by two different spirits; so that half of the visage shall express one mood, and the other half another.

A rich man left by will his mansion and estate to a poor couple. They remove into it, and find there a darksome servant, whom they are forbidden by will to turn away. He becomes a torment to them; and, in the finale, he turns out to be the former master of the estate.

Two persons to be expecting some occurrence, and watching for the two principal actors in it, and to find that the occurrence is even then passing, and that they themselves are the two actors.

There is evil in every human heart, which may remain latent, perhaps, through the whole of life; but circumstances may rouse it to activity. To imagine such circumstances. A woman, tempted to be false to her husband, apparently through mere whim — or a young man to feel

an instinctive thirst for blood, and to commit murder.
This appetite may be traced in the popularity of criminal
trials. The appetite might be observed first in a child,
and then traced upwards, manifesting itself in crimes
suited to every stage of life.

The good deeds in an evil life — the generous, noble,
and excellent actions done by people habitually wicked
— to ask what is to become of them.

A satirical article might be made out of the idea of an
imaginary museum, containing such articles as Aaron's
rod, the petticoat of General Harrison, the pistol with
which Benton shot Jackson — and then a diorama, con-
sisting of political or other scenes, or done in wax-work.
The idea to be wrought out and extended. Perhaps it
might be the museum of a deceased old man.[1]

An article might be made respecting various kinds of
ruin — ruin as regards property — ruin of health —
ruin of habits, as drunkenness and all kinds of debauchery
— ruin of character, while prosperous in other respects —
ruin of the soul. Ruin, perhaps, might be personified as a
demon, seizing its victims by various holds.

July 5, 1837 [*Augusta, Maine*]
Here I am, settled since night before last with Bridge,
and living very singularly. He leads a bachelor's life in
his paternal mansion, only a small part of which is occupied by a family who do his washing, make the beds,

[1] 'A Virtuoso's Collection.'

etc. He provides his own breakfast and supper, and occasionally his dinner; though this is oftener, I believe,
taken at a hotel, or an eating-house, or with some of his
relatives. I am his guest, and my presence makes no
alteration in his way of life. Our fare, thus far, has consisted of bread, butter, and cheese, crackers, herrings,
boiled eggs, coffee, milk, and claret wine. He has another
inmate, in the person of a queer little Frenchman, who
has his breakfast, tea, and lodging here, and finds his
dinner elsewhere. Monsieur Schaeffer does not appear to
be more than twenty-one years old — a diminutive figure,
with eyes askew, and otherwise of ungainly physiognomy; he is ill-dressed also, in a coarse blue coat, thin
cotton pantaloons, and unbrushed boots; altogether with
as little of French coxcombry as can well be imagined,
though with something of the monkey aspect inseparable
from a little Frenchman. He is, nevertheless, an intelligent and well-informed man, apparently of extensive
reading in his own language — a philosopher, Bridge tells
me, and an infidel. His insignificant personal appearance
stands in the way of his success, and prevents him from
receiving the respect which is really due to his talents and
acquirements, wherefore he is bitterly dissatisfied with
the country and its inhabitants, and often expresses his
feelings to Bridge (who has gained his confidence to a
certain degree) in very strong terms.

Thus here are three characters, each with something
out of the common way, living together somewhat like
monks. Bridge, our host, combines more high and admirable qualities, of that sort which make up a gentleman,
than any other that I have met with. Polished, yet

natural, frank, open, and straightforward, yet with a
delicate feeling for the sensitiveness of his companions; of
excellent temper and warm heart; well acquainted with
the world, with a keen faculty of observation, which he
has had many opportunities of exercising, and never
varying from a code of honor and principle which is really
nice and rigid in its way. There is a sort of philosophy
developing itself in him which will not impossibly cause
him to settle down in this or some other equally singular
course of life. He seems almost to have made up his mind
never to be married, which I wonder at; for he has strong
affections, and is fond both of women and children.

The little Frenchman impresses me very strongly, too,
so lonely as he is here, struggling against the world, with
bitter feelings in his breast, and yet talking with the
vivacity and gayety of his nation; making this his home
from darkness to daylight, and enjoying here what little
domestic comfort and confidence there is for him; and
then going about the livelong day, teaching French to
blockheads who sneer at him, and returning at about ten
o'clock in the evening (for I was wrong in saying he
supped here — he eats no supper) to his solitary room and
bed. Before retiring, he goes to Bridge's bedside, and, if
he finds him awake, stands talking French, expressing
his dislike of the Americans — '*Je hais, je hais les
Yankees!*' — thus giving vent to the stifled bitterness of
the whole day. In the morning I hear him getting up
early, at sunrise or before, humming to himself, scuffling
about his chamber with his thick boots, and at last taking
his departure for a solitary ramble till breakfast. Then
he comes in, cheerful and vivacious enough, eats pretty

heartily, and is off again, singing a French *chanson* as he goes down the gravel walk. The poor fellow has nobody to sympathize with him but Bridge; and thus a singular connection is established between two utterly different characters.

Then here is myself, who am likewise a queer character in my way, and have come to spend a week or two with my friend of half a lifetime — the longest space, probably, that we are ever destined to spend together; for Fate seems to be preparing changes for both of us. My circumstances, at least, cannot long continue as they are and have been; and Bridge, too, stands between high prosperity and utter ruin.

I think I should soon become strongly attached to our way of life, so independent and untroubled by the forms and restrictions of society.

July 26

Dined at Barker's yesterday. Before dinner, sat with several other persons on the stoop of the tavern. There were Bridge, J. A. Chandler, Clerk of the Court, a dilapidated man of middle age or beyond, two or three stage people, and, near by, a negro, whom they call 'the doctor,' a crafty-looking fellow, one of whose occupations is that of agent. In presence of this goodly company, a man of a depressed, neglected air, a soft, simple-looking fellow, with an anxious expression, in a laborer's dress, approached and inquired for Mr. Barker. Mine host being gone to Portland, the stranger was directed to the barkeeper, who stood at the door. The man asked where he should find one Mary Ann Russell — a question which

excited general and hardly suppressed mirth; for the said
Mary Ann is one of a knot of women who were routed on
Sunday evening by Barker and a constable. The man
was told that the black fellow would give him all the information he wanted. The black fellow asked —

'Do you want to see her?'

Others of the by-standers or by-sitters put various
questions as to the nature of the man's business with
Mary Ann and the connection between them. One
asked —

'Is she your daughter?'

'Why, a little nearer than that, I calkilate,' said the
poor devil.

Here the mirth was increased, it being evident that the
woman was his wife. The man seemed too simple and
obtuse to comprehend the ridicule of his situation, or to
be rendered very miserable by it. Nevertheless, he made
some touching points.

'A man generally places some little dependence on his
wife,' said he, 'whether she's good or bad.'

He meant, probably, that he rests some affection on
her. He told us that she had behaved well, till committed
to jail for striking a child; and I believe he was absent
from home at the time, and had not seen her since. And
now he was in search of her, intending, doubtless, to do
his best to get her out of her troubles, and then to take
her back to his bosom. Some advised him not to look after
her; others recommended him to pay 'the doctor' aforesaid for guiding him to her haunt; which finally 'the
doctor' did, in consideration of a treat; and the fellow
went off, having heard little but gibes and not one word

of sympathy. I would have given considerable to witness his meeting with his wife.

On the whole, there was a moral picturesqueness in the contrasts of this scene — a man moved as deeply as his nature would admit, in the midst of hardened, gibing spectators, heartless towards him. It is worth thinking over and studying out. He seemed rather hurt and pricked by the jests thrown at him, yet bore it patiently, and sometimes almost joined in the laugh. He was cowed by his situation, being of an easy, unenergetic temper.

Hints for characters: Nancy, a pretty, black-eyed, intelligent servant-girl, living in Captain Harriman's family. She comes daily to make the beds in our part of the house, and exchanges a good-morning with me, in a pleasant voice, and with a glance and smile — somewhat shy, because we are not well acquainted, yet capable of being made conversable. She washes once a week, and may be seen standing over her tub, with her handkerchief somewhat displaced from her white bosom, because it is hot. Often she stands with her bare arms in the water, talking with Mrs. Harriman, or looks through the window, perhaps, at Bridge, or somebody else crossing the yard — rather thoughtfully, but soon smiling or laughing. Then goeth she for a pail of water. In the afternoon, very probably, she dresses herself in silks, looking not only pretty, but lady-like, and strolls round the house, not unconscious that some gentleman may be staring at her from behind our green blinds. After supper, she walks to the village. Morning and evening, she goes a-milking. And thus passes her life, cheerfully, usefully, virtuously, with hopes, doubtless, of a husband and children. — Mrs. Harriman is a particularly plump, soft-fleshed, fair-complexioned, comely woman enough, with rather a simple countenance, not near so piquant as Nancy's. Her walk has something of the roll or waddle of a fat woman, though it were too much to call her fat. Her bosom swells out round and soft, being abundant with milk for a little brat of three or four months old — her first child, though she is not a very young woman. She seems to be a sociable body, probably laughter-loving. Captain Harriman himself has commanded a steamboat, and has a certain knowledge of life.

Query, in relation to the man's wife, how much desire and resolution of doing her duty by her husband can a wife retain, while injuring him in what is deemed the most essential point?

July 28

Saw my classmate and formerly intimate friend, Cilley, for the first time since we graduated. He has met with good success in life, and that in spite of circumstance, having struggled upward against bitter opposition, by the force of his own abilities, to be a member of Congress, after having been some time the leader of his party in the State Legislature. We met like old friends, and conversed almost as freely as we used to do in college days, twelve years ago and more. He is a singular person, shrewd, crafty, insinuating, with wonderful tact, seizing on each man by his manageable point, and using him for his own purpose, often without the man's suspecting that he is made a tool of; and yet, artificial as his character would seem to be, his conversation, at least to myself, was full of natural feeling, the expression of which can hardly be mistaken, and his revelations with regard to himself had really a great deal of frankness. He spoke of his ambition, of the obstacles which he had encountered, of the means by which he had overcome them, imputing great efficacy to his personal intercourse with his people, and study of their characters; then of his course as a member of the Legislature and Speaker, and of his style of speaking and its effects; of the dishonorable things which had been imputed to him, and in what manner he had repelled the charges. In short, he would have seemed to have opened himself very freely as to his public life. Then, as to private affairs, he spoke of his marriage, of his wife, his children, and told me, with tears in his eyes, of the death of a dear little girl, and how it had affected him, and how impossible it had been for him to believe that she was really to die. A man of the most open nature might well have been more reserved to a friend, after twelve years' separation, than Cilley was to me. Nevertheless, he is really a crafty man, concealing, like a murder-secret, anything that it is not good for him to have known. He by no means feigns the good-feeling that he professes, nor is there anything affected in the frankness of his conversation; and it is this that makes him so very fascinating. There is such a quantity of truth and kindliness and warm affections, that a man's heart opens to him, in spite of himself; he deceives by truth. And not only is he crafty, but, when occasion demands, bold and fierce as a tiger, determined, and even straightforward and undisguised in his measures — a daring fellow as well as a sly one. Yet notwithstanding his consummate art, the general estimate of his character seems to be pretty just; hardly anybody, probably, thinks him better than he is, and many think him worse. Nevertheless, unless he should fall into some great and overwhelming discovery of rascality, he will always possess influence; though I should hardly think that he would take any prominent part in Congress. As to any rascality, I rather believe that he has thought out for himself a much higher system of morality than any natural integrity would have prompted him to adopt; that he has seen the thorough advantage of morality and honesty; and the sentiment of these qualities has now got into his mind and spirit, and pretty well impregnated them. I believe him to be about as honest, now, as the great run of the world, with something even approaching to high-mindedness. His person in some degree accords with his character — thin and with a thin face, sharp features, sallow, a projecting brow, not very high, deep-set eyes, an insinuating smile and look, when he meets you, or is about to address you. I should think that he would do away with this peculiar expression, for it reveals more of himself than can be detected in any other way, in personal intercourse with him. Upon the whole, I have quite a good liking for him, and mean to go to Thomaston to see him.

August 22 [*Salem*]

A young man and girl meet together, each in search of a person to be known by some particular sign. They watch and wait a great while for that person to pass. At last some casual circumstance discloses that each is the one that the other is waiting for. Moral — that what we need for our happiness is often close at hand, if we knew but how to seek for it.

Distrust to be thus exemplified: Various good and desirable things to be presented to a young man, and offered to his acceptance — as a friend, a wife, a fortune; but he to refuse them all, suspecting that it is merely a delusion. Yet all to be real, and he to be told so, when too late.

A man tries to be happy in love; he cannot sincerely give his heart, and the affair seems all a dream. In domestic life, the same; in politics, a seeming patriot; but still he is sincere, and all seems like a theatre.[1]

An idle man's pleasures and occupations and thoughts during a day spent by the sea-shore: among them, that of sitting on the top of a cliff, and throwing stones at his own shadow, far below.[2]

A blind man to set forth on a walk through ways unknown to him, and to trust to the guidance of anybody who will take the trouble; the different characters who would undertake it: some mischievous, some well-meaning, but incapable; perhaps one blind man undertakes to lead another. At last, possibly, he rejects all guidance, and blunders on by himself.

Suppose a married couple fondly attached to one an-

[1] 'The Christmas Banquet.'   [2] 'Footprints on the Sea-shore.'

other, and to think that they lived solely for one another; then it to be found out that they were divorced, or that they might separate if they chose. What would be its effect?

October 7

How exceeding bright looks the sunshine, casually reflected from a looking-glass into a gloomy region of the chamber, distinctly marking out the figures and colors of the paper-hangings, which are scarcely seen elsewhere. It is like the light of mind thrown on an obscure subject.

Man's finest workmanship, the closer you observe it, the more imperfections it shows; as in a piece of polished steel a microscope will discover a rough surface. Whereas, what may look coarse and rough in Nature's workmanship will show an infinitely minute perfection, the closer you look into it. The reason of the minute superiority of Nature's work over man's is, that the former works from the innermost germ, while the latter works merely superficially.

A whirlwind, whirling the dried leaves round in a circle, not very violently.

To well consider the characters of a family of persons in a certain condition — in poverty, for instance — and endeavor to judge how an altered condition would affect the character of each.

The aromatic odor of peat-smoke in the sunny autumnal air is very pleasant.

October 14

The prospect from the hill [Browne's Hill] is wide and interesting; but methinks it is pleasanter in the more immediate vicinity of the hill than miles away. It is agreeable to look down at the square patches of cornfield, or of potato-ground, or of cabbages still green, or of beets looking red — all a man's farm, in short — each portion of which he considers separately so important, while you take in the whole at a glance. Then to cast your eye over so many different establishments at once and rapidly compare them — here a house of gentility, with shady old yellow-leaved elms hanging around it; there a new little white dwelling; there an old farm-house; to see the barns and sheds and all the out-houses clustered together; to comprehend the oneness and exclusiveness and what constitutes the peculiarity of each of so many establishments, and to have in your mind a multitude of them, each of which is the most important part of the world to those who live in it — this really enlarges the mind, and you come down the hill somewhat wiser than you go up. Pleasant to look over an orchard far below, and see the trees, each casting its own shadow; the white spires of meeting-houses; a sheet of water, partly seen among swelling lands.

An article to be made of telling the stories of the tiles of an old-fashioned chimney-piece to a child.[1]

[1] 'Grandfather's Chair' (modified).

A person conscious that he was soon to die, the humor in which he would pay his last visit to familiar persons and things.

A description of the various classes of hotels and taverns, and the prominent personages in each. There should be some story connected with it — as of a person commencing with boarding at a great hotel, and gradually, as his means grew less, descending in life, till he got below ground into a cellar.

A person to be in the possession of something as perfect as mortal man has a right to demand; he tries to make it better, and ruins it entirely.[1]

A person to spend all his life and splendid talents in trying to achieve something naturally impossible — as to make a conquest over Nature.

Meditations about the main gas-pipe of a great city — if the supply were to be stopped, what would happen? How many different scenes it sheds light on? It might be made emblematical of something.

December 6

A house to be built over a natural spring of inflammable gas, and to be constantly illuminated therewith. What moral could be drawn from this? It is carburetted hydrogen gas, and is cooled from a soft shale or slate, which is sometimes bituminous, and contains more or less

---

[1] 'The Birthmark.'

carbonate of lime. It appears in the vicinity of Lockport and Niagara Falls, and elsewhere in New York. I believe it indicates coal. At Fredonia, the whole village is lighted by it. Elsewhere, a farm-house was lighted by it, and no other fuel used in the coldest weather.

A man will undergo great toil and hardship for ends that must be many years distant — as wealth or fame — but none for an end that may be close at hand — as the joys of heaven.

Insincerity in a man's own heart must make all his enjoyments, all that concerns him, unreal; so that his whole life must seem like a merely dramatic representation. And this would be the case, even though he were surrounded by true-hearted relatives and friends.[1]

A company of men, none of whom have anything worth hoping for on earth, yet who do not look forward to anything beyond earth!

Sorrow to be personified, and its effect on a family represented by the way in which the members of the family regard this dark-clad and sad-browed inmate.

A story to show how we are all wronged and wrongers, and avenge one another.

A man living a wicked life in one place, and simultaneously a virtuous and religious one in another.

[1] 'The Scarlet Letter.'

An ornament to be worn about the person of a lady —
as a jewelled heart. After many years, it happens to
be broken or unscrewed, and a poisonous odor comes
out.

Some very famous jewel or other thing, much talked
of all over the world. Some person to meet with it, and
get possession of it in some unexpected manner, amid
homely circumstances.[1]

To poison a person or a party of persons with the
sacramental wine.

On being transported to strange scenes, we feel as if all
were unreal. This is but the perception of the true un-
reality of earthly things, made evident by the want of
congruity between ourselves and them. By and by we
become mutually adapted, and the perception is lost.

An old looking-glass. Somebody finds out the secret of
making all the images that have been reflected in it pass
back again across its surface.

Our Indian races having reared no monuments, like
the Greeks, Romans, and Egyptians, when they have
disappeared from the earth their history will appear a
fable, and they misty phantoms.

A woman to sympathize with all emotions, but to have
none of her own.

[1] 'The Great Carbuncle' (modified).

A portrait of a person in New England to be recognized as of the same person represented by a portrait in Old England. Having distinguished himself there, he had suddenly vanished, and had never been heard of till he was thus discovered to be identical with a distinguished man in New England.

Men of cold passions have quick eyes.

A virtuous but giddy girl to attempt to play a trick on a man. He sees what she is about, and contrives matters so that she throws herself completely into his power, and is ruined — all in jest.

A partially insane man to believe himself the Provincial Governor or other great official of Massachusetts. The scene might be the Province House.[1]

A dreadful secret to be communicated to several people of various characters — grave or gay, and they all to become insane, according to their characters, by the influence of the secret.

Stories to be told of a certain person's appearance in public, of his having been seen in various situations, and of his making visits in private circles; but finally, on looking for this person, to come upon his old grave and mossy tombstone.

The influence of a peculiar mind, in close communion with another, to drive the latter to insanity.

[1] 'Old Esther Dudley' (modified).

To look at a beautiful girl, and picture all the lovers, in different situations, whose hearts are centred upon her.

May 11, 1838

At Boston last week. Items: — A young man, with a small mustache, dyed brown, reddish from its original light color. He walks with an affected gait, his arms crooked outwards, treading much on his toes. His conversation is about the theatre, where he has a season ticket — about an amateur who lately appeared there, the actresses, theatrical scandal. — In the smoking-room, two checker and backgammon boards; the landlord a great player, seemingly a stupid man, but with considerable shrewdness and knowledge of the world. — F——, the comedian, a stout, heavy-looking Englishman, of grave deportment, with no signs of wit or humor, yet aiming at both in conversation, in order to support his character. Very steady and regular in his life, and parsimonious in his disposition — worth $50,000 made by his profession. — A clergyman, elderly, with a white neckcloth, very unbecoming, an unworldly manner, unacquaintance with the customs of the house, and learning them in a childlike way. A ruffle to his shirt, crimped. — A gentleman, young, handsome, and sea-flushed, belonging to Oswego, New York, but just arrived in port from the Mediterranean: he inquires of me about the troubles in Canada, which were first beginning to make a noise when he left the country — whether they are all over. I tell him all is finished, except the hanging of the prisoners. Then we talk over the matter, and I tell him the fates of the principal men — some banished to New South Wales, one hanged, others in prison, others, conspicuous at first, now almost forgotten. — Apartments of private families in the hotel — what sort of domesticity there may be in them; eating in public, with no board of their own. The gas that lights the rest of the house lights them also, in the chandelier from the ceiling. — A shabby-looking man, quiet, with spectacles, at first wearing an old, coarse brown frock, then appearing in a suit of elderly black, saying nothing unless spoken to, but talking intelligently when addressed. He is an editor, and I suppose printer, of a country paper. Among the guests, he holds intercourse with gentlemen of much more respectable appearance than himself, from the same part of the country. — Bill of fare; wines printed on the back, but nobody calls for a bottle. Chairs turned down for expected guests. Three-pronged steel forks. Cold supper from nine to eleven P.M. Great, round, mahogany table, in the sitting-room, covered with papers. In the morning, before and soon after breakfast, gentlemen reading the morning papers, while others wait for their chance, or try to pick out something from the papers of yesterday or longer ago. In the forenoon, the Southern papers are brought in, and thrown damp and folded on the table. The eagerness with which those who happen to be in the room start up and make prize of them. Play-bills, printed on yellow paper, laid upon the table. Towards evening comes the 'Transcript.'

June 15

The situation of a man in the midst of a crowd, yet as completely in the power of another, life and all, as if they two were in the deepest solitude.[1]

---

[1] 'The Scarlet Letter.'

July 10

Ladurlad, in 'The Curse of Kehama,' on visiting a certain celestial region, the fire in his heart and brain died away for a season, but was rekindled again on returning to earth. So may it be with me in my projected three months' seclusion from old associations.

July 13

A series of strange, mysterious, dreadful events to occur, wholly destructive of a person's happiness. He to impute them to various persons and causes, but ultimately finds that he is himself the sole agent. Moral, that our welfare depends on ourselves.

The strange incident in the court of Charles IX of France: he and five other maskers being attired in coats of linen covered with pitch and bestuck with flax to represent hairy savages. They entered the hall dancing, the five being fastened together, and the king in front. By accident the five were set on fire with a torch. Two were burned to death on the spot, two afterwards died; one fled to the buttery, and jumped into a vessel of water. It might be represented as the fate of a squad of dissolute men.

A perception, for a moment, of one's eventual and moral self, as if it were another person — the observant faculty being separated, and looking intently at the qualities of the character. There is a surprise when this happens — this getting out of one's self — and then the observer sees how queer a fellow he is.

July 27 [*North Adams*]

Left home [Salem] Monday, 23d instant. To Boston
by stage, and took the afternoon cars for Worcester.
Little boy returning from the city, several miles, with a
basket of empty custard-cups, which probably, their
contents, he had sold at the depot. Stopped at the Tem-
perance House.   An old gentleman, Mr. Phillips, of
Boston, got into conversation with me, and inquired very
freely as to my character, tastes, habits, and circumstances — a freedom sanctioned by his age, his kindly
and beneficent spirit, and the wisdom of his advice. It is
strange how little impertinence depends on what is
actually said, but on the manner and motives of saying it.
'I want to do you good,' said he with warmth, after becoming, apparently, moved by our communications.
'Well, sir,' replied I, 'I wish you could, for both our
sakes; for I have no doubt it would be a great satisfaction
to you.' He asked the most direct questions of another
young man; for instance, 'Was he married?' having before
ascertained that point with regard to myself. He told
me by all means to act, in whatever way; observing that
he himself would have no objection to be a servant, if no
other mode of action presented itself. . . .

On the road to Northampton, we passed a tame crow,
which was sitting on the peak of a barn. The crow flew
down from its perch, and followed us a great distance,
hopping along the road, and flying with its large, black,
flapping wings, from post to post of the fence, or from
tree to tree. At last he gave up the pursuit with a croak
of disappointment. The driver said, perhaps correctly,
that the crow had scented some salmon which was in a

basket under the seat, and that this was the secret of his pursuing us. This would be a terrific incident if it were a dead body that the crow scented, instead of a basket of salmon. Suppose, for instance, in a coach travelling along, that one of the passengers suddenly should die, and that one of the indications of his death was this deportment of the crow.

July 29

Remarkable characters: — A disagreeable figure, waning from middle age, clad in a pair of tow homespun pantaloons, and a very dirty shirt, barefoot, and with one of his feet maimed by an axe; also an arm amputated two or three inches below the elbow. His beard of a week's growth, grim and grisly, with a general effect of black; altogether a filthy and disgusting object. Yet he has the signs of having been a handsome man in his idea, though now such a beastly figure that probably no living thing but his great dog would touch him without an effort. Coming to the stoop, where several persons were sitting, 'Good morning, gentlemen,' said this wretch. Nobody answered for a time, till at last one said, 'I don't know who you speak to: not to me, I'm sure' (meaning that he did not claim to be a gentleman). 'Why I thought you [would] all speak at once,' replied the figure, laughing. So he sat himself down on the lower step of the stoop, and began to talk; and, the conversation being turned upon his bare feet by one of the company, he related the story of his losing his toes by the glancing aside of an axe, and with what grim fortitude he bore it. Thence he made a transition to the loss of his arm, and, setting his teeth and drawing in his breath, said that the pain was dreadful; but this, too, he seems to have borne like an Indian; and a person testified to his fortitude by saying that he did not suppose there was any feeling in him, from observing how he bore it. The man spoke of the pain of cutting the muscles, and the particular agony at one moment, while the bone was being sawed asunder; and there was a strange expression of remembered agony, as he shrugged his half-limb, and described the matter. Afterwards, in a reply to a question of mine, whether he still seemed to feel the hand that had been amputated, he answered that he did, always; and, baring the stump, he moved the severed muscles, saying, 'There is the thumb, there the forefinger,' and so on. Then he talked to me about phrenology, of which he seems a firm believer and skilful practitioner, telling how he had hit upon the true characters of many people. There was a great deal of sense and acuteness in his talk, and something of elevation in his expressions — perhaps a studied elevation — and a sort of courtesy in his manner; but his sense had something out of the way in it; something wild and ruined and desperate in his talk, though I can hardly say what it was. There was something of the gentleman and man of intellect through his deep degradation; and a pleasure in intellectual pursuits, and an acuteness and trained judgment, which bespoke a mind once strong and cultivated. 'My study is man,' said he. And, looking at me, 'I do not know your name,' said he, 'but there is something of the hawk-eye about you, too.'

This man was formerly a lawyer in good practice; but,

taking to drinking, was reduced to this lowest state. Yet not the lowest; for after the amputation of his arm, being advised by divers persons to throw himself upon the public for support, he told them that, even if he should lose his other arm, he would still be able to support himself and a waiter. Certainly he is a strong-minded and iron-constitutioned man; but, looking at the stump of his arm, he said 'that the pain of the mind was a thousand times greater than the pain of the body.' 'That hand could make the pen go fast,' said he. Among people in general, he does not seem to have any greater consideration in his ruin because of his former standing in society. He supports himself by making soap; and, on account of the offals used in that business, there is probably rather an evil smell in his domicile. Talking about a dead horse near his house, he said that he could not bear the scent of it. 'I should not think you could smell carrion in that house,' said a stage agent. Whereupon the soap-maker dropped his head, with a little snort, as it were, of wounded feeling; but immediately said that he took all in good part. There was an old squire of the village, a lawyer probably, whose demeanor was different — with a distance, yet a kindliness; for he remembered the times when they met on equal terms. 'You and I,' said the squire, alluding to their respective troubles and sicknesses, 'would have died long ago, if we had not had the courage to live.' The poor devil kept talking to me long after everybody else had left the stoop, giving vent to much practical philosophy, and just observation on the ways of men, mingled with rather more assumption of literature and cultivation than belonged to the present condition of his mind. Meantime his great dog, a cleanly looking and not ill-bred dog, being the only decent attribute appertaining to his master — a well-natured dog, too, and receiving civilly any demonstrations of courtesy from other people, though preserving a certain distance of deportment — this great dog grew weary of his master's lengthy talk, and expressed his impatience to be gone by thrusting himself between his legs, rolling over on his back, seizing his ragged trousers, or playfully taking his maimed, bare foot into his mouth — using, in short, the kindly and humorous freedom of a friend, with a wretch to whom all are free enough, but none other kind. His master rebuked him, but with kindness too, and not so that the dog felt himself bound to desist, though he seemed willing to allow his master all the time that could possibly be spared. And at last, having said many times that he must go and shave and dress himself — and as his beard had been at least a week growing, it might have seemed almost a week's work to get rid of it — he rose from the stoop and went his way — a forlorn and miserable thing in the light of the cheerful summer Sabbath morning. Yet he seems to keep his spirits up, and still preserves himself a man among men, asking nothing from them; nor is it clearly perceptible what right they have to scorn him, though he seems to acquiesce, in a sort, in their doing so. And yet he cannot wholly have lost his self-respect; and doubtless there were persons on the stoop more grovelling than himself.

July 30

Remarkable character: — A travelling 'Surgeon-Dentist,' who has taken a room in the North Adams House, and sticks up his advertising bills on the pillars of the piazza, and all about the town. He is a tall, slim young man, six feet two, dressed in a country-made coat of light blue (taken, as he tells me, in exchange for dental operations), black pantaloons, and clumsy, cowhide boots. Self-conceit is very strongly expressed in his air; and a doctor once told him that he owed his life to that quality; for, by keeping himself so stiffly upright, he opens his chest, and counteracts a consumptive tendency. He is not only a dentist, which trade he follows temporarily, but a licensed preacher of the Baptist persuasion, and is now on his way to the West to seek a place of settlement in his spiritual vocation. Whatever education he possesses, he has acquired by his own exertions, since the age of twenty-one — he being now twenty-four. We talk together very freely; and he has given me an account, among other matters, of all his love-affairs, which are rather curious, as illustrative of the life of a smart young country fellow as relates to the gentle sex. Nothing can exceed the exquisite self-conceit which characterizes these confidences, and which is expressed inimitably in his face, his upturned nose, and mouth, so as to be truly a caricature; and he seems strangely to find as much food for this passion in having been jilted once or twice as in his conquests. It is curious to notice his revengeful feeling against the false ones — hidden from himself under the guise of religious interest, and desire that they may be cured of their follies.

September 7

Mr. Leach and I took a walk by moonlight, last evening, on the road that leads over the mountain. Remote
from houses, far up on the hill-side, we found a lime-kiln,[1]
burning near the roadside; and, approaching it, a watcher
started from the ground, where he had been lying at his
length. There are several of these lime-kilns in this
vicinity; they are built circular, with stones, like a round
tower, eighteen or twenty feet high; having a hillock
heaped around in a considerable portion of their circum-
ference, so that the marble may be brought and thrown
in by cart-loads at the top. At the bottom there is a
doorway, large enough to admit a man in a stooping
posture. Thus an edifice of great solidity is composed,
which will endure for centuries, unless needless pains are
taken to tear it down. There is one on the hill-side, close
to the village, wherein weeds grow at the bottom, and
grass and shrubs too are rooted in the interstices of the
stones, and its low doorway has a dungeon-like aspect,
and we look down from the top as into a roofless tower.
It apparently has not been used for many years, and the
lime and weather-stained fragments of marble are scattered about.

But in the one we saw last night a hard-wood fire was
burning merrily beneath the superincumbent marble —
the kiln being heaped full; and shortly after we came,
the man (a dark, black-bearded figure, in shirt-sleeves)
opened the iron door, through the chinks of which the
fire was gleaming, and thrust in huge logs of wood, and
stirred the immense coals with a long pole; and showed

[1] 'Ethan Brand.'

us the glowing limestone — the lower layer of it. The glow of the fire was powerful, at the distance of several yards from the open door. He talked very sociably with us, being doubtless glad to have two visitors to vary his solitary night-watch; for it would not do for him to get asleep, since the fire should be refreshed as often as every twenty minutes. We ascended the hillock to the top of the kiln; and the marble was red-hot, and burning with a bluish, lambent flame, quivering up, sometimes nearly a yard high, and resembling the flame of anthracite coal, only, the marble being in larger fragments, the flame was higher. The kiln was perhaps six or eight feet across. Four hundred bushels of marble were then in a state of combustion. The expense of converting this quantity into lime is about fifty dollars, and it sells for 25 cts. per bushel at the kiln. We talked with the man about whether he would run across the top of the intensely burning kiln for a thousand dollars bare-footed; and he said he would for ten; he said that the lime had been burning forty-eight hours, and would be finished in thirty-six more, and cooled sufficiently to handle in twelve more. He liked the business of watching it better by night than day; because the days were often hot, but such a mild and beautiful night as the last was just right. . . . Here a poet might make verses with moonlight in them, and a gleam of fierce fire-light flickering through them. It is a shame to use this brilliant, white, almost transparent marble in this way. A man said of it, the other day, that into some pieces of it, when polished, one could see a considerable distance; and instanced a certain gravestone.

October 24 [*Boston*]

View from a chamber of the Tremont of the brick edifice opposite, on the other side of Beacon Street. At one of the lower windows a woman at work; at one above, a lady hemming a ruff or some such lady-like thing. She is pretty young, and married; for a little boy comes to her knees, and she parts his hair, and caresses him in a motherly way. A note on colored paper is brought her, and she reads it, and puts it in her bosom. At another window, at some depth within the apartment, a gentleman in a dressing-gown, reading, and rocking in an easy-chair, etc., etc., etc. A rainy day, and people passing with umbrellas disconsolately between the spectator and these various scenes of indoor occupation and comfort. With this sketch might be mingled and worked up some story that was going on within the chamber where the spectator was situated.[1]

Undated [*Salem*]

Singular character of a gentleman (H. H——, Esq.) living in retirement in Boston — esteemed a man of nicest honor, and his seclusion attributed to wounded feelings on account of the failure of his firm in business. Yet it was discovered that this man had been the mover of intrigues by which men in business had been ruined, and their property absorbed, none knew how or by whom; love-affairs had been broken off, and much other mischief done; and for years he was not in the least suspected. He died suddenly, soon after suspicion fell upon him. Probably it was the love of management, of having an influence on affairs, that produced these phenomena.

[1] 'The Blithedale Romance.'

Character of a man who, in himself and his external circumstances, shall be equally and totally false; his fortune resting on baseless credit — his patriotism assumed — his domestic affections, his honor and honesty, all a sham. His own misery in the midst of it — it making the whole universe, heaven and earth alike an unsubstantial mockery to him.[1]

Dr. Johnson's penance in Uttoxeter Market. A man who does penance in what might appear to lookers-on the most glorious and triumphal circumstance of his life. Each circumstance of the career of an apparently successful man to be a penance and torture to him on account of some fundamental error in early life.[2]

A person to catch fire-flies, and try to kindle his household fire with them. It would be symbolical of something.

Thanksgiving at the Worcester Lunatic Asylum. A ball and dance of the inmates in the evening — a furious lunatic dancing with the principal's wife. Thanksgiving in an almshouse might make a better sketch.

A person, while awake and in the business of life, to think highly of another, and place perfect confidence in him, but to be troubled with dreams in which this seeming friend appears to act the part of a most deadly enemy. Finally it is discovered that the dream-character is the true one. The explanation would be — the soul's instinctive perception.

[1] 'The Scarlet Letter.' [2] *Ibid.*

Pandora's box for a child's story.

A person to look back on a long life ill-spent, and to picture forth a beautiful life which he would live, if he could be permitted to begin his life over again. Finally to discover that he had only been dreaming of old age — that he was really young, and could live such a life as he had pictured.

H. L. Conolly heard from a French Canadian a story of a young couple in Acadie. On their marriage day, all the men of the Province were summoned to assemble in the church to hear a proclamation. When assembled, they were all seized and shipped off to be distributed through New England — among them the new bride-groom. His bride set off in search of him — wandered about New England all her lifetime, and at last, when she was old, she found her bridegroom on his deathbed. The shock was so great that it killed her likewise.[1]

[1] It is well known that this story, the 'source' of 'Evangeline,' was turned over to Longfellow by Hawthorne, who indeed reviewed the poem with enthusiasm on its appearance in 1847. 'I received [Mr. Conolly's] paper containing your notice of the book,' wrote Longfellow to Hawthorne, 'and thank you both for such friendly service. Still more do I thank you for resigning to me that legend of Acady. This success I owe entirely to you, for being willing to forego the pleasure of writing a prose tale which many people would have taken for poetry, that I might write a poem which many people take for prose.'

1839–1841

[EARLY in January, 1839, Hawthorne assumed his active duties at the Boston Custom House; and for something more than two years, in spite of a distaste for those duties which beset him almost from the beginning, he continued to spend his days supervising the measurement of coal and salt on dingy coastwise schooners in Boston Harbor. During all that time his literary activity was practically in abeyance, though 'Grandfather's Chair' belongs to this Boston period; even his journal, save for a few brief notes for tales, and a series of entries in February, 1839, was suspended; and its place was taken by the letters which he appears to have written with much the same regularity to Sophia Peabody.

When, in April, 1841, Hawthorne, anticipating the probable vengeance of a new Whig administration, resigned from his federal appointment, he found himself under the necessity of making some other practical arrangements in view of his still-deferred marriage. In this juncture, a suggestion from George Ripley that he throw in his lot with the experimenters at Brook Farm, appealed to both his practical and his adventurous impulses; and from April to November he was a colonist at West Roxbury, abandoning the experiment only when it threatened to be, for him, wholly quixotic. The letters to Sophia continue during the summer and fall at Brook Farm, and the journal is not resumed until late in September, continuing intermittently up to his last days among the communists.]

January 4, 1839

The strange sensation of a person who feels himself an object of deep interest, and close observation, and various construction of all his actions, by another person.[1]

A young man in search of happiness — to be personified by a figure whom he expects to meet in a crowd, and is to be recognized by certain signs. All these signs are given by a figure in various garbs and actions, but he does not recognize that this is the sought-for person till too late.

'A story there passeth of an Indian king that sent unto Alexander a fair woman, fed with aconite and other poisons, with this intent complexionally to destroy him!' — *Sir T. Browne.*[2]

A mortal symptom for a person being to lose his own aspect and to take the family lineaments, which were hidden deep in the healthful visage. Perhaps a seeker might thus recognize the man he had sought, after long intercourse with him unknowingly.

To have ice in one's blood.

The semblance of a human face to be formed on the side of a mountain, or in the fracture of a small stone, by a *lusus naturæ*. The face is an object of curiosity for years or centuries, and by and by a boy is born, whose features gradually assume the aspect of that portrait.

[1] 'The Scarlet Letter.'   [2] 'Rappaccini's Daughter.'

At some critical juncture, the resemblance is found to be perfect. A prophecy may be connected.[1]

A person to be the death of his beloved in trying to raise her to more than mortal perfection; yet this should be a comfort to him for having aimed so highly and holily.[2]

February 7 [*Boston*] [3]

Yesterday and day before, measuring a load of coal from the schooner Thomas Lowder, of St. John, N.B. A little, black, dirty vessel. The coal stowed in the hold, so as to fill the schooner full, and make her a solid mass of black mineral. The master, Best, a likely young man; his mate a fellow jabbering in some strange gibberish, English I believe — or nearer that than anything else — but gushing out all together — whole sentences confounded into one long, unintelligible word. Irishmen shoveling the coal into the two Custom House tubs, to be craned out of the hold, and others wheeling it away in barrows, to be laden into wagons. The first day, I walked the wharf, suffering not a little from cold; yesterday, I sat in the cabin whence I could look through the interstices of the bulkhead, or whatever they call it, into the hold. My eyes, what a cabin! Three paces would more than measure it in any direction, and it was filled with barrels, not clean and new, but black, and containing probably the provender of the vessel; jugs,

---

[1] 'The Great Stone Face.'   [2] 'The Birthmark.'

[3] For pp. 50–54, see 'Memories of Hawthorne': R. H. Lathrop, pp. 35–45.

firkins, the cook's utensils and kitchen furniture — everything grimy and sable with coal dust. There were two or three tiers of berths; and the blankets, etc., are not to be thought of. A cooking stove, wherein was burning some of the coal — excellent fuel, burning as freely as wood, and without the bituminous melting of Newcastle coal. The cook of the vessel, a grimy, unshaven, middle-aged man, trimming the fire at need, and sometimes washing his dishes in water that seemed to have cleansed the whole world beforehand — the draining of gutters, or caught at sink-spouts. In the cessation of labor, the Irishmen in the hold would poke their heads through the open space into the cabin and call 'Cook!' — for a drink of water or a pipe — whereupon Cook would fill a short black pipe, put a coal into it, and stick it into the Irishman's mouth. Here sat I on a bench before the fire, the other guests of the cabin being the stevedore, who takes the job of getting the coal ashore, and the owner of the horse that raised the tackle — the horse being driven by a boy. The cabin was lined with slabs — the rudest and dirtiest hole imaginable, yet the passengers had been accommodated here in the trip from New Brunswick. The bitter zero atmosphere came down the companionway, and threw its chill over me sometimes, but I was pretty comfortable — though, on reaching home, I found that I had swaggered through several thronged streets with coal streaks on my visage.

February 19

The City-Crier, talking in a familiar style to his auditors — delivering various messages to them, intermixed with his own remarks. He then runs over his memory to see whether he has omitted anything, and recollects a lost child — 'We've lost a child,' says he; as if, in his universal sympathy for all who have wants, and seek the gratification of them through his medium, he were one with the parents of the child. He then tells the people, whenever they find lost children, not to keep them overnight, but to bring them to his office. 'For it is a cruel thing' — to keep them; and at the conclusion of his lecture, he tells them that he has already worn out his lungs, talking to them of these things. He completely personifies the public, and considers it as an individual with whom he holds converse — he being as important on his side, as they on theirs.

Schooners more than any other vessels seem to have such names as Betsey, Emma-Jane, Sarah, Alice — being the namesakes of the owner's wife, daughter, or sweetheart. They are a sort of domestic concern, in which all the family take an interest. Not a cold, stately, unpersonified thing, like a merchant's tall ship, perhaps one of half a dozen in which he takes pride, but which he does not love, nor has a family feeling for. Now Betsey, or Sarah-Ann, seems like one of the family — something like a cow.

The mate of a coal-vessel — a leathern belt round his waist, sustaining a knife in a leathern sheath. Probably he uses it to eat his dinner with; perhaps also as a weapon.

An old seaman, seventy years of age — he has spent
seven years in the British Navy (being of English birth)
and nine in ours; has voyaged all over the world — for
instance, I asked if he had ever been in the Red Sea, and
he had, in the American sloop of war that carried General
Eaton, in 1803. His hair is brown — without a single
visible gray hair in it; and he would seem not much above
fifty. He is of particularly quiet demeanor — but observant of all things, and reflective — a philosopher in a
check shirt and sail-cloth trousers. Giving an impression
of the strictest integrity — of inability not to do his duty,
and his whole duty. Seemingly, he does not take a very
strong interest in the world, being a widower without
children; but he feels kindly towards it, and judges mildly
of it; and enjoys it very tolerably well, although he has so
slight a hold on it that it would not trouble him much to
give it up. He said he hoped he should die at sea, because
then it would be so little trouble to bury him. He is a
skeptic — and when I asked him if he would not wish
to live again, he spoke doubtfully and coldly. He said
that he had been in England within two or three years —
in his native county, Yorkshire — and finding his
brother's children in very poor condition, he gave them
sixty golden sovereigns. 'I have always had too many
poor friends,' he said, 'and that has kept me poor.' This
old man kept tally of the Alfred Tyler's cargo, on behalf
of the Captain, diligently marking all day long, and
calling 'tally, Sir,' to me at every sixth tub. Often would
he have to attend to some call of the stevedores, or
wheelers, or shovelers — now for a piece of spun-yarn —
now for a handspike — now for a hammer, or some nails

— now for some of the ship's molasses, to sweeten water
— the which the Captain afterwards reprehended him
for giving. These calls would keep him in about movement enough to give variety to his tallying — he moving
quietly about the decks, as if he belonged aboard ship
and nowhere else. Then sitting down he would converse
(though by no means forward to talk) about the weather,
about his recent or former voyages, etc., etc., etc., we
dodging the intense sun round the main mast.

July 3

I do not mean to imply that I am unhappy or discon-
tented; for this is not the case; my life only is a burthen,
in the same way that it is to every toilsome man, and mine
is a healthy weariness, such as needs only a night's sleep
to remove it. But from henceforth forever, I shall be en-
titled to call the sons of toil my brethren, and shall know
how to sympathize with them, seeing that I, likewise,
have risen at the dawn and borne the fervor of the midday
sun, nor turned my heavy footsteps homeward till even-
tide. Years hence, perhaps, the experience that my heart
is acquiring now will flow out in truth and wisdom.

August 27

Very dearest, your husband has been stationed all day
at the end of Long Wharf, and I rather think that he had
the most eligible situation of anybody in Boston. I was
aware that it must be intensely hot in the middle of the
city; but there was only a very short space of uncomfortable heat in my region, half-way towards the centre
of the harbor; and almost all the time there was a pure

and delightful breeze, fluttering and palpitating, sometimes shyly kissing my brow, then dying away, and then
rushing upon me in livelier sport, so that I was fain to
settle my straw hat tighter upon my head. Late in the
afternoon, there was a sunny shower, which came down
so like a benediction, that it seemed ungrateful to take
shelter in the cabin, or to put up an umbrella. Then there
was a rainbow, or a large segment of one, so exceedingly
brilliant, and of such long endurance, that I almost
fancied it was stained into the sky, and would continue
there permanently. And there were clouds floating all
about, great clouds and small, of all glorious and lovely
hues (save that imperial crimson, which was never revealed save to our united gaze), so glorious, indeed, and
so lovely, that I had a fantasy of Heaven's being broken
into fleecy fragments and dispersed throughout space,
with its blessed inhabitants yet dwelling blissfully upon
those scattered islands.

November 17

... How delightfully long the evenings are now! I do
not get intolerably tired any longer, and my thoughts
sometimes wander back to literature and I have momen-
tary impulses to write stories. But this will not be, at
present. The utmost that I can hope to do, will be to
portray some of the characteristics of the life which I
am now living, and of the people with whom I am brought
into contact, for future use.

December 1

Dearest, ... I have never had the good luck to profit

much, or indeed any, by attending lectures; so that I
think the ticket had better be bestowed on somebody who
can listen to Mr. Emerson more worthily. My evenings
are very precious to me; and some of them are unavoid-
ably thrown away in paying or receiving visits, or in
writing letters of business, and therefore I prize the rest
as if the sands of the hour-glass were gold or diamond
dust.

December 5

I was invited to dine at Mr. Bancroft's yesterday with
Miss Margaret Fuller; but Providence had given me
some business to do; for which I was very thankful.

February 11, 1840

Your husband has been measuring coal all day, aboard
of a black little British schooner, in a dismal dock at the
north end of the city. Most of the time, he paced the deck
to keep himself warm; for the wind (northeast, I believe
it was) blew up through the dock, as if it had been the
pipe of a pair of bellows. The vessel lying deep between
two wharves, there was no more delightful prospect, on
the right hand and on the left, than the posts and timbers,
half immersed in the water, and covered with ice, which
the rising and falling of successive tides had left upon
them; so that they looked like immense icicles. Across the
water, however, not more than half a mile off, appeared
the Bunker Hill monument; and what interested me considerably more, a church-steeple, with the dial of a clock
upon it, whereby I was enabled to measure the march of
the weary hours. Sometimes your husband descended

into the dirty little cabin of the schooner, and warmed
himself by a red-hot stove, among biscuit-barrels, pots
and kettles, sea-chests, and innumerable lumber of all
sorts — his olfactories, meanwhile, being greatly refreshed by the odor of a pipe, which the captain or some
of his crew were smoking. But at last came the sunset,
with delicate clouds, and a purple light upon the islands;
and your husband blessed it, because it was the signal of
his release; and so he came home to talk with his dearest
wife.

March 15

I do pray, that, in one year more, I may find some way
of escaping from this unblest Custom-House; for it is a
very grievous thraldom. I do detest all offices — all, at
least, that are held on a political tenure. And I want
nothing to do with politicians — they are not men; they
cease to be men, in becoming politicians. Their hearts
wither away, and die out of their bodies. Their con-
sciences are turned to india-rubber, or to some substance
as black as that, and which will stretch as much. One
thing, if no more, I have gained by my Custom-House
experience — to know a politician. It is a knowledge
which no previous thought, or power of sympathy, could
have taught me, because the animal, or the machine
rather, is not in nature.

March 26

Blessedest, I do think that it is the doom laid upon me,
of murdering so many of the brightest hours of the day
at that unblest Custom-House, that makes such havoc

with my wits; for here I am again, trying to write worthily
to my etherealest, and intellectualest, and feelingest, and
imaginativest wife, yet with a sense as if all the noblest
part of man had been left out of my composition — or
had decayed out of it since my nature was given to my
own keeping. . . . Never comes any bird of Paradise into
that dismal region. A salt, or even a coal-ship is ten
million times preferable; for there the sky is above me,
and the fresh breeze around me, and my thoughts, having hardly anything to do with my occupation, are as
free as air.

Nevertheless, belovedest, thou art not to fancy that
the above paragraph gives thee a correct idea of thy husband's mental and spiritual state; for he is sometimes
prone to the sin of exaggeration. It is only once in a
while that the image and desire of a better and happier
life makes him feel the iron of his chain; for, after all, a
human spirit may find no insufficiency of food fit for it,
even in the Custom-House. And, with such materials as
these, I do think, and feel, and learn things that are
worth knowing, and which I should not know unless I
had learned them there; so that the present portion of
my life shall not be quite left out of the sum of my real
existence. . . .

It is good for me, on many accounts, that my life has
had this passage in it. Thou canst not think how much
more I know than I did a year ago — what a stronger
sense I have of power to act as a man among men —
what worldly wisdom I have gained, and wisdom also
that is not altogether of this world. And when I quit this
earthly cavern, where I am now buried, nothing will cling

to me that ought to be left behind. Men will not perceive, I trust, by my look, or the tenor of my thoughts and feelings, that I have been a Custom-House officer.

April 3

Belovedest, thy husband has been busy all day, from early breakfast-time till late in the afternoon; and old Father Time has gone onward somewhat less heavily than is his wont when I am imprisoned within the walls of the Custom-House. It has been a brisk, breezy day, an effervescent atmosphere; and I have enjoyed it in all its freshness — breathing air which had not been breathed in advance by the hundred thousand pairs of lungs which have common and indivisible property in the atmosphere of this great city. My breath had never belonged to anybody but myself. It came fresh from the wilderness of ocean. . . . And, dearest, it was exhilarating to see the vessels, how they bounded over the waves, while a sheet of foam broke out around them. I found a good deal of enjoyment, too, in the busy scene around me; for several vessels were disgorging themselves (what an unseemly figure is this — 'disgorge,' quotha, as if the vessels were sick at their stomachs) on the wharf; and everybody seemed to be working with might and main. It pleased thy husband to think that he also had a part to act in the material and tangible business of this life, and that a part of all this industry could not have gone on without his presence. Nevertheless, my belovedest, pride not thyself too much on thy husband's activity and utilitarianism; he is naturally an idler, and doubtless soon will be pestering thee with bewailments at being compelled to earn his bread by taking some little share in the toils of mortal men.

April 7

My tenderest Dove, hast thou lived through the polar winter of to-day; for it does appear to me to have been the most uncomfortable day that ever was inflicted on poor mortals. . . . Besides the bleak, unkindly air, I have been plagued by *two* sets of coal-shovellers at the same time, and have had to keep two separate tallies simultaneously. But, dearest, I was conscious that all this was merely a vision and a phantasy, and that, in reality, I was not half frozen by the bitter blast, nor tormented by those grimy coal-heavers, but that I was basking quietly in the sunshine of eternity, with mine own Dove. Any sort of bodily and earthly torment may serve to make us sensible that we have a soul that is not within the jurisdiction of such shadowy demons — it separates the immortal within us from the mortal. But the wind has blown my brain into such confusion that I cannot philosophize now.

April 19

. . . Belovedest, what a beautiful day was yesterday. . . . Thy husband's spirit did rebel against being confined in his darksome dungeon at the Custom-House. It seemed a sin — a murder of the joyful young day — a quenching of the sunshine. Nevertheless, there he was kept a prisoner — till it was too late to fling himself on a gentle wind, and be blown away into the country. . . . When I shall be again free, I will enjoy all things with the fresh simplicity of a child of five years old; thou shalt find thine husband grown young again, made all over anew — he will go forth and stand in a summer shower, and all the worldly dust that has collected on him shall be washed away at once. . . .

6 P.M. — Thy husband went out to walk, dearest, about an hour ago, and found it very pleasant, though there was a somewhat cool wind. I went round and across the Common, and stood on the highest point of it, whence I could see miles and miles into the country. Blessed be God for this green tract, and the view which it affords; whereby we poor citizens may be put in mind, some-times, that all God's earth is not composed of brick blocks of houses, and of stone or wooden pavements. Blessed be God for the sky, too; though the smoke of the city may somewhat change its aspect — but still it is better than if each street were covered over with a roof. There were a good many people walking on the mall, mechanics apparently and shopkeepers' clerks, with their wives and sweethearts; and boys were rolling on the grass — and thy husband would have liked to lie down and roll too.

April 30

. . . I arose this morning feeling more elastic than I have throughout the winter; for the breathing of the ocean air has wrought a very beneficial effect. . . . What a beau-tiful, most beautiful afternoon this has been! It was a real happiness to live. If I had been merely a vegetable — a hawthorn-bush, for instance — I must have been happy in such an air and sunshine; but, having a mind and a soul, . . . I enjoyed somewhat more than mere vegetable happiness. . . . The footsteps of May can be traced upon the islands in the harbor, and I have been watching the tints of green upon them gradually deepening, till now they are almost as beautiful as they ever can be.

May 19

. . . Lights and shadows are continually flitting across my inward sky, and I know neither whence they come nor whither they go; nor do I inquire too closely into them. It is dangerous to look too minutely at such phenomena. It is apt to create a substance where at first there was a mere shadow. If at any time, dearest wife, there should seem — though to me there never does — but if there should ever seem to be an expression unintelligible from one of our souls to another, we will not strive to interpret it into earthly language, but wait for the soul to make itself understood; and were we to wait a thousand years, we need deem it no more time than we can spare. . . . It is not that I have any love for mystery; but because I abhor it — and because I have felt, a thousand times, that words may be a thick and darksome veil of mystery between the soul and the truth which it seeks. Wretched were we, indeed, if we had no better means of communicating ourselves, no fairer garb in which to array our essential selves, than these poor rags and tatters of Babel. Yet words are not without their use, even for purposes of explanation — but merely for explaining outward acts, and all sorts of external things, leaving the soul's life and action to explain itself in its own way.

My belovedest, what a misty disquisition I have scribbled! I would not read it over for sixpence.

May 29

Rejoice with thy husband, for he is free from a load of coal, which has been pressing upon his shoulders throughout all this hot weather. I am convinced that Christian's burthen consisted of coal; and no wonder he felt so much relieved when it fell off and rolled into the sepulchre. His load, however, at the utmost, could not have been more than a few bushels; whereas mine was exactly one hundred and thirty-five chaldrons and seven tubs.

Belovedest, I sometimes wish that thou couldst be with [me] on board my salt-vessels and colliers; because there are many things of which thou mightst make such pretty descriptions; and, in future years, when thy husband is again busy at the loom of fiction, he would weave in these little pictures. My fancy is rendered so torpid by my ungenial way of life, that I cannot sketch off the scenes and portraits that interest me; and I am forced to trust them to my memory, with the hope of recalling them at some more favorable period. For three or four days past, I have been observing a little Mediterranean boy, from Malaga, not more than ten or eleven years old, but who is already a citizen of the world, and seems to be just as gay and contented on the deck of a Yankee coal-vessel, as he could be while playing beside his mother's door. It is really touching to see how free and happy he is — how the little fellow takes the whole wide world for his home, and all mankind for his family. He talks Spanish — at least, that is his native tongue; but he is also very intelligible in English, and perhaps he likewise has smatterings of the speech of other countries, whither the winds may have wafted this little sea-bird. He is a Catholic; and yesterday, being Friday, he caught some fish and fried them for his dinner in sweet-oil, and really they looked so delicate that I almost wished he would invite me to partake. Every once in a while, he undresses himself and leaps overboard, plunging down beneath the waves, as if the sea were as native to him as the earth; then he runs up the rigging of the vessel, as if he meant to fly away through the air. Do thou remember this little boy, dearest, and tell me of him one of these days; and perhaps I may make something more beautiful of him than thou wouldst think from these rough and imperfect touches.

October

I was not at the end of Long Wharf to-day, but in a distant region — my authority having been put in requisition to quell a rebellion of the captain and 'gang' of shovellers aboard a coal-vessel. I would you could have beheld the awful sternness of my visage and demeanor in the execution of this momentous duty. Well — I have conquered the rebels, and proclaimed an amnesty; so to-morrow I shall return to that paradise of measurers, the end of Long Wharf — not to my former salt-ship, she being now discharged, but to another, which will probably employ me well-nigh a fortnight longer. . . . Salt is white and pure — there is something holy in salt. . . .

October 4 [*Salem*]

Here sits thy husband in his old accustomed chamber,
where he used to sit in years gone by, before his soul
became acquainted with thine. Here I have written many
tales — many that have been burned to ashes — many
that doubtless deserved the same fate. This deserves to
be called a haunted chamber, for thousands upon thousands of visions have appeared to me in it; and some few
of them have become visible to the world. If ever I
should have a biographer, he ought to make great mention
of this chamber in my memoirs, because so much of my
lonely youth was wasted here, and here my mind and
character were formed; and here I have been glad and
hopeful, and here I have been despondent; and here I
sat a long, long time, waiting patiently for the world to
know me, and sometimes wondering why it did not know
me sooner, or whether it would ever know me at all — at
least, till I were in my grave. And sometimes (for I had
no wife then to keep my heart warm) it seemed as if I
were already in the grave, with only life enough to be
chilled and benumbed. But oftener I was happy — at
least, as happy as I then knew how to be, or was aware
of the possibility of being. By and by, the world found
me out in my lonely chamber, and called me forth, not,
indeed, with a loud roar of acclamation, but rather with
a still, small voice; and forth I went, but found nothing
in the world that I thought preferable to my old solitude,
till at length a certain Dove was revealed to me, in the
shadow of a seclusion as deep as my own had been. And
I drew nearer and nearer to the Dove, and opened my
bosom to her, and she flitted into it, and closed her wings

there — and there she nestles now and forever, keeping my heart warm, and renewing my life with her own. So now I begin to understand why I was imprisoned so many years in this lonely chamber, and why I could never break through the viewless bolts and bars; for if I had sooner made my escape into the world, I should have grown hard and rough, and been covered with earthly dust, and my heart would have become callous by rude encounters with the multitude; so that I should have been all unfit to shelter a heavenly Dove in my arms. But living in solitude till the fulness of time was come, I still kept the dew of my youth and the freshness of my heart, and had these to offer to my Dove. . . .

Ownest, in the times that I have been speaking of, I used to think that I could imagine all passions, all feelings, all states of the heart and mind; but how little did I know what it is to be mingled with another's being! Thou only hast taught me that I have a heart — thou only hast thrown a light deep downward, and upward, into my soul. Thou only hast revealed me to myself; for without thy aid, my best knowledge of myself would have been merely to know my own shadow — to watch it flickering on the wall, and mistake its fantasies for my own real actions. Indeed, we are but shadows — we are not endowed with real life, and all that seems most real about us is but the thinnest substance of a dream — till the heart is touched. That touch creates us — then we begin to be — thereby we are beings of reality, and inheritors of eternity. Now, dearest, dost thou comprehend what thou hast done for me?

Undated

A man, unknown, conscious of temptation to secret crimes, puts up a note in church, desiring the prayers of the congregation for one so tempted.

Some most secret thing, valued and honored between lovers, to be hung up in public places, and made the subject of remark by the city — remarks, sneers, and laughter.

To make a story out of a scarecrow, giving it odd attributes. From different points of view, it should appear to change — now an old man, now an old woman — a gunner, a farmer, or the Old Nick.

A coroner's inquest on a murdered man — the gathering of the jury to be described, and the characters of the members — some with secret guilt upon their souls.

To represent a man as spending life and the intensest labor in the accomplishment of some mechanical trifle — as in making a miniature coach to be drawn by fleas, or a dinner-service to be put into a cherry-stone.

A bonfire to be made of the gallows and of all symbols of evil.[1]

The device of a sundial for a monument over a grave, with some suitable motto.

A man with the right perception of things — a feeling

[1] 'Earth's Holocaust.'

within him of what is true and what is false. It might be symbolized by the talisman with which, in fairy tales, an adventurer was enabled to distinguish enchantments from realities.

A phantom of the old royal governors, or some such shadowy pageant, on the night of the evacuation of Boston by the British.[1]

—— taking my likeness, I said that such changes would come over my face that she would not know me when we met again in heaven. 'See if I do not!' said she, smiling. There was the most peculiar and beautiful humor in the point itself, and in her manner, that can be imagined.

Selfishness is one of the qualities apt to inspire love. This might be thought out at great length.

April 13, 1841 [*Brook Farm, Oak Hill*]

... Here is thy poor husband in a polar Paradise! I know not how to interpret this aspect of Nature — whether it be of good or evil omen to our enterprise. But I reflect that the Plymouth pilgrims arrived in the midst of storm and stepped ashore upon mountain snow-drifts; and, nevertheless, they prospered, and became a great people — and doubtless it will be the same with us. I laud my stars, however, that thou wilt not have thy first impressions of our future home from such a day as this. ... Through faith, I persist in believing that spring and

[1] ' Howe's Masquerade.'

summer will come in their due season; but the unregenerated man shivers within me, and suggests a doubt whether I may not have wandered within the precincts of the Arctic Circle, and chosen my heritage among everlasting snows. Dearest, provide thyself with a good stock of furs, and, if thou canst obtain the skin of a polar bear, thou wilt find it a very suitable summer dress for this region. . . .

Belovedest, I have not yet taken my first lesson in agriculture, as thou mayst well suppose — except that I went to see our cows foddered, yesterday afternoon. We have eight of our own; and the number is now increased by a transcendental heifer belonging to Miss Margaret Fuller. She is very fractious, I believe, and apt to kick over the milk-pail. Thou knowest best, whether in these traits of character, she resembles her mistress. Thy husband intends to convert himself into a milkmaid this evening, but I pray Heaven that Mr. Ripley may be moved to assign him the kindliest cow in the herd, otherwise he will perform [his] duty with fear and trembling.

Ownest wife, I like my brethren in affliction very well; and, couldst thou see us sitting round our table, at mealtimes, before the great kitchen fire, thou wouldst call it a cheerful sight. Mrs. Parker is a most comfortable woman to behold. She looks as if her ample person were stuffed full of tenderness — indeed, as if she were all one great, kind heart.

April 14, 10 A.M.

Sweetest, I did not milk the cows last night, because Mr. Ripley was afraid to trust them to my hands, or me

to their horns — I know not which. But this morning I
have done wonders. Before breakfast, I went out to the
barn, and began to chop hay for the cattle, and with such
'righteous vehemence' (as Mr. Ripley says) did I labor,
that in the space of ten minutes, I broke the machine.
Then I brought wood and replenished the fires; and
finally sat down to breakfast, and ate up a huge mound
of buckwheat cakes. After breakfast, Mr. Ripley put a
four-pronged instrument into my hands, which he gave
me to understand was called a pitchfork; and he and Mr.
Farley being armed with similar weapons, we all three
commenced a gallant attack upon a heap of manure.
This office being concluded, and thy husband having
purified himself, he sits down to finish this letter to his
most beloved wife. . . .

Belovedest, Miss Fuller's cow hooks the other cows, and
has made herself ruler of the herd, and behaves in a very
tyrannical manner. . . . Dearest, I shall make an excellent
husbandman. I feel the original Adam reviving within
me.

April 16

Ownest wife, thy husband has milked a cow! ! !
Belovedest, the herd has rebelled against the usurpa-
tion of Miss Fuller's cow; and whenever they are turned
out of the barn, she is compelled to take refuge under our
protection. So much did she impede thy husband's labors, by keeping close to him, that he found it necessary
to give her two or three gentle pats with a shovel; but
still she preferred to trust herself to my tender mercies,
rather than venture among the horns of the herd. She is

not an amiable cow; but she has a very intelligent face, and seems to be of a reflective cast of character. I doubt not that she will soon perceive the expediency of being on good terms with the rest of the sisterhood. I have not yet been twenty yards from our house and barn; but I begin to perceive that this is a beautiful place. The scenery is of a mild and placid character, with nothing bold in its character; but I think its beauties will grow upon us, and make us love it the more, the longer we live here. There is a brook, so near the house that we shall [be] able to hear it ripple in the summer evenings; but, for agricultural purposes, it has been made to flow in a straight and rectangular fashion, which does it infinite damage, as a picturesque object.

Naughtiest, it was a moment or two before I could think whom thou didst mean by Mr. Dismal View. Why, he is one of the best of the brotherhood, so far as cheerfulness goes; for, if he do not laugh himself, he makes the rest of us laugh continually. He is the quaintest and queerest personage thou didst ever see — full of dry jokes, the humor of which is so incorporated with the strange twistifications of his physiognomy, that his sayings ought to be written down, accompanied with illustrations by Cruikshank. Then he keeps quoting innumerable scraps of Latin, and makes classical allusions, while we are turning over the gold-mine; and the contrast between the nature of his employment and the character of his thoughts is irresistibly ludicrous.

April 22

. . . What an abominable hand do I scribble! but I have

been chopping wood, and turning a grindstone all the forenoon; and such occupations are likely to disturb the
equilibrium of the muscles and sinews. It is an endless
surprise to me how much work there is to be done in the
world; but, thank God, I am able to do my share of it —
and my ability increases daily. What a great, broad-
shouldered, elephantine personage I shall become by and
by!

April 28

I read no newspapers, and hardly remember who is
President; and feel as if I had no more concern with what
other people trouble themselves about, than if I dwelt in
another planet.

May 1

. . . Every day of my life makes me feel more and more
how seldom a fact is accurately stated; how, almost
invariably, when a story has passed through the mind of a
third person, it becomes, so far as regards the impression
that it makes in further repetitions, little better than a
falsehood, and this, too, though the narrator be the most
truth-seeking person in existence. How marvellous the
tendency is! . . . Is truth a fantasy which we are to pursue
forever and never grasp? . . .

My cold has almost entirely departed. Were it a sunny
day, I should consider myself quite fit for labors out of
doors; but as the ground is so damp, and the atmosphere
so chill, and the sky so sullen, I intend to keep myself on
the sick-list this one day longer, more especially as I wish
to read Carlyle on Heroes.

May 4

My cold no longer troubles me; and all this morning, I have been at work under the clear blue sky, on a hill-side. Sometimes it almost seemed as if I were at work in the sky itself; though the material in which I wrought was the ore from our gold-mine. Nevertheless, there is nothing so unseemly and disagreeable in this sort of toil as thou wouldst think. It defiles the hands, indeed, but not the soul. This gold ore is a pure and wholesome substance; else our Mother Nature would not devour it so readily, and derive so much nourishment from it, and return such a rich abundance of good grain and roots in requital of it.

The farm is growing very beautiful now — not that we yet see anything of the pease or potatoes, which we have planted; but the grass blushes green on the slopes and hollows. I wrote that word blush almost unconsciously; so we will let it go as an inspired utterance. When I go forth afield, I think of my Dove, and look beneath the stone-walls, where the verdure is richest, in hopes that a little company of violets, or some solitary bud, prophetic of the summer, may be there. . . . But not a wild-flower have I yet found. One of the boys gathered some yellow cowslips, last Sunday; but I am well content not to have found them; for they are not precisely what I should like to send my Dove, though they deserve honor and praise, because they come to us when no others will. We have our parlor here dressed in evergreen as at Christmas. That beautifullest little flower-vase of thine stands on Mr. Ripley's study-table, at which I am now writing. It contains some daffodils and some willow-blossoms. I brought it here, rather than kept it in my chamber, because I never sit there, and it gives me many pleasant emotions to look round and be surprised (for it is often a surprise, though I well know that it is there) by something which is connected with the idea of thee. . . .

We had some tableaux last evening, the principal characters being sustained by Mr. Farley and Miss Ellen Slade. They went off very well. . . .

June 1

I have been too busy to write thee a long letter by this opportunity; for I think this present life of mine gives me an antipathy to pen and ink, even more than my Custom-House experience did. . . . In the midst of toil, or after a hard day's work in the gold-mine, my soul obstinately refuses to be poured out on paper. That abominable gold-mine! Thank God, we anticipate getting rid of its treasures, in the course of two or three days! Of all hateful places, that is the worst; and I shall never comfort myself for having spent so many days of blessed sunshine there. It is my opinion, dearest, that a man's soul may be buried and perish under a dung-heap or in a furrow of the field, just as well as under a pile of money. Well, that giant, Mr. George Bradford, will probably be here to-day; so there will be no danger of thy husband being under the necessity of laboring more than he likes, hereafter. Meantime my health is perfect, and my spirits buoyant, even in the gold-mine.

August 13

Belovedest, I am very well, and not at all weary; for yesterday's rain gave us a holiday; and moreover the labors of the farm are not so pressing as they have been. And — joyful thought! — in a little more than a fortnight, thy husband will be free from his bondage — free to think of his Dove — free to enjoy Nature — free to think and feel! I do think that a greater weight will then be removed from me, than when Christian's burthen fell off at the foot of the Cross. Even my Custom-House experience was not such a thraldom and weariness; my mind and heart were freer. Oh, belovedest, labor is the curse of the world, and nobody can meddle with it, without becoming proportionably brutified! Dost thou think it a praiseworthy matter that I have spent five golden months in providing food for cows and horses? Dearest, it is not so. Thank God, my soul is not utterly buried under a dungheap. I shall yet retain it, somewhat defiled, to be sure, but not utterly unsusceptible of purification.

August 18

Dearest, I am very well; only somewhat tired with walking half a dozen miles immediately after breakfast, and raking hay ever since. We shall quite finish haying this week; and then there will be no more very hard or constant labor, during the one other week that I shall remain a slave.

August 22

I should have been reprehensible in not writing, the last time Mr. and Mrs. Ripley went to town; but I had an indispensable engagement in the bean-field, whither, indeed, I was glad to betake myself, in order to escape a parting scene with poor Mr. Farley. He was quite out of his wits, the night before, and thy husband sat up with him till long past midnight. The farm is pleasanter now that he is gone; for his unappeasable wretchedness threw a gloom over everything. Since I last wrote to thee, we have done haying; and the remainder of my bondage will probably be light. It will be a long time, however, before I shall know how to make a good use of leisure, either as regards enjoyment or literary occupation. . . .

Dearest wife, it is extremely doubtful whether Mr. Ripley will succeed in locating his community on this farm. He can bring Mr. Ellis to no terms; and the more they talk about the matter, the farther they appear to be from a settlement. Thou and I must form other plans for ourselves; for I can see few or no signs that Providence purposes to give us a home here. I am weary, weary, thrice weary of waiting so many ages. Yet what can be done? Whatever may be thy husband's gifts, he has not hitherto shown a single one that may avail to gather gold. I confess that I have strong hopes of good from this arrangement with Munroe; but when I look at the scanty avails of my past literary efforts, I do not feel authorized to expect much from the future. Well; we shall see. Other persons have bought large estates and built splendid mansions with such little books as I mean to write; so perhaps it is not unreasonable to hope that mine may enable me to build a little cottage — or, at least, to buy or hire one. But I am becoming more and more convinced, that we must not lean upon the community. Whatever is to be done, must be done by thy husband's own undivided strength. Most beloved, I shall not remain here through the winter, unless with an absolute certainty that there will be a home ready for us in the spring. Otherwise I shall return to Boston — still, however, considering myself an associate of the community; so that we may take advantage of any more favorable aspect of affairs. Dearest, how much depends on these little books! Methinks, if anything could draw out my whole strength, it would be the motives that now press upon me. Yet, after all, I must keep these considerations out of my mind, because an external pressure always disturbs, instead of assisting me.

September 3 [*Salem*]

. . . But really I should judge it to be twenty years since I left Brook Farm; and I take this to be one proof that my life there was an unnatural and unsuitable, and therefore an unreal one. It already looks like a dream behind me. The real Me was never an associate of the community; there has been a spectral Appearance there, sounding the horn at daybreak, and milking the cows, and hoeing potatoes, and raking hay, toiling and sweating in the sun, and doing me the honor to assume my name. But be thou not deceived, Dove of my heart. This Spectre was not thy husband. Nevertheless, it is somewhat remarkable that thy husband's hands have, during the past summer, grown very brown and rough; insomuch that many people persist in believing that he, after all, was the aforesaid spectral horn-sounder, cow-milker, potato-hoer, and hay-raker. But such people do not know a reality from a shadow.

September 10

Sweetest, thou dost please me much by criticising thy

husband's stories, and finding fault with them. I do not very well recollect Monsieur du Miroir; but, as to Mrs. Bullfrog ['Mosses from an Old Manse'], I give her up to thy severest reprehension. The story was written as a mere experiment in that style; it did not come from any depth within me — neither my heart nor mind had anything to do with it. I recollect that the Man of Adamant seemed a fine idea to me, when I looked at it prophetically; but I failed in giving shape and substance to the vision which I saw. I don't think it can be very good.

September 22 [Brook Farm]

Dearest love, here is thy husband again, slowly adapting himself to the life of this queer community, whence he seems to have been absent half a lifetime — so utterly has he grown apart from the spirit and manners of the place. ... Nevertheless, I was most kindly received; and the fields and woods looked very pleasant, in the bright sunshine of the day before yesterday. I had a friendlier disposition towards the farm, now that I am no longer obliged to toil in its stubborn furrows. Yesterday and to-day, however, the weather has been intolerable — cold, chill, sullen, so that it is impossible to be on kindly terms with Mother Nature. ...

Belovedest, I doubt whether I shall succeed in writing another volume of Grandfather's Library, while I remain at the farm. I have not the sense of perfect seclusion, which has always been essential to my power of producing anything. It is true, nobody intrudes into my room; but still I cannot be quiet. Nothing here is settled — everything is but beginning to arrange itself — and though thy husband would seem to have little to do with aught beside his own thoughts, still he cannot but partake of the ferment around him. My mind will not be abstracted. I must observe, and think, and feel, and content myself with catching glimpses of things which may be wrought out hereafter. Perhaps it will be quite as well that I find myself unable to set seriously about literary occupation for the present. It will be good to have a longer interval between my labor of the body and that of the mind. I shall work to the better purpose, after the beginning of November. Meantime, I shall see these people and their enterprise under a new point of view, and perhaps be able to determine whether thou and I have any call to cast in our lot among them. . . .

September 23

Belovedest, I do wish the weather would put off this sulky mood. Had it not been for the warmth and brightness of Monday, when I arrived here, I should have supposed that all sunshine had left Brook Farm forever. I have no disposition to take long walks, in such a state of the sky; nor have I any buoyancy of spirit. Thy husband is a very dull person just at this time.

September 25

. . . One thing is certain. I cannot and will not spend the winter here. The time would be absolutely thrown away so far as regards any literary labor to be performed — and then to suffer this famished yearning for thee, all winter long! It is impossible.

This intrusion of an outward necessity into labors of the imagination and intellect is, to me, very painful. . . .

I had rather a pleasant walk to a distant meadow, a day or two ago; and we found white and purple grapes in great abundance, ripe, and gushing with rich juice when the hand pressed the clusters. Didst thou know what treasures of wild grapes there are in this land? If we dwell here, we will make our own wine — of which, I know, my Dove will want a great quantity.

September 28

A picnic party in the woods, yesterday, in honor of Frank Dana's birthday, he being six years old.[1] I strolled into the woods, after dinner, with Mr. Bradford, and in a lonesome glade we met the apparition of an Indian chief, dressed in appropriate costume of blankets, feathers, and paint, and armed with a musket. Almost at the same time, a young gypsy fortune-teller came from among the trees, and proposed to tell my fortune; which while she was doing, the goddess Diana, known on earth as Miss Ellen Slade, let fly an arrow, and hit me smartly in the hand. The fortune-teller and goddess were a fine contrast, Diana being a blonde, fair, quiet, with a moderate composure; and the gypsy (Ora Gennett) a bright, vivacious, dark-haired, rich-complexioned damsel — both of them very pretty, at least pretty enough to make fifteen years enchanting. Accompanied by these denizens of the wild wood, we went onward, and came to a company of fantastic figures, arranged in a ring for a dance or game. There was a Swiss girl, an Indian squaw, a negro

---

[1] 'The Blithedale Romance,' chap. xxiv.

of the Jim Crow order, one or two foresters, and several people in Christian attire, besides children of all ages. Then followed childish games, in which the grown people took part with mirth enough — while I, whose nature it is to be a mere spectator both of sport and serious business, lay under the trees and looked on. Meanwhile, Mr. Emerson and Miss Fuller, who arrived an hour or two before, came forth into the little glade where we were assembled. Here followed much talk. The ceremonies of the day concluded with a cold collation of cakes and fruit. All was pleasant enough — an excellent piece of work — 'would 'twere done!' It has left a fantastic impression on my memory, this intermingling of wild and fabulous characters with real and homely ones, in the secluded nook of the woods. I remember them, with the sunlight breaking through overshadowing branches, and they appearing and disappearing confusedly — perhaps starting out of the earth; as if the every-day laws of nature were suspended for this particular occasion. There were the children, too, laughing and sporting about, as if they were at home among such strange shapes — and anon bursting into loud uproar of lamentation, when the rude gambols of the merry archers chanced to overturn them. And apart, with a shrewd, Yankee observation of the scene, stands our friend Orange, a thickset, sturdy figure, in his blue frock, enjoying the fun well enough, yet rather laughing with a perception of its nonsensicalness, than at all entering into the spirit of the thing.

October 8

In my walk yesterday forenoon I passed an old house

which seemed to be quite deserted. It was a two-story, wooden house, dark and weather-beaten. The front windows, some of them, were shattered and open, and others were boarded up. Trees and shrubbery were growing neglected, so as quite to block up the lower part. There was an aged barn near at hand, so ruinous that it had been necessary to prop it up. There were two old carts, both of which had lost a wheel. Everything was in keeping. At first I supposed that there would be no inhabitants in such a dilapidated place; but, passing on, I looked back, and saw a ruinous and infirm old man at the angle of the house, its fit occupant. The grass, however, was very green and beautiful around this dwelling, and, the sunshine falling brightly on it, the whole effect was cheerful and pleasant. It seemed as if the world was so pleasant that this desolate old place, where there was never to be any more hope and happiness, could not at all lessen the general effect of joy.

October 9

Still dismal weather. Our household, being composed in great measure of children and young people, is generally a cheerful one enough, even in gloomy weather. For a week past we have been especially gladdened with a little seamstress from Boston, about seventeen years old; but of such a *petite* figure, that, at first view, one would take her to be hardly in her teens.[1] She is very vivacious and smart, laughing and singing and talking all the time — talking sensibly; but still, taking the view of matters that a city girl naturally would. If she were larger than she is,

[1] Priscilla in 'The Blithedale Romance.'

and of less pleasing aspect, I think she might be intolerable; but being so small, and with a fair skin, and as healthy
as a wild-flower, she is really very agreeable; and to look
at her face is like being shone upon by a ray of the sun.
She never walks, but bounds and dances along, and this
motion, in her diminutive person, does not give the idea
of violence. It is like a bird, hopping from twig to twig,
and chirping merrily all the time. Sometimes she is rather
vulgar, but even that works well enough into her character,
and accords with it. On continued observation, one dis-
covers that she is not a little girl, but really a little woman,
with all the prerogatives and liabilities of a woman. This
gives a new aspect to her, while the girlish impression still
continues, and is strangely combined with the sense that
this frolicsome maiden has the material for that sober character, a wife. She romps with the boys, runs races with
them in the yard, and up and down the stairs, and is
heard scolding laughingly at their rough play. She asks
William Allen to place her 'on top of that horse,' whereupon he puts his large brown hands about her waist, and,
swinging her to and fro, places her on horseback. William
threatens to rivet two horse shoes round her neck, for
having clambered, with the other girls and boys, upon a
load of hay, whereby the said load lost its balance and slid
off the cart. She strings the seed-berries of roses together,
making a scarlet necklace of them, which she wears
about her neck. She gathers flowers of everlasting to
wear in her bonnet, arranging them with the skill of a
dress-maker. In the evening, she sits singing by the hour,
with the musical part of the establishment, often breaking
into laughter, whereto she is incited by the tricks of the

boys. The last thing you hear of her, she is tripping up stairs to bed, talking lightsomely or singing; and you meet her in the morning, the very image of bright morn itself, smiling briskly at you, so that one takes her for a promise of cheerfulness through the day. Be it said, with all the rest, that there is a perfect maiden modesty in her deportment, though I doubt whether the boys, in their rompings with her, do not feel that she has passed out of her childhood. This lightsome little maid has left us this morning, and the last thing I saw of her was her vivacious face peeping through the curtain of the cariole, and nodding a gay farewell to the family, who were shouting their adieus at the door. With her other merits, she is an excellent daughter, and supports her mother by the labor of her hands. It would be difficult to conceive beforehand how much can be added to the enjoyment of a household by mere sunniness of temper and smartness of disposition; for her intellect is very ordinary, and she never says anything worth hearing, or even laughing at, in itself. But she herself is an expression well worth studying.

October 18

Belovedest, my spirit is moved to talk to thee to-day about these magnetic miracles and to beseech thee to take no part in them. I am unwilling that a power should be exercised on thee of which we know neither the origin nor the consequence, and the phenomena of which seem rather calculated to bewilder us, than to teach us any truths about the present or future state of being. . . . Supposing that this power arises from the transfusion of one spirit into another, it seems to me that the sacredness of an individual is violated by it; there would be an intrusion into thy holy of holies. . . . Now, ownest wife, I have no faith whatever that people are raised to the seventh heaven, or to any heaven at all, or that they gain any insight into the mysteries of life beyond death, by means of this strange science. Without distrusting that the phenomena which thou tellest me of, and others as remarkable, have really occurred, I think that they are to be accounted for as the result of a physical and material, not of a spiritual, influence. *Opium* has produced many a brighter vision of heaven (and just as susceptible of proof) than those which thou recountest. . . . And what delusion can be more lamentable and mischievous, than to mistake the physical and material for the spiritual? What so miserable as to lose the soul's true, though hidden, knowledge and consciousness of heaven, in the mist of an earth-born vision? Thou shalt not do this. If thou wouldst know what heaven is, before thou comest thither hand in hand with thy husband, then retire into the depths of thine own spirit, and thou wilt find it there among holy thoughts and feelings; but do not degrade high Heaven and its inhabitants into any such symbols and forms as those which Miss Larned describes — do not let an earthly effluence from Mrs. Park's corporeal system bewilder thee and perhaps contaminate something spiritual and sacred. I should as soon think of seeking revelations of the future state in the rottenness of the grave — where so many do seek it. . . .

Thou wilt know that the view which I take of this matter is caused by no want of faith in mysteries, but from a deep reverence of the soul, and of the mysteries which it knows within itself, but never transmits to the earthly eye and ear. Keep thy imagination sane — that is one of the truest conditions of communion with Heaven.

October 27

Fringed gentians — I found the last, probably, that will be seen this year, growing on the margin of the brook. [Last Brook Farm entry.]

1842–1845

[OF the early months of 1842, little or no record remains, either in the form of journals or of letters, and we know of no literary work that was certainly done at this time. In July, Hawthorne and Sophia Peabody were married in Boston, and removed at once to Concord, where, until late in 1845, they were occupants of the Ripley homestead, the Old Manse. These years, in spite of increasing financial anxieties, were the happiest of Hawthorne's life; and the journals which he kept in Concord, especially during the summers when literary work was too uncongenial to be persevered in, reflect, as if in the cool light of early morning or the rich light of a late summer afternoon, the mellow pastoral contentment which he and his wife enjoyed.

As a resident of Concord, Hawthorne of course had for neighbors several of the Greeks who at that time stood out against the general barbarism of American life; he himself was now an author of some little reputation, and it was but natural that Emerson, Thoreau, Margaret Fuller, Ellery Channing, and the Hoars, should make overtures toward social intercourse. What Hawthorne himself made of these eminent or near-eminent contemporaries is recorded with quiet candor and considerable insight in his journals for these years.]

Undated [*Salem or Boston*]

To trace out the influence of a frightful and disgraceful

crime in debasing and destroying a character naturally high and noble, the guilty person being alone conscious of the crime.[1]

A man, virtuous in his general conduct, but committing habitually some monstrous crime — as murder — and doing this without the sense of guilt, but with a peaceful conscience. Habit, probably, has reconciled him to it; but something (for instance, discovery) occurs to make him sensible of his enormity. His horror then.

A prophecy, somewhat in the style of Swift's about Partridge, but embracing various events and personages.

An incident that befell Dr. Harris, while a Junior at college. Being in great want of money to buy shirts or other necessaries, and not knowing how to obtain it, he set out on a walk from Cambridge to Boston. On the way he cut a stick, and, after walking a short distance, perceived that something had become attached to the end of it. It proved to be a gold ring, with the motto, 'God speed thee, friend.'

People with false hair and other artifices may be supposed to deceive Death himself, so that he does not know when their hour is come.

Bees are sometimes drowned in the honey which they collect — so some writers lost in their collected learning.

[1] 'The Scarlet Letter'; 'The Marble Faun.'

A father confessor — his reflections on character and the contrast of the inward man with the outward, as he looks around on his congregation, all whose secret sins are known to him.

A person with an ice-cold hand — his right hand, which people ever afterwards remember when once they have grasped it.

The famous characters of history — to imagine their spirits now extant on earth, in the guise of various public or private personages.

The case quoted in Combe's 'Physiology' of a young man of great talents and profound knowledge of chemistry, who had in view some new discovery of importance. In order to put his mind into the highest possible activity, he shut himself up for several successive days, and used various methods of excitement. He had a singing-girl, he drank spirits, smelled penetrating odors, sprinkled Cologne-water round the room, etc., etc. Eight days thus passed, when he was seized with a fit of frenzy which terminated in mania.

A spendthrift — in one sense he has his money's worth by the purchase of large lots of repentance and other dolorous commodities.

To symbolize moral or spiritual disease by disease of the body; as thus — when a person committed any sin, it might appear in some form on the body — this to be wrought out.

A physician for the cure of moral diseases.

To point out the moral slavery of one who deems himself a free man.

A stray leaf from the book of fate, picked up in the street.

August 5, 1842 [*Concord*]

A rainy day — a rainy day — and I do verily believe there is no sunshine in this world, except what beams from my wife's eyes. At present she has laid her strict command on me to take pen in hand, and I am therefore banished to the little ten-foot-square apartment misnamed my study; but perhaps the dismalness of the day and the dulness of my solitude will be the prominent characteristics of what I write. And what is there to write about? Happiness has no succession of events, because it is a part of eternity; and we have been living in eternity ever since we came to this old manse. Like Enoch, we seem to have been translated to the other state of being without having passed through death. Our spirits must have flitted away unconsciously in the deep and quiet rapture of some long embrace, and we can only perceive that we have cast off our mortal part by the more real and earnest life of our souls. Externally, our Paradise has very much the aspect of a pleasant old domicile on earth. This antique house — for it looks antique, though it was created by Providence expressly for our use, and at the precise time when we wanted it — stands behind a noble avenue of balm-of-Gilead trees; and when we chance to observe a passing traveller through the sunshine and the shadow of this long avenue, his figure appears too dim and remote to disturb our sense of blissful seclusion. Few, indeed, are the mortals who venture within our sacred precincts. George Prescott, who has not yet grown earthly enough, I suppose, to be debarred from occasional visits to Paradise, comes daily to bring three pints of milk from some ambrosial cow; occasionally, also, he makes an offering of mortal flowers at the shrine of a certain angelic personage. Mr. Emerson comes sometimes, and has been so far favored as to be feasted (with a gnome, yclept Ellery Channing) on our nectar and ambrosia. Mr. Thoreau has twice listened to the music of the spheres, which, for our private convenience, we have packed into a musical-box. Elizabeth Hoar, who is much more at home among spirits than among fleshly bodies, came hither a few times merely to welcome us to the ethereal world; but latterly she has vanished into some other region of infinite space. One rash mortal, on the second Sunday after our arrival, obtruded himself upon us in a gig. There have since been three or four callers, who preposterously think that the courtesies of the lower world are to be responded to by people whose home is in Paradise. I must not forget to mention that the butcher comes twice or thrice a week; and we have so far improved upon the custom of Adam and Eve, that we generally furnish forth our feasts with portions of some delicate calf or lamb, whose unspotted innocence entitles them to the happiness of becoming our sustenance. Would that I were permitted to record the celestial dainties that kind Heaven provided for us on the first day of our arrival! Never, surely, was such food heard of on earth — at least, not by me. Well, the above-mentioned persons are nearly all that have intruded into the hallowed shade of our avenue; except, indeed, a certain sinner who came to bargain for the grass in our orchard, and another who came with a new cistern. For it is one of the drawbacks upon our Eden that it contains no water fit either to drink or to bathe in; so that the showers have become, in good truth, a godsend. I wonder why Providence does not cause a clear, cold fountain to bubble up at our doorstep; methinks it would not be unreasonable to pray for such a favor. At present we are under the ridiculous necessity of sending to the outer world for water. Only imagine Adam trudging out of Paradise with a bucket in each hand, to get water to drink, or for Eve to bathe in! Intolerable! I shall absolutely think myself wronged, unless I find the aforesaid fountain bubbling at our doorstep, the next time I look out. In other respects Providence has treated us pretty tolerably well; but here I shall expect something further to be done. Also, in the way of future favors, a kitten would be very acceptable. Animals (except, perhaps, a pig) seem never out of place, even in the most paradisiacal spheres. And, by the bye, a young colt comes up our avenue, now and then, to crop the seldom-trodden herbage; and so does a company of cows, whose sweet breath well repays us for the food which they obtain. There are likewise a few hens, whose quiet cluck is heard pleasantly about the house. A black dog sometimes stands at the farther extremity of the avenue, and looks wistfully towards the house; but when I whistle to him, he puts his tail between his legs, and trots away. Foolish dog! if he had more faith, he should have bones enough.

August 6

I bathe once, and often twice a day, in our river; but
one dip into the salt sea would be worth more than a
whole week's soaking in such a lifeless tide. I have read of
a river somewhere (whether it be in classic regions, or
among our Western Indians, I know not) which seemed
to dissolve and steal away the vigor of those who bathed
in it. Perhaps our stream will be found to have this
property. Its water, however, is pleasant in its immediate
effect, being as soft as milk, and always warmer than the
air. Its hue has a slight tinge of gold; and my limbs, when
I behold them through its medium, look tawny. I am not
aware that the inhabitants of Concord resemble their
native river in any of their moral characteristics; their
forefathers, certainly, seem to have had the energy and
impetus of a mountain torrent, rather than the torpor of
this listless stream — as was proved by the blood with
which they stained their River of Peace. There are said to
be plenty of fish in it; but my most important captures
have been a mud-turtle and an enormous eel. The former
made his escape to his native element — the latter we ate;
and truly he had the taste of the whole river in his flesh,
with a very prominent flavor of mud. On the whole,
Concord River is no great favorite of mine; but I am glad
to have any river at all so near at hand, being just at the
bottom of our orchard. Neither is it without a degree and
kind of picturesqueness, both in its nearness and in the
distance, when a blue gleam from its surface, among the
green meadows and woods, seems like an open eye in
earth's countenance. Pleasant it is, too, to behold a little
flat-bottomed skiff gliding along its quiet bosom, which

yields lazily to the stroke of the paddle, and allows the boat to go against its current almost as freely as with it. Pleasant, too, to watch an angler, as he strays along the margin, sometimes sheltering himself behind a tuft of bushes, and trailing his line along the water, in hopes to catch a pickerel. But, taking the river for all in all, I can find nothing more fit to compare it with, than one of the half-torpid earthworms, which I dig up for the purpose of bait. The worm is sluggish, and so is the river — the river is muddy, and so is the worm — you hardly know whether either of them is alive or dead; but still, in the course of time, they both manage to creep away. The best aspect of our river is when there is a northwest breeze curling its surface, in a bright, sunshiny day; it then assumes a vivacity not its own. Moonlight, also, gives it beauty — as it does to all scenery of earth or water.

August 9

My fancy has always found something very interesting in an orchard — especially an old orchard. Apple-trees, and all fruit-trees, have a domestic character, which brings them into relationship with man; they have lost, in a great measure, the wild nature of the forest-tree, and have grown humanized, by receiving the care of man, and by contributing to his wants. They have become a part of the family; and their individual characters are as well understood and appreciated as those of the human members. One tree is harsh and crabbed — another mild — one is churlish and illiberal — another exhausts itself with its free-hearted bounties. Even the shapes of apple-

trees have great individuality, into such strange pos-
tures do they put themselves, and thrust their contorted
branches so grotesquely in all directions. And when they
have stood around a house for many years, and held converse with successive dynasties of occupants, and gladdened their hearts so often in the fruitful autumn, then it
would seem almost sacrilege to cut them down. . . .

I have serious thoughts of inducting a new incumbent
in this part of the parsonage [the pig-sty]. It is our duty
to support a pig, even if we have no design of feasting
upon him; and, for my own part, I have a great sympathy
and interest for the whole race of porkers, and should
have much amusement in studying the character of a pig.
Perhaps I might try to bring out his moral and intellectual
nature, and cultivate his affections. A cat, too, and perhaps a dog, would be desirable additions to our household.

August 13

My life, at this time, is more like that of a boy, externally, than it has been since I was really a boy. It is
usually supposed that the cares of life come with matri-
mony; but I seem to have cast off all care, and live on
with as much easy trust in Providence as Adam could
possibly have felt before he had learned that there was a
world beyond Paradise. My chief anxiety consists in
watching the prosperity of my vegetables, in observing
how they are affected by the rain or sunshine, in lament-
ing the blight of one squash and rejoicing at the luxurious
growth of another. It is as if the original relation between
Man and Nature were restored in my case, and that I
were to look exclusively to her for the support of my Eve

and myself — to trust to her for food and clothing, and all things needful, with the full assurance that she would not fail me. The fight with the world — the struggle of a man among men — the agony of the universal effort to wrench the means of living from a host of greedy competitors — all this seems like a dream to me. My business is merely to live and to enjoy; and whatever is essential to life and enjoyment will come as naturally as the dew from heaven. This is, practically at least, my faith. And so I awake in the morning with a boyish thoughtlessness as to how the outgoings of the day are to be provided for, and its incomings rendered certain. After breakfast, I go forth into my garden, and gather whatever the bountiful Mother has made fit for our present sustenance; and of late days she generally gives me two squashes and a cucumber, and promises me green corn and shell-beans very soon. Then I pass down through our orchard to the riverside, and ramble along its margin in search of flowers. Usually I discern a fragrant white lily, here and there along the shore, growing, with sweet prudishness, beyond the grasp of mortal arm. But it does not escape me so. I know what is its fitting destiny better than the silly flower knows for itself; so I wade in, heedless of wet trousers, and seize the shy lily by its slender stem. Thus I make prize of five or six, which are as many as usually blossom within my reach in a single morning; — some of them partially worm-eaten or blighted, like virgins with an eating sorrow at the heart; others as fair and perfect as Nature's own idea was, when she first imagined this lovely flower. A perfect pond-lily is the most satisfactory of flowers. Besides these, I gather whatever else of beauti-

ful chances to be growing in the moist soil by the riverside — an amphibious tribe, yet with more richness and
grace than the wild-flowers of the deep and dry woodlands
and hedgerows — sometimes the white arrow-head, always the blue spires and broad green leaves of the pickerel
flower, which contrast and harmonize so well with the
white lilies. For the last two or three days, I have found
scattered stalks of the cardinal-flower, the gorgeous scarlet of which it is a joy even to remember. The world is
made brighter and sunnier by flowers of such a hue; even
perfume, which otherwise is the soul and spirit of a flower,
may be spared when it arrays itself in this scarlet glory.
It is a flower of thought and feeling, too; it seems to have
its roots deep down in the hearts of those who gaze at it.
Other bright flowers sometimes impress me as wanting
sentiment; but it is not so with this.

Well, having made up my bunch of flowers, I return
with them to my wife. . . . I ascend to my study, and
generally read, or perchance scribble in this journal, and
otherwise suffer Time to loiter onward at his own pleasure,
till the dinner-hour. In pleasant days, the chief event of
the afternoon, and the happiest one of the day, is our
walk. She must describe these walks; for where she and I
have enjoyed anything together, I always deem my pen
unworthy and inadequate to record it. So comes the
night; and I look back upon a day spent in what the world
would call idleness, and for which I myself can suggest no
more appropriate epithet; and which, nevertheless, I cannot feel to have been spent amiss. True, it might be a sin
and shame, in such a world as ours, to spend a lifetime in
this manner; but for a few summer weeks it is good to live

as if this world were heaven. And so it is, and so it shall be, although, in a little while, a flitting shadow of earthly care and toil will mingle itself with our realities.

August 15

... About nine o'clock, Hillard and I set out for a walk to Walden Pond, calling by the way at Mr. Emerson's, to obtain his guidance or directions. He, from a scruple of his external conscience, detained us till after the people had got into church, and then accompanied us in his own illustrious person. We turned aside a little from our way, to visit Mr. Edmund Hosmer, a yeoman, of whose homely and self-acquired wisdom Mr. Emerson has a very high opinion. We found him walking in his fields, a short but stalwart and sturdy personage of middle age, with a face of shrewd and kind expression, and manners of natural courtesy. He seemed to have a very free flow of talk, and not much diffidence about his own opinions; for, with a little induction from Mr. Emerson, he began to discourse about the state of the nation, agriculture, and business in general, uttering thoughts that had come to him at the plough, and which had a sort of flavor of the fresh earth about them. I was not impressed with any remarkable originality in his views, but they were sensible and characteristic, and had grown in the soil where we found them. Methought, however, the good yeoman was not quite so natural as he may have been at a former period; the simplicity of his character has probably suffered, in some degree, by his detecting the impression which he makes on those around him. There is a circle, I suppose, who look up to him as an oracle; and so

he inevitably assumes the oracular manner, and speaks as
if truth and wisdom were uttering themselves by his voice.
Mr. Emerson has risked the doing him much mischief, by
putting him in print — a trial which few persons can sus-
tain, without losing their unconsciousness. But, after all,
a man gifted with thought and expression, whatever his
rank in life, and his mode of uttering himself, whether by
pen or tongue, cannot be expected to go through the
world without finding himself out — and as all such self-
discoveries are partial and imperfect, they do more harm
than good to the character. Mr. Hosmer is more natural
than ninety-nine men out of a hundred; and he is certainly a man of intellectual and moral substance, a sturdy
fact, a reality, something to be felt and touched. It
would be amusing to draw a parallel between him and
his admirer, Mr. Emerson — the mystic, stretching his
hand out of cloud-land, in vain search for something
real; and the man of sturdy sense, all whose ideas seem
to be dug out of his mind, hard and substantial, as
he digs potatoes, beets, carrots, and turnips, out of the
earth. Mr. Emerson is a great searcher for facts; but
they seem to melt away and become insubstantial in his
grasp.

After leaving Mr. Hosmer, we proceeded through
wood-paths to Walden Pond, picking blackberries of
enormous size along the way. . . . After Mr. Emerson left
us, Hillard and I bathed in the pond, and it does really
seem as if not only my corporeal person, but my moral
self had received a cleansing from that bath. A good deal
of mud and river slime had accumulated on my soul; but
these bright waters washed it all away.

August 22

I took a walk through the woods, yesterday afternoon [Sunday], to Mr. Emerson's, with a book which Margaret Fuller had left behind her, after a call on Saturday eve. I missed the nearest way, and wandered into a very secluded portion of the forest — for forest it might justly be called, so dense and sombre was the shade of oaks and pines. Once I wandered into a tract so overgrown with bushes and underbrush that I could scarcely force a passage through. Nothing is more annoying than a walk of this kind — to be tormented by an innumerable host of petty impediments; it incenses and depresses me at the same time. Always when I flounder into the midst of a tract of bushes, which cross and intertwine themselves about my legs, and brush my face, and seize hold of my clothes with a multitudinous gripe — always, in such a difficulty, I feel as if it were almost as well to lie down and die in rage and despair as to go one step further. It is laughable, after I have got out of the scrape, to think how miserably it affected me for the moment; but I had better learn patience betimes, for there are many such bushy tracts in this vicinity, on the margins of meadows; and my walks will often lead me into them. Escaping from the bushes, I soon came to an open space among the woods — a very lonely spot, with the tall old trees standing around, as quietly as if nobody had intruded there throughout the whole summer. A company of crows were holding their sabbath in the tops of some of the trees; apparently they felt themselves injured or insulted by my presence; for, with one consent, they began to caw — caw — caw — and, launching themselves sullenly on the air, took flight

to some securer solitude. Mine, probably, was the first
human shape that they had seen, all day long — at least,
if they had been stationary in that spot; but perhaps they
had winged their way over miles and miles of country —
had breakfasted on the summit of Graylock, and dined at
the base of Wachusett, and were merely come to sup and
sleep among the quiet woods of Concord. But it was my
impression, at the time, that they had sat still and silent
in the tops of the trees, all through the Sabbath day; and
I felt like one who should unawares disturb an assembly
of worshippers. A crow, however, has no real pretension
to religion, in spite of their gravity of mien and black attire; they are certainly thieves, and probably infidels.
Nevertheless, their voices, yesterday, were in admirable
accordance with the influences of the quiet, sunny, warm,
yet autumnal afternoon; they were so far above my head,
that their loud clamor added to the quiet of the scene, instead of disturbing it. There was no other sound, except
the song of the crickets, which is but an audible stillness;
for, though it be very loud, and heard afar, yet the mind
does not take note of it as a sound, so entirely does it
mingle and lose its individuality among the other characteristics of coming autumn. Alas, for the summer! The
grass is still verdant on the hills and in the valleys; the
foliage of the trees is as dense as ever, and as green; the
flowers are abundant along the margin of the river, and in
the hedge-rows, and deep among the woods; the days,
too, are as fervid as they were a month ago — and yet in
every breath of wind, and in every beam of sunshine,
there is an autumnal influence. I know not how to describe it; — methinks there is a sort of coolness amid all

the heat, and a mildness in the brightest of the sunshine. A breeze cannot stir without thrilling me with the breath of autumn, and I behold its pensive glory in the far, golden gleams among the long shadows of the trees. The flowers, even the brightest of them — the golden-rod and the gorgeous cardinals — all the most glorious flowers of the year — have this gentle sadness amid their pomp. Pensive autumn is expressed in the glow of every one of them. I have felt this influence earlier in some years than in others. Sometimes autumn may be perceived even in the early days of July. There is no other feeling like that caused by this faint, doubtful, yet real perception, or rather prophecy, of the year's decay — so deliciously sweet and sad in the same breath.

After leaving the book at Mr. Emerson's I returned through the woods, and, entering Sleepy Hollow, I perceived a lady reclining near the path which bends along its verge. It was Margaret herself. She had been there the whole afternoon, meditating or reading; for she had a book in her hand, with some strange title, which I did not understand and have forgotten. She said that nobody had broken her solitude, and was just giving utterance to a theory that no inhabitant of Concord ever visited Sleepy Hollow, when we saw a whole group of people entering the sacred precincts. Most of them followed a path that led them remote from us; but an old man passed near us, and smiled to see Margaret lying on the ground, and me sitting by her side. He made some remark about the beauty of the afternoon, and withdrew himself into the shadow of the wood. Then we talked about autumn, and about the pleasures of getting lost in the woods, and

about the crows, whose voices Margaret had heard, and
about the experiences of early childhood, whose influence
remains upon the character after the recollection of them
has passed away — and about the sight of mountains
from a distance, and the view from their summits — and
about other matters of high and low philosophy. In the
midst of our talk, we heard footsteps above us, on the
high bank; and while the intruder was still hidden among
the trees, he called to Margaret, of whom he had gotten a
glimpse. Then he emerged from the green shade; and,
behold, it was Mr. Emerson, who, in spite of his clerical
consecration, had found no better way of spending the
Sabbath than to ramble among the woods. He appeared
to have had a pleasant time; for he said that there were
Muses in the woods to-day, and whispers to be heard in
the breezes. It being now nearly six o'clock, we separated
— Mr. Emerson and Margaret towards his house, and I
towards mine, where my little wife was very busy getting
tea. By the bye, Mr. Emerson gave me an invitation
to dinner to-day, to be complied with or not, as might
suit my convenience at the time; and it happens not to
suit. . . .

Last evening there was the most beautiful moonlight
that ever hallowed this earthly world; and when I went to
bathe in the river, which was as calm as death, it seemed
like plunging down into the sky. But I had rather be on
earth than even in the seventh heaven, just now.

August 27

George Bradford, my old fellow-laborer at the Community, called on me last evening, and dined here to-

day. He has been cultivating vegetables at Plymouth
this summer, and selling them in the market. What a
singular mode of life for a man of education and refinement — to spend his days in hard and earnest bodily
toil, and then to convey the products of his labor, in a
wheelbarrow, to the public market, and there retail them
out — a peck of peas or beans, a bunch of turnips, a
squash, a dozen ears of green corn! Few men, without
some eccentricity of character, would have the moral
strength to do this; and it is very striking to find such
strength combined with the utmost gentleness, and an
uncommon regularity of nature. Occasionally he returns
for a day or two to resume his place among scholars and
idle people, as, for instance, the present week, when he has
thrown aside his spade and hoe to attend the Commencement at Cambridge. He is a rare man — a perfect original, yet without any one salient point; a character to be
felt and understood, but almost impossible to describe;
for, should you seize upon any characteristic, it would inevitably be altered and distorted in the process of writing
it down.

August 30

In the afternoon Mr. Emerson called, bringing Mr.
Frost, the colleague and successor of Mr. Ripley. He is a
good sort of humdrum parson enough, and well fitted to
increase the stock of manuscript sermons, of which there
must be a fearful quantity already in the world. I find
that my respect for clerical people, as such, and my faith
in the utility of their office, decreases daily. We certainly
do need a new revelation — a new system — for there

seems to be no life in the old one. Mr. Frost, however, is
probably one of the best and most useful of his class, because no suspicion of the necessity of his profession, constituted as it now is, to mankind, and of his own useful-
ness and success in it, has hitherto disturbed him; and
therefore he labors with faith and confidence, as ministers
did a hundred years ago, when they had really something
to do in the world. . . .

I have a liking for vagrants of all sorts, and never, that
I know of, refused my mite to a wandering beggar, when I
had anything in my own pocket. There is so much
wretchedness in the world, that we may safely take the
word of any mortal professing to need our assistance; and,
even should we be deceived, still the good to ourselves re-
sulting from a kind act is worth more than the trifle by
which we purchase it. It is desirable, I think, that such
persons should be permitted to roam through our land of
plenty, scattering the seeds of tenderness and charity, as
birds of passage bear the seeds of precious plants from
land to land, without even dreaming of the office which
they perform.

September 1

Mr. Thoreau dined with us yesterday. He is a singular
character — a young man with much of wild original nature still remaining in him; and so far as he is sophisticated, it is in a way and method of his own. He is as
ugly as sin, long-nosed, queer-mouthed, and with uncouth
and rustic, although courteous manners, corresponding
very well with such an exterior. But his ugliness is of an
honest and agreeable fashion, and becomes him much

better than beauty. He was educated, I believe, at Cambridge, and formerly kept school in this town; but for two or three years back, he has repudiated all regular modes of getting a living, and seems inclined to lead a sort of Indian life among civilized men — an Indian life, I mean, as respects the absence of any systematic effort for a livelihood. He has been for some time an inmate of Mr. Emerson's family; and, in requital, he labors in the garden, and performs such other offices as may suit him — being entertained by Mr. Emerson for the sake of what true manhood there is in him. Mr. Thoreau is a keen and delicate observer of nature — a genuine observer — which, I suspect, is almost as rare a character as even an original poet; and Nature, in return for his love, seems to adopt him as her especial child, and shows him secrets which few others are allowed to witness. He is familiar with beast, fish, fowl, and reptile, and has strange stories to tell of adventures and friendly passages with these lower brethren of mortality. Herb and flower, likewise, wherever they grow, whether in garden or wildwood, are his familiar friends. He is also on intimate terms with the clouds, and can tell the portents of storms. It is a characteristic trait, that he has a great regard for the memory of the Indian tribes, whose wild life would have suited him so well; and, strange to say, he seldom walks over a ploughed field without picking up an arrow-point, spear-head, or other relic of the red man, as if their spirits willed him to be the inheritor of their simple wealth.

With all this he has more than a tincture of literature — a deep and true taste for poetry, especially the elder poets, although more exclusive than is desirable, like all other Transcendentalists, so far as I am acquainted with them. He is a good writer — at least he has written one good article, a rambling disquisition on Natural History, in the last Dial, which, he says, was chiefly made up from journals of his own observations. Methinks this article gives a very fair image of his mind and character — so true, innate, and literal in observation, yet giving the spirit as well as the letter of what he sees, even as a lake reflects its wooded banks, showing every leaf, yet giving the wild beauty of the whole scene. Then there are passages in the article of cloudy and dreamy metaphysics, partly affected, and partly the natural exhalations of his intellect; and also passages where his thoughts seem to measure and attune themselves into spontaneous verse, as they rightfully may, since there is real poetry in him. There is a basis of good sense and of moral truth, too, throughout the article, which also is a reflection of his character; for he is not unwise to think and feel, however imperfect is his own mode of action. On the whole, I find him a healthy and wholesome man to know.

After dinner (at which we cut the first watermelon and muskmelon that our garden has grown), Mr. Thoreau and I walked up the bank of the river, and at a certain point he shouted for his boat. Forthwith a young man paddled it across, and Mr. Thoreau and I voyaged farther up the stream, which soon became more beautiful than any picture, with its dark and quiet sheet of water, half shaded, half sunny, between high and wooded banks. The late rains have swollen the stream so much that many trees are standing up to their knees, as it were, in the water, and boughs, which lately swung high in air, now dip and drink deep of the passing wave. As to the poor cardinals which glowed upon the bank a few days since, I could see only a few of their scarlet caps, peeping above the tide. Mr. Thoreau managed the boat so perfectly, either with two paddles or with one, that it seemed instinct with his own will, and to require no physical effort to guide it. He said that, when some Indians visited Concord a few years ago, he found that he had acquired, without a teacher, their precise method of propelling and steering a canoe. Nevertheless being in want of money, the poor fellow was desirous of selling the boat of which he was so fit a pilot, and which was built by his own hands; so I agreed to give him his price (only seven dollars), and accordingly became the possessor of the Musketaquid. I wish I could acquire the aquatic skill of the original owner at as reasonable a rate.

September 2

In the evening, Ellery Channing called to see us, wishing to talk with me about a Boston periodical, of which he had heard that I was to be editor, and to which he desired to contribute. He is one of those queer and clever young men whom Mr. Emerson (that everlasting rejector of all that is, and seeker for he knows not what) is continually picking up by way of a genius. There is nothing very peculiar about him—some originality and self-inspiration in his character, but none, or very little, in his intellect. Nevertheless, the lad himself seems to feel as if he were a genius, and ridiculously enough looks upon his own verses as too sacred to be sold for money. Prose he will sell to the highest bidder; but measured feet and jingling lines are not to

be exchanged for gold — which, indeed, is not very likely
to be offered for them. I like him well enough, however;
but, after all, these originals in a small way, after one has
seen a few of them, become more dull and commonplace
than even those who keep the ordinary pathway of life.
They have a rule and routine, which they follow with as
little variety as other people do their rule and routine; and
when once we have fathomed their mystery, nothing can
be more wearisome. An innate perception and reflection
of truth give the only sort of originality that does not
finally grow intolerable.

September 4

I made a voyage in the Pond-Lily all by myself yesterday morning, and was much encouraged by my success in
causing the boat to go whither I would. I have always
liked to be afloat, but I think I have never adequately
conceived of the enjoyment till now, when I begin to feel
a power over that which supports me. I suppose I must
have felt something like this sense of triumph when I first
learned to swim; but I have forgotten it. Oh that I could
run wild! — that is, that I could put myself into a true
relation with Nature, and be on friendly terms with all
congenial elements.

October 10

A week or two ago (September 27 and 28) I went on a
pedestrian excursion with Mr. Emerson, and was gone two
days and one night, it being the first and only night that
I have slept away from my belovedest wife. We spent the
night at the village of Harvard, and the next morning

walked three miles farther, to the Shaker village, where we breakfasted. Mr. Emerson had a theological discussion with two of the Shaker brethren; but the particulars of it have faded from my memory; and all the other adventures of the tour have now so lost their freshness that I cannot adequately recall them. Wherefore let them rest untold. I recollect nothing so well as the aspect of some fringed gentians, which we saw growing by the roadside, and which were so beautiful that I longed to turn back and pluck them. After an arduous journey, we arrived safe home in the afternoon of the second day — the first time that I ever came home in my life; for I never had a home before.

12 *o'clock*, M.

Just now I heard a sharp tapping at the window of my study, and, looking up from my book (a volume of Rabelais), behold! the head of a little bird, who seemed to demand admittance! He was probably attempting to get a fly, which was on the pane of glass against which he rapped; and on my first motion the feathered visitor took wing. This incident had a curious effect on me. It impressed me as if the bird had been a spiritual visitant, so strange was it that this little wild thing should seem to ask our hospitality.

March 31, 1843

. . . Every day, I trudge through snow and slosh to the village, look into the post-office, and spend an hour at the reading-room; and then return home, generally without having spoken a word to a human being. My wife is, in

the strictest sense, my sole companion; and I need no
other — there is no vacancy in my mind, any more than
in my heart. In truth, I have spent so many years in total
seclusion from all human society, that it is no wonder if I
now feel all my desires satisfied by this sole intercourse.
But my Dove has come to me from the midst of many
friends, and a large circle of acquaintance; yet she lives
from day to day in this solitude, seeing nobody but myself and our Molly, while the snow of our avenue is un-
trodden for weeks by any footstep save mine; yet she is
always cheerful, and far more than cheerful. Thank God
that I suffice for her boundless heart! In the way of exercise I saw and split wood, and, physically, I never was in
so good condition as now. This is chiefly owing, doubtless, to a satisfied heart, in aid of which comes the exercise
above mentioned, and about a fair proportion of intellectual labor.

On the 9th of this month, we left home again on a visit
to Boston and Salem. I alone went to Salem, where I resumed all my bachelor habits for nearly a fortnight, leading the same life in which ten years of my youth flitted
away like a dream. But how much changed was I! At last
I had caught hold of a reality which never could be taken
from me. It was good thus to get apart from my happiness, for the sake of contemplating it. On the 21st, I returned to Boston, and went out to Cambridge to dine with
Longfellow, whom I had not seen since his return from
Europe. The next day we came back to our old house,
which had been deserted all this time; for our Molly
Bryan had gone with us to Boston.

April 7

My belovedest wife has deserted her poor husband; she has this day gone to Boston to see her sister Mary, who is to marry Mr. Mann in two or three weeks, and then immediately to visit Europe for six months. . . . I betook myself to sawing and splitting wood; there being an inward unquietness which demanded active exercise, and I sawed, I think, more briskly than ever before. When I reentered the house, it was with somewhat of a desolate feeling; yet not without an intermingled pleasure, as being the more conscious that all separation was temporary and scarcely real, even for the little time that it may last. After my solitary dinner, I lay down, with the Dial in my hand, and attempted to sleep; but sleep would not come, for the sufficient reason, perhaps, that my little wife was at that very moment jolting most uncomfortably over a rough road. So I arose, and began this record in the journal, almost at the commencement of which I was interrupted by a visit from Mr. Thoreau, who came to return a book, and to announce his purpose of going to reside at Staten Island, as private tutor in the family of Mr. Emerson's brother. We had some conversation upon this subject, and upon the spiritual advantages of change of place, and upon the Dial, and upon Mr. Alcott, and other kindred or concatenated subjects. I am glad, on Mr. Thoreau's own account, that he is going away; as he is physically out of health, and, morally and intellectually, seems not to have found exactly the guiding clue; and in all these respects he may be benefited by his removal; — also it is one step towards a circumstantial position in the world. On my account, I should like to have him remain

here; he being one of the few persons, I think, with whom
to hold intercourse is like hearing the wind among the
boughs of a forest-tree; and, with all this wild freedom,
there is high and classic cultivation in him too. He says
that Ellery Channing is coming back to Concord, and
that he (Mr. Thoreau) has concluded a bargain, in his behalf, for the hire of a small house, with land attached, at
$55 per year. I am rather glad than otherwise; but
Ellery, so far as he has been developed to my observation,
is but a poor substitute for Mr. Thoreau.

April 8

Mr. Emerson came, with a sunbeam in his face; and
we had as good a talk as I ever remember experiencing
with him. My little wife, I know, will demand to know
every word that was spoken; but she knows me too well to
anticipate anything of the kind. He seemed fullest of
Margaret Fuller, who, he says, has risen perceptibly into
a higher state since their last meeting. He apotheosized
her as the greatest woman, I believe, of ancient or modern
times, and the one figure in the world worth considering.
[There rings the supper-bell.]   Then we spoke of Ellery
Channing, a volume of whose poems is to be immediately
published, with revisions by Mr. Emerson himself and
Mr. Sam G. Ward. He seems to anticipate no very wide
reception for them; he calls them 'poetry for poets,' and
thinks that perhaps a hundred persons may admire them
very much; while, to the rest of the world, they will be
little or nothing. Next Mr. Thoreau was discussed, and
his approaching departure; in respect to which we agreed
pretty well; but Mr. Emerson appears to have suffered
some inconveniency from his experience of Mr. Thoreau

as an inmate. It may well be that such a sturdy and un-compromising person is fitter to meet occasionally in the open air, than to have as a permanent guest at table and fireside. We talked of Brook Farm, and the singular moral aspects which it presents, and the great desirability that its progress and developments should be observed and its history written; also of Charles Newcomb, who, it appears, is passing through a new moral phasis. He is silent, inexpressive, talks little or none, and listens without response, except a sardonic laugh; and some of his friends think that he is passing into permanent eclipse. Various other matters were discussed or glanced at, and finally, between five and six o'clock, Mr. Emerson took his leave, threatening to come again, unless I call on him very soon. I then went out to chop wood, my allotted space for which had been very much abridged by his visit; but I was not sorry. I went on with the journal for a few minutes before supper, and have finished the present record in the setting sunshine and gathering dusk. I would like to see my wife.

April 10

I sat till eight o'clock, meditating upon this world and the next, and my dear little wife, as connected with both, and sometimes dimly shaping out scenes of a tale. Then lighted the lamp and betook myself to the German phrase-book. Ah, dearest! these are but dreary evenings. The lamp would not brighten my spirits, though Molly had duly filled it. Nevertheless, lacking energy to bathe, I deferred that duty later than usual, and did not get to bed till ten o'clock. What is the use of going to bed at all, in solitude? I dreamed a good deal, but to no good purpose, for all the characters and incidents have vanished. . . . This forenoon was spent in scribbling, by no means to my satisfaction, until past eleven, when I went to the village. Nothing in our box at the post-office. I read during the customary hour, or more, at the Athenæum, and returned without saying a word to mortal. I gathered from some conversation that I heard, that a son of Adam is to be buried this afternoon from the meeting-house; but the name of the deceased escaped me. It is no great matter, so it be but written in the Book of Life.

April 11

Just when I was on the point of choking with a huge German word, Molly announced Mr. Thoreau. He wished to take a row in the boat, for the last time, perhaps, before he leaves Concord. So we emptied the water out of her, and set forth on our voyage. She leaks, but not more than she did in the autumn. We rowed to the foot of the hill which borders the North Branch, and there landed, and climbed the moist and snowy hill-side for the sake of the prospect. Looking down the river, it might well have been mistaken for an arm of the sea, so broad is now its swollen tide; and I could have fancied that, beyond one other headland, the mighty ocean would outspread itself before the eye. On our return we boarded a large cake of ice, which was floating down the river, and were borne by it directly to our own landing-place, with the boat towing behind.

Parting with Mr. Thoreau, I spent half an hour in chopping wood, when Molly informed me that Mr. Emer-

son wished to see me. He had brought a letter of Ellery
Channing, written in a style of very pleasant humor. This
being read and discussed, together with a few other matters, he took his leave, since which I have been attending
to my journalizing duty; and thus this record is brought
down to the present moment, ten minutes past six.
To-night — to-night — yes, within an hour — this Eden,
which is no Eden to a solitary Adam, will regain its
Eve.

April 25

Spring is advancing, sometimes with sunny days, and
sometimes, as is the case now, with chill, moist, sullen
ones. There is an influence in the season that makes it
almost impossible for me to bring my mind down to
literary employment; perhaps because several months'
pretty constant work has exhausted that species of energy
— perhaps because in spring it is more natural to labor
actively than to think. But my impulse now is to be idle
altogether — to lie in the sun or wander about and look
at the revival of Nature from her deathlike slumber, or
to be borne down the current of the river in my boat. If I
had wings, I would gladly fly; yet would prefer to be
wafted along by a breeze, sometimes alighting on a patch
of green grass, then gently whirled away to a still sunnier
spot. . . . But here I linger on earth, very happy, it is true,
at bottom, but a good deal troubled with the sense of
imbecility — one of the dismallest sensations, methinks,
that mortal man can experience — the consciousness of a
blunted pen, benumbed fingers, and a mind no longer
capable of vigorous grasp. My torpidity of intellect makes

me irritable. .... O, how blest should I be were there nothing to do! Then I would watch every inch and hair's-
breadth of the progress of the season; and not a leaf
should put itself forth, in the vicinity of our old mansion,
without my noting it. But now, with the burden of a
continual task upon me, I have not freedom of mind to
make such observations.

April 26

Winter and Spring are now struggling for the mastery
in my study; and I yield somewhat to each, and wholly to
neither. The window is open, and there is a fire in the
stove. The day when the window is first thrown open
should be an epoch in the year; but I have forgotten to
record it. Seventy or eighty springs have visited this old
house; and sixty of them found old Dr. Ripley here —
not always old, it is true, but gradually getting wrinkles
and gray hairs, and looking more and more the picture of
winter. But he was no flower-shrub, but one of those
fruit-trees or timber-trees that acquire a grace with their
old age. Last spring found the house solitary for the
first time since it was built; and now again she peeps into
our open windows and finds new faces here. Methinks my
little wife is twin-sister of the spring; so they should greet
one another tenderly — for they both are fresh and dewy,
both full of hope and cheerfulness; both have bird-voices,
always singing out of their hearts; both are sometimes
overcast with flitting mists, which only make the flowers
bloom brighter; and both have power to renew and re-
create the weary spirit. I have married the spring! I am
husband to the month of May!

June 23

Summer has come at last — the longest days, with blazing sunshine, and fervid heat. Yesterday glowed like molten brass. Last night was the most uncomfortably and unsleepably sultry that we have experienced since our residence in Concord; and to-day it scorches again. I have a sort of enjoyment in these seven-times-heated furnaces of midsummer, even though they make me droop like a thirsty plant. The sunshine can scarcely be too intense for my taste; but I am no enemy to summer showers. Could I only have the freedom to be perfectly idle now — no duty to fulfil, no mental or physical labor to perform — I should be as happy as a squash, and much in the same mode; but the necessity of keeping my brain at work eats into my comfort, as the squash-bugs do into the heart of the vines. I keep myself uneasy and produce little, and almost nothing that is worth producing.

July 9

Dearest love, I know not what to say, and yet cannot be satisfied without marking with a word or two this holiest anniversary of our life. But life now heaves and swells beneath me like a brim-full ocean; and the endeavor to comprise any portion of it in words is like trying to dip up the ocean in a goblet. We were never so happy as now — never such wide capacity for happiness, yet overflowing with all that the day and every moment brings us. Methinks this birthday of our married life is like a cape, which we have now doubled, and find a more infinite ocean of love stretching out before us. God bless and keep us! for there is something more awful in happi-

ness than in sorrow — the latter being earthly and finite,
the former composed of the texture and substance of
eternity, so that spirits still embodied may well tremble
at it.

October 6

Yesterday afternoon (leaving my wife with my sister
Louisa, who has been with us two or three days) I took
a solitary walk to Walden Pond. It was a cool, windy
day, with heavy clouds rolling and tumbling about the
sky, but still a prevalence of genial autumn sunshine.
The fields are still green, and the great masses of the
woods have not yet assumed their many-colored garments; but here and there are solitary oaks of deep, substantial red, or maples of a more brilliant hue, or chest-
nuts either yellow or of a tenderer green than in summer.
Some trees seem to return to their hue of May or early
June before they put on the brighter autumnal tints. In
some places, along the borders of low and moist land, a
whole range of trees were clothed in the perfect gorgeous-
ness of autumn, of all shades of brilliant color, looking like
the palette on which Nature was arranging the tints
wherewith to paint a picture. These hues appeared to be
thrown together without design; and yet there was perfect
harmony among them, and a softness and a delicacy made
up of a thousand different brightnesses. There is not, I
think, so much contrast among these colors as might at
first appear. The more you consider them, the more they
seem to have one element among them all, which is the
reason that the most brilliant display of them soothes the
observer, instead of exciting him. And I know not

whether it be more a moral effect or a physical one, operating merely on the eye; but it is a pensive gayety, which causes a sigh often, but never a smile. We never fancy, for instance, that these gayly clad trees should be changed into young damsels in holiday attire, and betake themselves to dancing on the plain. If they were to undergo such a transformation, they would surely arrange themselves in funeral procession, and go sadly along, with their purple and scarlet and golden garments trailing over the withering grass. When the sunshine falls upon them, they seem to smile; but it is as if they were heart-broken. But it is in vain for me to attempt to describe these autumnal brilliancies, or to convey the impression which they make on me. I have tried a thousand times, and always without the slightest self-satisfaction. Luckily there is no need of such a record, for Nature renews the picture year after year; and even when we shall have passed away from the world, we can spiritually create these scenes, so that we may dispense with all further efforts to put them into words.

Walden Pond was clear and beautiful as usual. It tempted me to bathe; and, though the water was thrillingly cold, it was like the thrill of a happy death. Never was there such transparent water as this. I threw sticks into it, and saw them float suspended on an almost invisible medium. It seemed as if the pure air were beneath them, as well as above. If I were to be baptised, it should be in this pond; but then one would not wish to pollute it by washing off his sins into it. None but angels should bathe there. . . .

In a small and secluded dell that opens upon the most

beautiful cove of the whole lake, there is a little hamlet of huts or shanties inhabited by the Irish people who are at work upon the railroad. There are three or four of these habitations, the very rudest, I should imagine, that civilized men ever made for themselves — constructed of rough boards, with the protruding ends. Against some of them the earth is heaped up to the roof, or nearly so; and when the grass has had time to sprout upon them, they will look like small natural hillocks, or a species of ant-hills — something in which Nature has a larger share than man. These huts are placed beneath the trees, oaks, walnuts, and white-pines, wherever the trunks give them space to stand; and by thus adapting themselves to natural interstices, instead of making new ones, they do not break or disturb the solitude and seclusion of the place. Voices are heard, and the shouts and laughter of children, who play about like the sunbeams that come down through the branches. Women are washing in open spaces, and long lines of whitened clothes are extended from tree to tree, fluttering and gambolling in the breeze. A pig, in a sty even more extemporary than the shanties, is grunting and poking his snout through the clefts of his habitation. The household pots and kettles are seen at the doors; and a glance within shows the rough benches that serve for chairs, and the bed upon the floor. The visitor's nose takes note of the fragrance of a pipe. And yet, with all these homely items, the repose and sanctity of the old wood do not seem to be destroyed or profaned; she overshadows these poor people, and assimilates them somehow or other to the character of her natural inhabitants. Their presence did not shock me any more than if I had merely discovered a squirrel's nest in a tree. To be sure, it is a torment to see the great, high, ugly embankment of the railroad, which is here thrusting itself into the lake, or along its margin, in close vicinity to this picturesque little hamlet. I have seldom seen any-thing more beautiful than the cove on the border of which the huts are situated; and the more I looked, the lovelier it grew. The trees overshadowed it deeply; but on one side there was some brilliant shrubbery which seemed to light up the whole picture with the effect of a sweet and melancholy smile. I felt as if spirits were there — or as if these shrubs had a spiritual life. In short, the impres-sion was indefinable; and, after gazing and musing a good while, I retraced my steps through the Irish hamlet, and plodded on along a wood-path.

According to my invariable custom, I mistook my way, and, emerging upon the road, I turned my back in-stead of my face towards Concord, and walked on very diligently till a guide-board informed me of my mistake. I then turned about, and was shortly overtaken by an old yeoman in a chaise, who kindly offered me a ride, and soon set me down in the village.

April 14, 1844 [*Salem*]

. . . I went to George Hillard's office, and he spoke with immitigable resolution of the necessity of my going to dine with Longfellow before returning to Concord; but I have an almost miraculous power of escaping from necessities of this kind. Destiny itself has often been worsted in the attempt to get me out to dinner. Possibly, however, I may go.

Undated [Concord]

A moral philosopher to buy a slave, or otherwise get possession of a human being, and to use him for the sake of experiment, by trying the operation of a certain vice on him.

When the reformation of the world is complete, a fire shall be made of the gallows; and the Hangman shall come and sit down by it, in solitude and despair. To him shall come the Last Thief, the Last Prostitute, the Last Drunkard, and other representatives of past crime and vice; and they shall hold a dismal merrymaking, quaffing the contents of the Drunkard's last Brandy Bottle.[1]

The human heart to be allegorized as a cavern; at the entrance there is sunshine, and flowers growing about it. You step within, but a short distance, and find yourself surrounded with a terrible gloom, and monsters of divers kinds; it seems like hell itself. You are bewildered, and wander long without hope. At last, a light strikes upon you. You press towards it, and find yourself in a region that seems, in some sort, to reproduce the flowers and sunny beauty of the entrance — but all perfect. These are the depths of the heart, or of human nature, bright and beautiful; the gloom and terror may lie deep, but deeper still is this eternal beauty.

A man, in his progress through life, picks up various matters, sin, care, habit, riches, etc., until at last he struggles along under a heavy burden.

[1] 'Earth's Holocaust.'

To have a life-long desire for a certain object, which shall appear to be the one thing essential to happiness. At last this object is attained, but proves to be merely incidental to a more important affair; and that affair is the greatest evil fortune that can occur. For instance, all through the winter I had wished to sit in the dusk of evening, by the flickering firelight, with my wife, instead of beside a dismal stove. At last, this has come to pass; but it was owing to her illness, and our having no chamber with a stove, fit to receive her.

An Auction (perhaps in Vanity Fair) of offices, honors, and all sorts of things considered desirable by mankind; together with things eternally valuable, which shall be considered by most people as worthless lumber.

The greater picturesqueness and reality of back-yards, and everything appertaining to the rear of a house; as compared with the front, which is fitted up for the public eye. There is much to be learnt, always, by getting a glimpse at rears. When the direction of a road has been altered, so as to pass the rear of farm-houses, instead of the front, a very noticeable aspect is presented.[1]

An essay on the various kinds of death, together with the just-before and the just-after.

The majesty of death to be exemplified in a beggar, who, after being seen, humble and cringing, in the streets of a city, for many years, at length, by some means or

[1] 'The Blithedale Romance,' chap. XVII.

other, gets admittance into a rich man's mansion, and
there dies — assuming state, and striking awe into the
hearts of those who had looked down upon him.

To allegorize life as a masquerade, and represent mankind generally as masquers. Here and there, a natural
face may appear.

Sketch of a personage with the malignity of a witch,
and doing the mischief attributed to one — but by natural means; breaking off love-affairs, teaching children
vices, ruining men of wealth, etc.

The emerging from their lurking-places of evil characters on some occasion suited to their action — they having been quite unknown to the world hitherto. For
instance, the French Revolution brought out such
wretches.

Pearl — the English of Margaret — a pretty name
for a girl in a story.[1]

In moods of heavy despondency, one feels as if it would
be delightful to sink down in some quiet spot, and lie
there forever, letting the soil gradually accumulate and
form a little hillock over us, and the grass and perhaps
flowers gather over it. At such times, death is too much
of an event to be wished for; — we have not spirits to
encounter it; but choose to pass out of existence in this
sluggish way.

[1] 'The Scarlet Letter.'

A dream, the other night, that the world had become dissatisfied with the inaccurate manner in which facts are reported, and had employed me, with a salary of a thousand dollars, to relate things of public importance exactly as they happen.

Summer and Fall

The search of an investigator for the Unpardonable Sin — he at last finds it in his own heart and practice.

The Unpardonable Sin might consist in a want of love and reverence for the Human Soul; in consequence of which, the investigator pried into its dark depths, not with a hope or purpose of making it better, but from a cold philosophical curiosity — content that it should be wicked in whatever kind or degree, and only desiring to study it out. Would not this, in other words, be the separation of the intellect from the heart? [1]

Biographies of Eminent American Merchants; it would be a work likely to have a great circulation in our commercial country. If successful, there might be a second volume of Eminent Foreign Merchants. Perhaps it had better be adapted to the capacity of young clerks and apprentices.

Sketch of a person, who, by strength of character, or assistant circumstances, has reduced another to absolute slavery and dependence on him. Then show, that the person who appears to be the master, must inevitably be

[1] 'Ethan Brand.'

at least as much a slave, if not more, than the other. All slavery is reciprocal, on the supposition most favorable to the rulers.[1]

To represent a man in the midst of all sorts of cares and annoyances — with impossibilities to perform — and almost driven distracted by his inadequacy. Then quietly comes Death, and releases him from all his troubles; and at his last gasp, he smiles, and congratulates himself on escaping so easily.

The life of a woman, who, by the old colony law, was condemned always to wear the letter A, sewed on her garment, in token of her having committed adultery.

March or April, 1845

Perhaps there are higher intelligences that look upon all the manifestations of the human mind — metaphysics, ethics, histories, politics, poems, stories, etc., etc. — with the same interest as we do on flowers, or any other humble production of nature; finding a beauty and fitness even in the poorest of them which we cannot see in the best.

[1] 'The Scarlet Letter.'

1847–1853

[LATE in 1845, the owners of the Manse being about to re-occupy it, Hawthorne and his wife removed, with their baby daughter, to Salem, where, from the spring of 1846 to the summer of 1849, Hawthorne was chiefly engaged in his duties as surveyor of the port. It was a sterile period creatively, and his journals, save for descriptions of his children's life and for the few pages written in his mother's last illness, are comparatively silent. Only when, after his dismissal from office, and after the writing of 'The Scarlet Letter,' Hawthorne was a leisured man again, do they recommence. A short stay in Boston in the spring of 1850 was fruitful in journalistic entries of which several were to be woven, with changes, into the fabric of 'The Blithedale Romance.'

From the late spring of 1850 to the fall of 1851, the Hawthornes made their home in the country near Lenox, Massachusetts, and here 'The House of the Seven Gables' and 'A Wonder Book' were written. The journal is continued, but only intermittently, being partly occupied with new notes for tales, partly with observations of wood and hill, partly with the doings and sayings of Hawthorne's children, Una and Julian.

The winter of 1851–52 was spent in West Newton, where 'The Blithedale Romance' was written. For more than a year, Hawthorne was again in Concord, where he now had a house of his own, the Wayside, and where he wrote 'Tanglewood Tales' and the campaign biography

of Franklin Pierce. Shortly after Pierce's inauguration as
President, Hawthorne was appointed American consul in
Liverpool, and in July, 1853, the family set sail for
England.]

Undated

Nothing comes amiss to Nature — all is fish that comes
to her net. If there be a living form of perfect beauty
instinct with soul — why, it is all very well, and suits
Nature well enough. But she would just as lief have that
same beautiful, soul-illumined body, to make worm's
meat of, and to manure the earth with.

Some men have no right to perform great deeds, or
think high thoughts — and when they do so, it is a kind
of humbug. They had better keep within their own
propriety.

November 17, 1847

A story of the effects of revenge, in diabolizing him
who indulges in it.[1]

March, 1848 [Salem]

I have just been for a walk round Buffum's corner, and
returning, after some half an hour's absence, find Una and
Julian gone to bed. Thus ends the day of these two
children — one of them four years old, the other some
months less than two. But the days and the years melt
away so rapidly that I hardly know whether they are still
little children at their parents' knees, or already a maiden

[1] 'The Scarlet Letter.'

and a youth, a woman and a man. This present life has hardly substance and tangibility enough to be the image of eternity. The future too soon becomes the present, which, before we can grasp it, looks back upon us as the past. It must, I think, be only the image of an image. Our next state of existence, we may hope, will be more real — that is to say, it may be only one remove from reality. But, as yet, we dwell in the shadow cast by time, which is itself the shadow cast by eternity.

October 13

An angel comes from Heaven, commissioned to gather up, put into a basket, and carry away, everything good that is not improved by mankind, for whose benefit it was intended. She distributes the articles where they will be appreciated.

A benevolent person going about the world, and endeavoring to do good to everybody; in pursuance of which object, for instance, he gives a pair of spectacles to a blind man — and does all such ill-suited things. Beautiful pictures or statues to one intellectually blind. . . .

A man, arriving at the extreme point of old age, grows young again, at the same pace at which he has grown old; returning upon his path, throughout the whole of life, and thus taking the reverse view of matters. Methinks it would give rise to some odd concatenations.

January, 1849

Her [Una's] beauty is the most flitting, transitory, most uncertain and unaccountable affair, that ever had a real existence; it beams out when nobody expects it; it has mysteriously passed away when you think yourself sure of it. If you glance sideways at her, you perhaps think it is illuminating her face, but, turning full round to enjoy it, it is gone again. When really visible, it is rare and precious as the vision of an angel. It is a transfiguration — a grace, delicacy, or ethereal fineness — which at once, in my secret soul, makes me give up all severe opinions that I may have begun to form about her. It is but fair to conclude that on these occasions we see her real soul. When she seems less lovely, we merely see something external. But, in truth, one manifestation belongs to her as much as another; for, before the establishment of principles, what is character but the succession of moods?

The sentiment of a picture, tale, or poem is seldom lost upon her; and when her feelings are thus interested, she will not bear to have them interfered with by any ludicrous remark or other discordance. Yet she has, often, a rhinoceros-armor against sentiment or tenderness; you would think she were marble or adamant. It seems to me that, like many sensitive people, her sensibilities are more readily awakened by fiction than realities.[1]

March 16

A story, the principal personage of which shall seem always on the point of entering on the scene, but shall never appear.

Between March 16 *and September* 17

A modern magician to make the semblance of a human

[1] 'The Scarlet Letter,' chap. VI.

being, with two laths for legs, a pumpkin for a head, etc.
— of the most modest and meagre materials. Then a
tailor helps him to finish his work, and transforms this
scarecrow into quite a fashionable figure. At the end of
the story, after deceiving the world for a long time, the
spell should be broken, and the gay dandy be discovered
to be nothing but a suit of clothes, with these few sticks
inside of it. All through his seeming existence as a human
being, there shall be some characteristics, some tokens,
that, to the man of close observation and insight, betray
him to be a mere thing of laths and clothes, without
heart, soul, or intellect. And so this wretched old thing
shall become the symbol of a large class.[1]

July 29

Una is describing grandmamma's sickness to Julian.
'Oh, you don't know how sick she is, Julian; she is as sick
as I was when I had scarlet fever in Boston.' What a
contrast between that childish disease and these last
heavy throbbings — this funeral march — of my mother's heart. Death is never beautiful but in children.
How strange! For them Nature breaks her promise,
violates her pledge, and, like a pettish child, destroys her
own prettiest playthings; whereas the death of old age is
the consummation of life, and yet there is so much gloom
and ambiguity about it that it opens no vista for us into
Heaven. But we seem to see the flight of a dead child
upward, like a butterfly's . . .

At about five o'clock I went to my mother's chamber,
and was shocked to see such an alteration since my last

[1] 'Feathertop.'

visit. I love my mother; but there has been, ever since
my boyhood, a sort of coldness of intercourse between us,
such as is apt to come between persons of strong feelings
if they are not managed rightly. I did not expect to be
much moved at the time — that is to say, not to feel any
overpowering emotion struggling just then — though I
knew that I should deeply remember and regret her.
Mrs. Dike was in the chamber; Louisa pointed to a chair
near the bed, but I was moved to kneel down close by my
mother, and take her hand. She knew me, but could only
murmur a few indistinct words; among which I understood an injunction to take care of my sisters. Mrs. Dike
left the chamber, and then I found the tears slowly
gathering in my eyes. I tried to keep them down, but it
would not be; I kept filling up, till, for a few moments, I
shook with sobs. For a long time I knelt there, holding
her hand; and surely it is the darkest hour I ever lived.
Afterwards I stood by the open window and looked
through the crevice of the curtain. The shouts, laughter,
and cries of the two children had come up into the
chamber from the open air, making a strange contrast
with the death-bed scene. And now, through the crevice
of the curtain, I saw my little Una of the golden locks,
looking very beautiful, and so full of spirit and life that
she was life itself. And then I looked at my poor dying
mother, and seemed to see the whole of human existence
at once, standing in the dusty midst of it. Oh, what a
mockery, if what I saw were all — let the interval between extreme youth and dying age be filled up with what
happiness it might! But God would not have made the
close so dark and wretched, if there were nothing beyond;

for then it would have been a fiend that created us and measured out our existence, and not God. It would be something beyond wrong, it would be insult, to be thrust out of life and annihilated in this miserable way. So, out of the very bitterness of death, I gather the sweet assurance of a better state of being.

July 30

Another bright forenoon, warmer than yesterday, with flies buzzing through the sunny air. Mother still lives, but is gradually growing weaker, and appears to be scarcely sensible. Julian is playing quietly about, and is now out of doors, probably hanging on the gate. Una takes a strong and strange interest in poor mother's condition, and can hardly be kept out of the chamber — endeavoring to thrust herself in at the door whenever it is opened, and continually teasing me to be permitted to go up. This is partly the intense curiosity of her active mind; partly, I suppose, natural affection. I know not what she supposes to be the final result to which grandmamma is approaching. She talks of her being soon to go to God, and probably thinks that she will be taken away bodily. Would to God it were to be so! Faith and trust would be far easier than they are now. But, to return to Una, there is something that almost frightens me about the child — I know not whether elfish or angelic, but, at all events, supernatural. She steps so boldly into the midst of everything, shrinks from nothing, has such a comprehension of everything, seems at times to have but little delicacy, and anon shows that she possesses the finest essence of it — now so hard, now so tender; now so perfectly unreasonable, soon again so wise. In short, I now and then catch an aspect of her in which I cannot believe her to be my own human child, but a spirit strangely mingled with good and evil, haunting the house where I dwell. The little boy is always the same child, and never varies in his relation to me.

February 16, 1850

The sunbeam that comes through a round-hole in the shutter of a darkened window, where a dead man sits in solitude.

May 5 [Boston]

Mr. [Charles] Folsom carried me to Mr. [George] Ticknor's, the historian of Spanish literature. He has a fine house, at the corner of Park and Beacon Streets, perhaps the very best position in Boston. A marble hall, a wide and easy staircase, a respectable old man-servant, evidently long at home in the mansion, to admit us. We entered the library, Mr. Folsom considerably in advance, as being familiar with the house; and I heard Mr. Ticknor greet him in friendly tones, their scholar-like and bibliographical pursuits, I suppose, bringing them into frequent conjunction. Then I was introduced, and received with great distinction, but yet without any ostentatious flourish of courtesy. Mr. Ticknor has a great head and a queer face, with a nose the reverse of aquiline, though not exactly a pug or snub; his hair is gray or grizzly; he has a comfortable roundness of person. You recognize in him at once the man who knows the world, the scholar, too, which probably is his more distinctive character, though

a little more under the surface. He was in his slippers;
a volume of his book was open on a table, and apparently
he had been engaged in revising or annotating it. His
library is a noble and beautiful room for a private dwelling, and itself looks large and rich. The fireplace has a
white marble frame about it, richly sculptured with
figures and reliefs. Over it hung a portrait of Sir Walter
Scott, a copy, I think, of the one that represents him in
Melrose Abbey.

Mr. Ticknor was most kind in his alacrity to solve the
point on which Mr. Folsom, in my behalf, had consulted
him (as to whether there had been any English transla-
tion of the Tales of Cervantes); and most liberal in his
offers of books from his library. I know not (never having
read any of his writings) what may [be] his claims and
standing as a productive man of intellect; but certainly
he is a fine example of a generous-principled scholar,
anxious to assist the human intellect in its efforts and re-
searches. Methinks he must have spent a happy life (as
happiness goes among mortals), writing his great three-
volumed book for twenty years; writing it, not for bread,
nor with any uneasy desire of fame, but only with a purpose to achieve something true and enduring. He is not,
I apprehend, one of the highest or profoundest of men,
but a man of great cultivation and refinement, and with
quite substance enough to be polished and refined, without being worn too thin in the process. Fond of good
dinners; appreciative of the quality of wine; a man of
society. There is something peculiar in his manner, and
odd and humorsome in his voice; as of one who knows his
own advantages and eminent social position, and so

superinduces a little oddity upon the manners of a gentleman. This, doubtless, was the more perceptible in the
presence of an old and familiar friend, like Mr. Folsom,
and might not have been visible, had I been alone with
him. He related a queer story of an attempt of his to
become acquainted with me years ago, when he mistook
my kinsman Eben for me.

May 6

I left Mr. Thompson before ten, and took my way
through the sloppy streets to the Athenæum, where I
looked over the newspapers and periodicals, and found
two of my old stories ('Peter Goldthwaite' and the
'Shaker Bridal') published as original in the last 'London
Metropolitan'! The English are ten times as unscrupulous
and dishonest pirates as ourselves. However, if they
are poor enough to perk themselves in such false feathers
as these, Heaven help them! I glanced over the stories,
and they seemed painfully cold and dull. It is the more
singular that these should be so published, inasmuch as
the whole book was republished in London, only a few
months ago. Mr. Fields tells me that two publishers in
London had advertised the 'Scarlet Letter' as in press,
each book at a shilling.

May 7

I did not go out yesterday afternoon, but after tea I
went to Parker's. The drinking and smoking shop is no
bad place to see one kind of life. The front apartment is
for drinking. The door opens into Court Square, and is
denoted, usually, by some choice specimens of dainties

exhibited in the windows, or hanging beside the door-post; as, for instance, a pair of canvas-back ducks, distinguishable by their delicately mottled feathers; an admirable cut of raw beefsteak; a ham, ready boiled, and with curious figures traced in spices on its outward fat; a half, or perchance the whole, of a large salmon, when in season; a bunch of partridges, etc., etc. A screen stands directly before the door, so as to conceal the interior from an outside barbarian. At the counter stand, at almost all hours — certainly at all hours when I have chanced to observe — tipplers, either taking a solitary glass, or treating all round, veteran topers, flashy young men, visitors from the country, the various petty officers connected with the law, whom the vicinity of the Court-House brings hither. Chiefly, they drink plain liquors, gin, brandy, or whiskey, sometimes a Tom and Jerry, a gin cocktail (which the bar-tender makes artistically, tossing it in a large parabola from one tumbler to another, until fit for drinking), a brandy-smash and numerous other concoctions. All this toping goes forward with little or no apparent exhilaration of spirits; nor does this seem to be the object sought — it being rather, I imagine, to create a titillation of the coats of the stomach and a general sense of invigoration, without affecting the brain. Very seldom does a man grow wild and unruly.

The inner room is hung round with pictures and engravings of various kinds — a painting of a premium ox, a lithograph of a Turk and of a Turkish lady, . . . various showily engraved tailors' advertisements, and other shop-bills; among them all, a small painting of a drunken toper, sleeping on a bench beside the grog-shop

— a ragged, half-hatless, bloated, red-nosed, jolly, miser-
able-looking devil, very well done, and strangely suitable
to the room in which it hangs. Round the walls are placed
some half a dozen marble-topped tables, and a centre-
table in the midst; most of them strewn with theatrical
and other show-bills; and the large theatre-bills, with
their type of gigantic solidity and blackness, hung against
the walls.

Last evening, when I entered, there was one guest
somewhat overcome with liquor, and slumbering with
his chair tipped against one of the marble tables. In the
course of a quarter of an hour, he roused himself (a plain,
middle-aged man), and went out with rather an unsteady
step, and a hot, red face. One or two others were smoking,
and looking over the papers, or glancing at a play-bill.
From the centre of the ceiling descended a branch with
two gas-burners, which sufficiently illuminated every
corner of the room. Nothing is so remarkable in these
bar-rooms and drinking-places, as the perfect order that
prevails there: if a man gets drunk, it is no otherwise
perceptible than by his going to sleep, or inability to
walk.

Walking the sidewalk in front of this grog-shop of
Parker's (or sometimes, in cold or rainy days, taking his
station inside), there is generally to be observed an
elderly ragamuffin,[1] in a dingy and battered hat, an old
surtout, and a more than shabby general aspect; a thin
face and red nose, a patch over one eye, and the other
half-drowned in moisture; he leans in a slightly stooping posture on a stick, forlorn and silent, addressing

[1] Old Moodie in 'The Blithedale Romance.'

nobody, but fixing his one moist eye on you with a certain
intentness. He is a man who has been in decent circumstances at some former period of his life, but, falling into
decay (perhaps by dint of too frequent visits at Parker's
bar), he now haunts about the place, as a ghost haunts
the spot where he was murdered, 'to collect his rents,' as
Parker says — that is, to catch an occasional ninepence
from some charitable acquaintances, or a glass of liquor
at the bar. The word 'ragamuffin,' which I have used
above, does not accurately express the man, because there
is a sort of shadow or delusion of respectability about
him; and a sobriety too, and a kind of decency in his
groggy and red-nosed destitution.

Underground, beneath the drinking and smoking rooms,
is Parker's eating-hall, extending all the way to Court
Street. All sorts of good eating may be had there, and a
gourmand may feast at what expense he will, and gladden
his heart with choice wines.

I take an interest in all the nooks and crannies and
every development of cities; so here I try to make a description of the view from the back windows of a house in
the centre of Boston, at which I glance in the intervals of
writing. The view is bounded, at perhaps thirty yards'
distance (or perhaps not so much) by a row of opposite
brick dwellings, standing, I think, on Temple Place;
houses of the better order, with tokens of genteel families
visible in all the rooms betwixt the basements and the attic windows in the roof; plate-glass in the rear drawing-
rooms, flower-pots in some of the windows of the upper
stories; occasionally, a lady's figure, either seated or appearing with a flitting grace, or dimly manifest farther

within the obscurity of the room.   A balcony, with a
wrought-iron fence running along under the row of drawing-room windows, above the basement.   In the space
betwixt the opposite row of dwellings and that in which I
am situated are the low outhouses of the above-described
dwellings, with flat roofs; or solid brick walls, with walks
on them, and high railings, for the convenience of the
washerwomen in hanging out their clothes.   In the intervals betwixt these ranges of outhouses or walks, are grassplots, already green, because so sheltered; and fruit-trees,
now beginning to put forth their leaves, and one of them, a
cherry-tree, almost in full blossom.   Birds flutter and sing
among these trees.   I should judge it a good site for the
growth of delicate fruit; for, quite enclosed on all sides by
houses, the blighting winds cannot molest the trees; they
have sunshine on them a good part of the day, though the
shadow must come early; and I suppose there is a rich soil
about the roots.   I see grapevines clambering against one
wall, and also peeping over another, where the main body
of the vine is invisible to me.   In another place, a frame is
erected for a grapevine, and probably it will produce as
rich clusters as the vines of Madeira, here in the heart of
the city, in this little spot of fructifying earth, while the
thunder of wheels rolls about it on every side.   The trees
are not all fruit-trees; one pretty well-grown button-
wood-tree aspires upward above the roofs of the houses.
In the full verdure of summer, there will be quite a mass
or curtain of foliage, between the hither and the thither
row of houses.

A thought to-day.   Great men have to be lifted upon

the shoulders of the whole world, in order to conceive their great ideas, or perform their great deeds. That is, there must be an atmosphere of greatness round about them; a hero cannot be a hero unless in an heroic world.

May 14 [The Tremont House]

The grassplots appertaining to each of the houses whose rears are opposite ours (standing in Temple Place) are perhaps ten or twelve feet broad, and three times as long. Were I a solitary prisoner, I should not doubt to find occupation of deep interest for my whole day in watching only one of the houses. One house seems to be quite shut up; all the blinds in the three windows of each of the four stories being closed, although in the roof-windows of the attic story the curtains are hung carelessly upward, instead of being drawn. I think the house is empty, perhaps for the summer. The visible side of the whole row of houses is now in the shade — they looking towards, I should say, the southwest. Later in the day, they are wholly covered with sunshine, and continue so through the afternoon; and at evening the sunshine showly withdraws upward, gleams aslant upon the windows, perches on the chimneys, and so disappears. The upper part of the spire and the weathercock of the Park Street Church appear over one of the houses, looking as if it were close behind. It shows the wind to be east now. At one of the windows of the third story sits a woman in a colored dress, diligently sewing on something white. She sews, not like a lady, but with an occupational air. Her dress, I observe, on closer observation, is a kind of loose morning sack, with, I think, a silky gloss on it; and she seems to have a silver comb in her hair — no, this latter item is a mistake. Sheltered as the space is between the two rows of houses, a puff of the east-wind finds its way in, and shakes off some of the withering blossoms from the cherry-trees.

July 16 [*Lenox*]

The queer gestures and sounds of a hen looking about for a place to deposit her egg; her self-important gait; the sideway turn of her head and cock of her eye, as she pries into one and another nook, croaking all the while — evidently with the idea that the egg in question is the most important thing that has been brought to pass since the world began. A speckled black and white and tufted hen of ours does it to most ludicrous perfection; and there is something laughably womanish in it too.[1]

August 4

Dined at hotel with J. T. Fields and wife. Afternoon, drove with them to Pittsfield and called on Dr. Holmes.

August 5

Drove with Fields and his wife to Stockbridge, being thereto invited by Mr. Field of Stockbridge, in order to ascend Monument Mountain. Found at Mr. Field's Dr. Holmes and Mr. Duyckinck of New York; also Mr. Cornelius Matthews and Herman Melville. Ascended the mountain: that is to say, Mrs. Fields and Miss Jenny Field, Mr. Field and Mr. Fields, Dr. Holmes, Messrs. Duyckinck, Matthews, Melville, Mr. Henry Sedgwick,

[1] 'The House of the Seven Gables,' chap. x.

and I, and were caught in a shower. Dined at Mr.
Field's. Afternoon, under guidance of J. T. Headley,
the party scrambled through the ice-glen.

August 24

In the afternoons, nowadays, this valley in which I
dwell seems like a vast basin filled with golden sunshine as
with wine.

August 31

J. R. Lowell called in the evening.

September 1

He and Mrs. Lowell called in the forenoon, on their
way to Stockbridge or Lebanon, to meet Miss Bremer.

September 7

In a wood, a heap or pile of logs and sticks, that had
been cut for firewood, and piled up square, in order to be
carted away to the house when convenience served — or,
rather, to be sledded in sleighing time. But the moss had
accumulated on them, and leaves falling over them from
year to year and decaying, a kind of soil had quite covered
them, although the softened outline of the woodpile was
perceptible in the green mound. It was perhaps fifty
years — perhaps more — since the woodman had cut and
piled those logs and sticks, intending them for his winter
fires. But he probably needs no fire now. There was
something strangely interesting in this simple circumstance. Imagine the long-dead woodman, and his long-
dead wife and family, and one old man who was a little

child when the wood was cut, coming back from their graves, and trying to make a fire with this mossy fuel.

October 13

One of the children, drawing a cow on the blackboard, says, 'I'll kick this leg out a little more' — a very happy energy of expression, completely identifying herself with the cow; or perhaps, as the cow's creator, conscious of full power over its movements.

October 16

There is a glen between our house and the lake, through which winds a little brook with pools and tiny waterfalls over the great roots of trees. The glen is deep and narrow, and filled with trees; so that, in the summer, it is all a dense shadow of obscurity. Now, the foliage of the trees being almost entirely a golden yellow, instead of being full of shadow, the glen is absolutely full of sunshine, and its depths are more brilliant than the open plain or the mountain-tops. The trees are sunshine, and, many of the golden leaves being freshly fallen, the glen is strewn with sunshine, amid which winds and gurgles the bright, dark little brook.[1]

October 16 (?)

A ray of sunshine searching for an old blood spot, through a lonely room.

December 19

If the world were crumbled to the finest dust, and scat-

[1] 'Tanglewood Tales.'

tered through the universe, there would not be an atom of the dust for each star.

December

The print in blood of a naked foot to be traced through the street of a town.[1]

Of a bitter satirist — of Swift, for instance — it might be said, that the person or thing on which his satire fell shrivelled up as if the Devil had spit on it.

For the virtuoso's collection — the pen with which Faust signed away his salvation, with a drop of blood dried in it.

An eating-house, where all the dishes served out, even to the bread and salt, shall be poisoned with the adulterations that are said to be practised. Perhaps Death himself might be the cook.

Mrs. Prescott has an ox whose visage bears a strong resemblance to Daniel Webster — a majestic brute.

The spells of witches have the power of producing meats and viands that have the appearance of a sumptuous feast, which the Devil furnishes. But a Divine Providence seldom permits the meat to be good, but it has generally some bad taste or smell — mostly wants salt — and the feast is often without bread.

If we consider the lives of the lower animals we shall see in them a close parallelism to those of mortals — toil,

[1] 'The Ancestral Footstep.'

struggle, danger, privation, mingled with glimpses of peace and ease; enmity, affection, a continual hope of bettering themselves, although their objects lie at less distance before them than ours can do. Thus, no argument for the imperfect character of our existence and its delusory promises, and its apparent injustice, can be drawn in reference to our immortality, without, in a degree, being applicable to our brute brethren.

July 31, 1851

At three o'clock, . . . I dressed [Julian] and myself for a walk to the village, and we set out at four. . . . Returning to the Post-office, I got Mr. Tappan's mail and my own, and proceeded homeward, but clambered over the fence and sat down in Love Grove, to read the papers. While thus engaged, a cavalier on horseback came along the road, and saluted me in Spanish; to which I replied by touching my hat, and went on with the newspaper. But the cavalier renewing his salutation, I regarded him more attentively, and saw that it was Herman Melville! Whereupon, Julian and I hastened to the road, when ensued a greeting, and we all went homeward together, talking as we went. Soon Mr. Melville alighted, and put Julian into the saddle; and the little man was highly pleased, and sat on the horse with the freedom and fearlessness of an old equestrian, and had a ride of at least a mile homeward.

I asked Mrs. Peters to make some tea for Herman Melville; and so she did, and he drank a cup, but was afraid to drink much, because it would keep him awake. After supper, I put Julian to bed; and Melville and I had

a talk about time and eternity, things of this world and
of the next, and all possible and impossible matters, that
lasted pretty deep into the night. [Sentence deleted.]
At last, he arose, and saddled his horse (whom he had put
into the barn) and rode off for his own domicile; and I
hastened to make the most of what little sleeping-time
remained for me.

August 5

It now lacks a quarter of eleven o'clock. The only remarkable event, thus far, has been a visit. I was sitting in
the boudoir, when a knock came to the front-door; and
Mrs. Peters said that a lady wished to see me; so I went
upstairs on tiptoe, and made myself as presentable as I
could, at short notice, and came down to the drawing-
room. The visitor was a lady,[1] rather young, and quite
comely, with pleasant and intelligent eyes, in a pretty
Quaker dress. She offered me her hand, and spoke with
much simplicity, but yet in a ladylike way, of her interest
in my works, and her not being able to resist a desire to
see me, on finding herself in my vicinity. I asked her into
the sitting-room, to enjoy our back view; and we talked
of the scenery, and of various persons and matters.
Lowell, Whittier, Mr. James, and Herman Melville were
more or less discussed; she seemed to be a particular friend
of Whittier, and had heard of his calling on me, two or
three years ago. Her manners were very agreeable in-

---

[1] This woman — whom, at the age of just forty, Hawthorne curiously
speaks of as 'rather young' — was Elizabeth Lloyd, with whom it is
now known that Whittier was in love, and with whom he carried on, for
many years, an affectionate correspondence.   (See 'Whittier's Unknown Romance,' edited by Marie V. Denervaud, Boston, 1922.)

deed; the Quaker simplicity and the little touch of Quaker phraseology gave piquancy to her refinement and air of society. She had a pleasant smile, and eyes that readily responded to one's thought, so that it was not difficult to talk with her; a singular, but yet a gentle freedom in expressing her own opinions; an entire absence of affectation. These were the traits that impressed me; and, on the whole, it was the only pleasant visit I ever experienced in my capacity as author. She did not bore me with laudations of my own writings, but merely said that there are some authors with whom we feel ourselves privileged to become acquainted, by the nature of our sympathy with their writings — or something to that effect.

All this time, Julian was climbing into my lap and off again. She smiled on him, and praised his healthy aspect, inquired whether he looked like his mother, observing that he had no resemblance to myself. Finally she rose to depart, and I ushered her to the gate, where, as she took leave, she told me her name — Elizabeth Lloyd — and, bidding me farewell, she went on her way, and I saw her no more.

October 13

How pleasant it is to see a human countenance which cannot be insincere — in reference to baby's smile.

The best of us being unfit to die, what an inexpressible absurdity to put the worst to death!

October 21

Going to the village yesterday afternoon, I saw the face

of a beautiful woman, gazing at me from a cloud. It was the full face, not the bust. It had a sort of mantle on the head, and a pleasant expression of countenance. The vision lasted while I took a few steps, and then vanished. I never before saw nearly so distinct a cloud-picture, or rather sculpture; for it came out in alto-rilievo on the body of the cloud.

Happiness in this world, when it comes, comes incidentally. Make it the object of pursuit, and it leads us a wild-goose chase, and is never attained. Follow some other object, and very possibly we may find that we have caught happiness without dreaming of it; but likely enough it is gone the moment we say to ourselves, 'Here it is!' like the chest of gold that treasure-seekers find.

April 13, 1852 [*West Newton*]

Wrote the last page (199th MS.) of 'The Blithedale Romance.'

May 1

Wrote Preface. Afterwards modified the conclusion, and lengthened it to 201 pages. First proof-sheets, May 14.

August 14 [*Concord*]

In a grim, weird story, a figure of a gay, laughing, handsome youth, or young lady, all at once, in a natural, unconcerned way, takes off its face like a mask, and shows the grinning, bare skeleton face beneath.

August 20

A piece of land contiguous to and connected with a

handsome estate, to the adornment and good appearance of which it was essential. But the owner of the strip of land was at variance with the owner of the estate, so he always refused to sell it at any price, but let it lie there, wild and ragged, in front of and near the mansion-house. When he dies, the owner of the estate, who has rejoiced at the approach of the event all through his enemy's illness, hopes at last to buy it; but, to his infinite discomfiture, the enemy enjoined in his will that his body should be buried in the center of this strip of land. All sorts of ugly weeds grow most luxuriantly out of the grave in poisonous rankness.

September 4 [*Isle of Shoals*]

In the afternoon I walked round the portion of the island that I had not previously visited; and, in the evening, went with Mr. Titcomb to Mr. Thaxter's to drink apple-toddy. We found Mrs. [Celia] Thaxter sitting in a neat little parlor, very simply furnished, but in good taste. She is not now, I believe, more than eighteen years old, very pretty, and with the manners of a lady — not prim and precise, but with enough of freedom and ease. The books on the table were 'Pre-Raphaelitism,' also a tract on spiritual mediums, etc., and one or two others. There were several shelves of books on one side of the room, and engravings hung about. Mr. Weiss was there, and I do not know but he is an inmate of Mr. Thaxter's — certainly, a familiar. By and by came in Mr. Thaxter's brother, with a young lady whose position I do not know — either a sister, or the brother's wife. Anon, too, came in the apple-toddy, a very rich and spicy compound; after which we had some glees and negro melodies, in which Mr. Thaxter sang a noble bass, and Mrs. Thaxter sang like a bird, and Mr. Weiss, I suppose, sang tenor, and the brother Thaxter took some other part, and all were very mirthful and jolly. At about ten o'clock Mr. Titcomb and myself took leave; and emerging into the open air, out of that room of song, and pretty youthfulness of woman, and gay young men, there was the sky, and the three-quarters waning moon, and the old sea moaning all round about the island.

March 9, 1853 [*Concord*]

Finished, this day, the last story of 'Tanglewood Tales.' They were written in the following order: 'The Pomegranate Seeds' — 'The Minotaur' — 'The Golden Fleece' — 'The Dragon's Teeth' — 'Circe's Palace' — 'The Pygmies.' The Introduction is yet to be written. Wrote it 13th March.

Caresses, expressions of one sort or another, are necessary to the life of the affections, as leaves are to the life of a tree. If they are wholly restrained, love will die at the roots.

June 9

I burned great heaps of old letters, and other papers, a little while ago, preparatory to going to England. Among them were hundreds of Sophia's maiden letters. The world has no more such, and now they are all ashes. What a trustful guardian of secret matters fire is! What should we do without Fire and Death?

1853-1857

[At no time in Hawthorne's life did he keep up his journal with so great assiduity as during the seven years of his residence abroad. From August, 1853, to July, 1857, Hawthorne was occupied during the greater part of the year with his official duties as consul in Liverpool, though his residence there was broken by a vacation in North Wales in September, 1854; by a trip to the Lakes in the summer, and a month's stay in London in the fall of 1855; by another stay in London in the spring of 1856, and trips to Scotland, Yorkshire, and the southern counties later in the year; and by stays at Southport and in London, and a second trip to Scotland and the eastern counties in 1857. From October, 1855, to June, 1856, Mrs. Hawthorne was in Lisbon for her health, Hawthorne meanwhile living as a widower with his small son at Mrs. Blodgett's boarding-house in Liverpool.

No month of this quadrennium went wholly unrecorded, and, though much of the record is in itself tedious — for Hawthorne seemed to aim at accumulating notes of travel that should be complete at any cost — the poet and the novelist in Hawthorne were too constantly arrested, on the one hand by the imaginative connotations of great scenes, and on the other by the current life of a foreign country, for his fluent account of these things to be anything but fascinating. Hawthorne on his walks through the dingier streets of Liverpool or through the great bustle of London; Hawthorne at Abbotsford or

Peterborough; Hawthorne in confrontation with the literary celebrities of London in the fifties — this is Hawthorne at very nearly his best as a diarist.]

August 15, 1853 [*Liverpool*]

On Friday, at 7 P.M., I went to dine with the Mayor. It was a dinner given to the Judges and the Grand Jury. The Judges of England, during the time of holding an Assize, are the persons first in rank in the kingdom. They take precedence of everybody else — of the highest military officers — of the Lord Lieutenants — of the Archbishops — of the Prince of Wales — of all except the Sovereign, whose authority and dignity they represent. In case of a royal dinner, the Judge would lead the Queen to the table.

The dinner was at the Town Hall; and the rooms, and the whole affair, were all in the most splendid style. Nothing struck me more than the footmen in the city livery; they really looked more magnificent, in their gold-lace and breeches and white silk stockings, than any officers of state whom I have ever seen. The rooms were beautiful; gorgeously painted and gilded, gorgeously lighted, gorgeously hung with paintings, gorgeously illuminated — the plate gorgeous, the dinner gorgeous, in the English fashion. As to the company, they had a kind of roughness, that seems to be the characteristic of all Englishmen so far as I have yet seen them; — elderly John Bulls — and there is hardly a less beautiful object than the elderly John Bull, with his large body, protruding paunch, short legs, and mottled, double-chinned, irregular-featured aspect. They are men of the world, at

home in society, easy in their manners, but without refinement; nor are they especially what one thinks of,
under the appellation of gentlemen.

After the removal of the cloth the Mayor gave various
toasts, prefacing each with some remarks — the first, of
course, the Sovereign, after which 'God save the Queen'
was sung; and there was something rather ludicrous in
seeing the company stand up and join in the chorus, their
ample faces glowing with wine, enthusiasm, perspiration,
and loyalty. There certainly is a vein of the ridiculous
running through these people; nor does it take away from
their respectability. Afterwards the Bar, and various
other dignities and institutions were toasted; and by and
by came the toast to the United States, and to me, as
their Representative. Hereupon either 'Hail Columbia,'
or 'Yankee Doodle,' or some other of our national tunes
(but Heaven knows which), was played; and at the conclusion, being cornered, and with no alternative, I got
upon my legs, and made a response. They received me
and listened to my nonsense with a good deal of rapping,
and my speech seemed to give great satisfaction. My
chief difficulty lay in not knowing how to pitch my voice
to the size of the room; as for the matter, it is not of the
slightest consequence. Anybody may make an after-
dinner speech who will be content to talk onward without
saying anything. My speech was not more than two or
three inches long; and, considering that I did not know a
soul there, except the Mayor himself, and that I am
wholly unpractised in all sorts of oratory, and that I had
nothing to say, it was quite successful. I hardly thought
it was in me; but, being once on my legs, I felt no em-

barrassment, and went through it as coolly as if I were going to be hanged.

August 20

. . . Almost every day, I take walks about Liverpool; preferring the darker and dingier streets, inhabited by the poorer classes. . . . I never walk through these streets without feeling as if I should catch some disease, but yet there is a strong interest in such walks; and moreover there is a bustle, a sense of being in the midst of life, and of having got hold of something real, which I do not find in the better streets of the city.

August 24

From 1 o'clock till 2, to-day, I have spent in rambling along the streets, Tithe Barn Street, Scotland Road, and that vicinity. I never saw, of course, nor imagined from any description, what squalor there is in the inhabitants of these streets, as seen along the side-walks. All these avenues (the quotation occurs to me continually; and I suppose I have made it two or three times already) are 'with dreadful faces thronged.' Women with young figures, but old and wrinkled countenances; young girls, without any maiden neatness and trimness, barefooted, with dirty legs [phrase deleted]. Women of all ages, even elderly, go along with great, bare, ugly feet; many have baskets and other burdens on their heads. All along the street, with their wares at the edge of the side-walk, and their own seats fairly in the carriage way, you see women with fruit to sell, or combs and cheap jewelry, or coarse crockery, or oysters, or the devil knows what; and sometimes the woman is sewing, meanwhile. This life and domestic occupation in the street is very striking, in all these meaner quarters of the city — nursing of babies, sewing and knitting, sometimes even reading. In a drama of low life, the street might fairly and truly be the one scene where everything should take place — courtship, quarrels, plot and counterplot, and what not besides. My God, what dirty, dirty children! And the grown people are the flowers of these buds, physically and morally. At every ten steps, too, there are 'spirit vaults,' and often 'Beds' are advertised on a placard, in connection with the liquor-trade.

Little children are often seen taking care of littler children; and it seems to me that they take good and faithful care of them. To-day, I heard a dirty mother laughing and priding herself on the pretty ways of her dirty infant — just as a Christian mother might in a nursery or drawing-room. I must study this street-life more, and think of it more deeply.

October 3

Saturday evening, at six, I went to dine with Mr. Aiken, a wealthy merchant here, to meet two of the sons of Burns. There was a party of ten or twelve, Mr. Aiken and his two daughters included. The two sons of Burns have both been in the Indian army, and have attained the ranks of Colonel and Major; one having spent thirty, and the other twenty-seven years in India. They are now old gentlemen of sixty and upwards; the elder with a gray head, the younger with a perfectly white one — rather under than above the middle stature, and with a British roundness of figure — plain, respectable, intelligent-looking persons, with quiet manners though not particularly refined. I saw no resemblance in either of them to any portrait of their father. After the ladies left the table, I sat next to the Major, the younger of the two, and had a good deal of talk with him. He seemed a very kindly and social man, and was quite ready to speak about his father, nor was at all reluctant to let it be seen how much he valued the glory of being descended from the poet. By and by, at Mr. Aiken's instance, he sang one of Burns's songs — the one about Annie and the rigs of barley. He sings in a perfectly simple style, so that it is little more than recitative; and yet the effect is very good as to humor, sense, and pathos. After rejoining the ladies, he sang another, 'A posie for my ain dear May,' and likewise 'A man's a man for a' that.' My admiration of his father, and partly, perhaps, my being an American, gained me some favor with him; and he promised to give me what he considered the best engraving of Burns, and some other remembrance of him. The Major is that son of Burns who spent an evening at Abbotsford with Sir Walter Scott, when, as Lockhart writes, 'The children sang the ballads of their sires.' He spoke with vast indignation of a recent edition of his father's works by Robert Chambers, in which the latter appears to have wronged the poet by some misstatements. Late in the evening, Mr. Aiken and most of the gentlemen retired to the smoking-room, where we found brandy, whiskey, and some good cigars. The sons of the poet showed, I think, an hereditary appreciation of good liquor, both at the dinner table (where they neglected neither sherry, port, hock,

champagne, nor claret) and here in the smoking-room.
Both of them, however, drank brandy, instead of the
liquor which their father immortalized. The Colonel
smoked cigars; the Major filled and refilled a German
pipe. Neither of them (nor, in fact, anybody else) was
at all the worse for liquor; but I thought I saw a little of
the coarser side of Burns, in the rapturous approbation
with which the Major responded to a very good but rather
indecorous story from one of the gentlemen. But I liked
them both, and they liked me, and asked me to go and
see them at Cheltenham, where they reside. We broke
up at about midnight.

The members of this dinner-party were of the more
liberal tone of thinking, here in Liverpool. The Colonel
and Major seemed to be of similar principles; and the
eyes of the latter glowed, when he sang his father's noble
verse, 'The rank is but the guinea's stamp,' etc. It would
have been too pitiable, if Burns had left a son who could
not feel the spirit of that verse.

October 19

I have had a good many visitors at the Consulate from
the United States within a short time — among others,
Mr. D. D. Barnard, our late minister to Berlin, returning
homeward to-day by the Arctic; and Mr. Sickles, Secretary of Legation to London, a fine-looking, intelligent,
gentlemanly young man.... With him came Judge
[Stephen A.] Douglas, the chosen man of Young America.
He is very short, extremely short, but has an uncom-
monly good head, and uncommon dignity without seeming to aim at it, being free and simple in manners. I judge

him to be a very able man, with the Western sociability
and free-fellowship. When I saw him in Washington, he
had on a very dirty shirt-collar. I believe it was clean
yesterday.... Generally I see no reason to be ashamed
of my countrymen who come out here in public position,
or otherwise assuming the rank of gentlemen.

October 22

At a dinner-party at Mr. Holland's last evening, a
gentleman, in instance of Charles Dickens's unweari-
ability, said that during some theatrical performances in
Liverpool he played in play and farce, spent the rest of the
night making speeches, feasting, and drinking at table,
and ended at seven o'clock in the morning by jumping
leap-frog over the backs of the whole company.

Wishing to send a letter to a dead man, who may be
supposed to have gone to Tophet — throw it into the
fire.

November 14

The other day, at the entrance of the market-house, I
saw a woman sitting in a small hand-wagon, apparently
for the purpose of receiving alms. There was no attendant at hand; but I noticed that one or two persons who
passed by seemed to inquire whether she wished her wagon
to be moved. Perhaps this is her mode of making progress
about the city, by the voluntary aid of boys and other
people who help to drag her. There is something in this —
I don't yet well know what — that has impressed me,
as if I could make a romance out of the idea of a woman

living in this manner a public life, and moving about by
such means.

December 13

What was the after life of the young man, whom Jesus,
looking on, 'loved,' and bade him sell all that he had, and
give to the poor, and take up his cross and follow him?
Something very deep and beautiful might be made out
of this.

January 6, *1854*

I was sent for to the police court, the other morning,
in the case of an American sailor, accused of robbing a
shipmate at sea. A large room, with a great coal-fire
burning on one side; and above it the portrait of a Mr.
Rushton, deceased, a magistrate of many years' continu-
ance. A long table, with chairs; on one side, the witness-
box. One of the borough magistrates, a merchant of the
city, sat at the head of the table, with paper and pen-and-
ink before him; but the real judge was the clerk of the
court, whose professional knowledge and experience gov-
erned all the proceedings. In the short time while I was
waiting, two cases were tried, in the first of which the
prisoner was discharged. The second case was of a
woman — a thin, sallow, hard-looking, careworn, young-
ish woman — for stealing a pair of slippers out of a shop.
The trial occupied five minutes or less; and she was
sentenced to twenty-one days' imprisonment — whereupon, without speaking, she looked up wildly first into
one policeman's face, then into another's, at the same
time wringing her hands, with no theatric gesture, but

because her torment took this outward shape — and was led away. The Yankee sailor was then brought up — an intelligent, but ruffian-like fellow; and as the case (being only for stealing a comforter) was out of the jurisdiction of the English magistrates, and as it was not worth my while to get him sent over to America for trial, he was forthwith discharged.

If mankind were all intellect, they would be continually changing, so that one age would be entirely unlike another. The great conservative is the heart, which remains the same in all ages; so that commonplaces of a thousand years' standing are as effective as ever.

February 13

Englishmen are not made of polishable substance — not of marble, but rather of red freestone. There is a kind of roughness and uncouthness in the most cultivated of them. After some conversance with them as a people, you learn to distinguish gentlemen among them; but at first it seems as if there were none.

February 23

There came to see me the other day a young gentleman with a moustache and a blue cloak, who announced himself as William Allingham, and handed me a copy of his poems, a thin volume, with paper covers, published by Routledge. I thought I remembered hearing his name, but had never seen any of his works. His face was intelligent, dark, pleasing, and not at all John-Bullish. He said that he had been employed in the Customs in Ireland,

and was now going to London to live by literature — to be connected with some newspaper, I imagine. He had been in London before, and was acquainted with some of the principal literary people — among others, Tennyson and Carlyle. He seemed to have been on rather intimate terms with Tennyson, and I gathered from what he said that Tennyson is a moody man, though genial with his friends. He says Tennyson told him that, if he were sure there were no hereafter, he would go and fling himself over London bridge; — a foolish thing to do or to say; but perhaps he might have said a wiser thing to a wise man. Tennyson is a very shy man, and thinks everybody stares at him on account of his strange appearance, on railways and everywhere else, even in the seclusion of his own garden. This, I judge, has no reference to the notice drawn on him by his poetry, but is the natural morbidness of a man who shirks society. We talked awhile in my dingy and dusky Consulate, and he then took leave. His manners are good, and he appears to possess independence of mind. On looking over his poems, I find some good things among them.

Yesterday, I saw a British regiment march down to George's Pier, to embark in the Niagara for Malta. The troops had nothing very remarkable about them; but the thousands of ragged and filthy wretches, who thronged the pier and streets to gaze at them, were what I had not seen before, in such masses. How unlike the well-dressed and well-washed multitude in an American city. This was the first populace I have beheld; for even the Irish, on the other side of the water, acquire respectability of aspect.

John Bull is going with his whole heart into this Turkish war. He is a great fool. Whatever the Czar may propose to himself, it is for the interest of democracy that he should not be easily put down.

The regiment, on its way to embark, carried the Queen's colors, and, side by side with them, the banner of the 28th, yellow, with the names of the Peninsular, and other battles in which it had been engaged, inscribed on it, in a double column. It is a very distinguished regiment; and Mr. Henry Bright mentioned as one of its distinctions, that Washington had formerly been an officer in it. I never heard of this, and don't believe it.

February 27

Aboard the ferry-boat yesterday, a laboring man eating oysters; he took them, one by one, from his pocket in interminable succession, opened them with his jack-knife, swallowed the oyster, threw the shell overboard — and then for another. Having concluded his meal, he took out a clay tobacco-pipe, filled, lighted it with a match, and smoked it — all this, while the other passengers were looking at him, and with a perfect coolness and independence, such as no single man can ever feel in America. Here, a man does not seem to consider what other people will think of his conduct, but whether it suits his own convenience to do so and so. It may be the better way.

March 16

THE DIARY OF A CORONER would be a work likely to meet with large popular acceptance. A dark passageway, only a few yards in extent, leads from the liveliest street in Liverpool to this coroner's court-room, where all the discussion is about murder and suicide. It seems, that, after a verdict of suicide, the corpse can only be buried at midnight, without religious rites.

A woman's chastity consists, like an onion, of a series of coats. You may strip off the outer ones without doing much mischief, perhaps none at all; but you keep taking off one after another, in expectation of coming to the inner nucleus, including the whole value of the matter. It proves, however, that there is no such nucleus, and that Chastity is diffused through the whole series of coats, is lessened with the removal of each, and vanishes with the final one, which you supposed would introduce you to the hidden pearl.

March 23

A son of General Arnold, named William Fitch Arnold, and born in 1794, now possesses the estate of Little Messenden Abbey, Bucks County, and is a magistrate for that county. He was formerly Captain of the 19th Lancers. He has now two sons and four daughters. The other three sons of General Arnold, all older than this one, and all military men, do not appear to have left children; but a daughter married to Colonel Phipps, of the Mulgrave family, has a son and two daughters. I question whether any of our true-hearted Revolutionary heroes have left a more prosperous progeny than this arch-traitor. I should like to know their feelings with respect to their ancestor.

April 3

I stood on the Exchange at noon, to-day, to see the
88th Regiment, or Connaught Rangers, marching down
to embark for the East. They were a body of young,
healthy, and cheerful-looking men; and looked greatly
better than the dirty crowd that thronged to gaze at
them. The royal banner of England, quartering the lion,
the leopard, and the harp, waved on the town-house, and
looked gorgeous and venerable. Here and there, a woman
exchanged greetings with an individual soldier, as he
marched along; and gentlemen shook hands with officers,
with whom they happened to be acquainted. Being a
stranger in the land, it seemed as if I could see the future
in the present, more than if I had been an Englishman;
so I questioned with myself how many of these ruddy-
cheeked young fellows, marching so stoutly away, would
ever tread English ground again!

The populace did not evince any enthusiasm; yet there
could not possibly be a war to which the country could
assent more fully than to this. I somewhat doubt whether
the English populace really feels a vital interest in the
nation.

Good Friday

Mrs. O'Sullivan's grandmother died fifty years ago, at
the age of twenty-eight. She had great personal charms,
and among them a beautiful head of chestnut hair. After
her burial (in a family tomb) the coffin of one of her
children was laid on her own coffin, so that the lid seems
to have decayed, or been broken from this cause; at any
rate, this was the case when the tomb was opened,

about a year ago. The grandmother's coffin was then found to be filled with beautiful, glossy, living chestnut ringlets, into which her whole substance seems to have been transformed, for there was nothing else but this coffin-full of shining ringlets, the growth of half a century in the tomb. An old man, with a ringlet of his youthful mistress treasured on his heart, might be supposed to witness this wonderful thing.

June 12

Barry Cornwall (alias Procter) called on me, a week or more ago; but I happened not to be in the office. Saturday last he called again, and as I had crossed to Rock Park, he followed me thither. A plain, middle-sized, rather smallish, English-looking gentleman, elderly (sixty or thereabouts) with short white hair. Particularly quiet in his manners; he talks in a somewhat feeble tone and emphasis, not at all energetic, scarcely distinct. An American of the same intellectual calibre would have more token of it in his manner and personal appearance, and would have a more refined aspect; his head, however, has a good outline, and would look well in marble; but the English complexion takes greatly from its chasteness and dignity. I liked him very well; he talked unaffectedly, showing an author's regard to his reputation, and evidently was pleased to hear of his American celebrity. Nothing remains on my mind of what he said, except that, in his younger days, he was a scientific pugilist, and once took a journey to have a sparring encounter with the Game-Chicken. Certainly, no one would have looked for a pugilist in this subdued old gentleman. He is now Com-

missioner of Lunacy, and makes periodical circuits
through the country, attending to the business of his
office. He is slightly deaf, and this may be the cause of
his feeble utterance — owing to his not being able to
regulate his voice exactly by his own ear. On the whole,
he made a pleasant and kindly, but not a powerful impression on me — as how should he? being a small, though
elegant poet, and a man of no passion or emphasized intellect. My wife and the children came into the drawing-
room to see him; and all parties seemed to be pleased with
one another. He is a good little man, and is much better
expressed by his real name, William [sic] Procter, than
by his poetical one, Barry Cornwall. Every Englishman
has an outward case of such undeniable flesh and blood
that I doubt whether it is best to see the poets of this
country. Our pale, thin, Yankee aspect is the fitter
garniture for poets. Mr. Procter took my hand in both
of his at parting, and walking with very short steps, left
the house, being in a hurry to get to the Adelphi, where
he expected a friend to dinner. I think the social rank of
Englishmen (always conscious of somebody above them)
prevents them from having any dignity in their manner.
Barry Cornwall looks like a man who may have kept
company with lords — not that he is mean, either, but
neither is he of the first rank.

August 8

Visiting the Zoölogical Gardens the other day with
Julian, it occurred to me what a fantastic kind of life a
person connected with them might be depicted as leading
— a child, for instance. The grounds are very extensive,

and include arrangements for all kinds of exhibitions, calculated to attract the idle people of a great city. In one
enclosure a bear, who climbs a pole to get cake and ginger-
bread from the spectators. Elsewhere, a circular building,
with compartments for lions, wolves, tigers, etc. In another part of the garden is a colony of monkeys; the
skeleton of an elephant; birds of all kinds. Swans, and
various rare water-fowl, swimming on a piece of water,
which was green, by the by; and when the fowls dived,
they stirred up black mud. A stork was parading along
the margin, with melancholy strides of its long legs, and
came slowly towards us, as if for companionship. In one
apartment, was an obstreperously noisy society of parrots,
macaws, etc., most gorgeous and diversified of hue. These
different colonies of birds and beasts were scattered about
in various parts of the grounds, so that you came upon
them unexpectedly. Also, there was an archery ground,
a shooting-ground, a swing, and other such things. A
theatre, also, at which a rehearsal was going on — we
standing at one of the exterior doors, and looking in
towards the dusky stage where the company, in their
ordinary dresses, were rehearsing something that had a
good deal of dance and action in it. In the open air, there
was an arrangement of painted scenery representing a
wide expanse of mountains, with a city at their feet, and
before it the sea, with actual water, and large vessels
upon it — the vessels having only the side that would be
presented to the spectator; but the scenery was so good
that at first casual glance I almost mistook it for reality.
There was a refreshment-room, with drinks, and cake and
pastry, but, so far as I saw, no substantial victual. About

in the centre of the garden there was an actual, homely-looking, small dwelling-house or cottage, where perhaps the overlookers of the concern live. Now, this might be wrought, in an imaginative description, into a pleasant sort of a fool's paradise, where all sorts of unreal delights should seem to cluster round some suitable personage; and it would relieve, in a very odd and effective way, the stern realities of life on the outside of the garden-walls. I saw a little girl, simply dressed, who seemed to have her habitat within the garden. There was also a daguerreotypist, with his wife and family, carrying on his business in a little shed or shanty, and perhaps having his home in its inner room. He seemed to be an honest, intelligent, pleasant young man, and his wife a pleasant woman; and I got Julian's daguerreotype taken for three shillings, in a little brass frame. In the description of the garden, the velvet turf, of a charming verdure, and the shrubbery, and shadowy walks under large trees, and the slopes and inequalities of ground, must not be forgotten. In one place, there was a maze and labyrinth, where a person might wander a long while in the vain endeavor to get out; although, all the time, looking at the exterior garden over the low hedges that border the walks of the maze. And this is like the inappreciable difficulties that often beset us in life.

I will see the garden again, before long, and get some additional record of it.

August 24

After all, the utmost force of man can do positively very little towards making grand things or beautiful

things. The imagination can do so much more, merely
on shutting one's eyes, that the actual effect seems
meagre; so that a new house, unassociated with the past,
is exceedingly unsatisfactory, especially when you have
heard that the wealth and skill of man has here done its
best.

At the railroad station [Chester], Sophia saw a small
edition of 'Twice-Told Tales,' forming a volume of the
Cottage Library; and, opening it, there was the queerest
imaginable portrait of myself — so very queer that we
could not but buy it. The shilling editions of 'The Scarlet
Letter' and 'Seven Gables' are at all the book-stalls and
shop-windows; but so is 'The Lamplighter,' and still
more trashy books.

August 26

All past affairs, all home conclusions, all people whom
I have known in America and meet again here, are
strangely compelled to undergo a new trial. It is not that
they suffer by comparison with circumstances of English
life and forms of English manhood or womanhood; but,
being free from my old surroundings, and the inevitable
prejudices of home, I decide upon them absolutely.

I think I neglected to record that I saw Miss Martineau
a few weeks since. She is a large, robust (one might almost
say, bouncing), elderly woman, very coarse of aspect, and
plainly dressed; but withal [she has] so kind, cheerful, and
intelligent a face that she is pleasanter to look at than
most beauties. Her hair is of a decided gray, and she does
not shrink from calling herself an old woman. She is the

most continual talker I ever heard; it is really like the
babbling of a brook, and very lively and sensible too;
and all the while she talks, she moves the bowl of her
ear-trumpet from one auditor to another, so that it becomes quite an organ of intelligence and sympathy between her and yourself. The ear-trumpet seems a sensible
part of her, like the feelers of some insects. If you have
any little remark to make, you drop it in; and she helps
you to make remarks by this delicate little appeal of the
trumpet, as she slightly directs it towards you; and if you
have nothing to say, the appeal is not strong enough to
embarrass you. All her talk was about herself and her
affairs; but it did not seem like egotism, because it was so
cheerful and free from morbidness. And this woman is
an Atheist, and thinks that the principle of life will become extinct when her great, fat, well-to-do body is laid
in the grave! I will not think so, were it only for her sake;
— only a few weeds to spring out of her fat mortality, instead of her intellect and sympathies flowering and fruit-
ing forever!

September 20 [North Wales]

I am getting tired of antiquity. It is certainly less interesting in the long run than novelty.

September 22 [Liverpool]

I dined on Wednesday evening at Mr. John Heywood's,
Norris Green. Mr. Monckton Milnes and lady were of
the company. Mr. Milnes is a very agreeable, kindly
man, resembling Longfellow a good deal in personal appearance; and he promotes, by his genial manners, the

same pleasant intercourse which is so easily established
with Longfellow. He is said to be a very kind patron of
literary men, and to do a great deal of good among young
and neglected people of that class. He is considered one
of the best conversationists at present in society: it may
very well be so; his style of talking being very simple and
natural, anything but obtrusive, so that you might enjoy
its agreeableness without suspecting it. He introduced me
to his wife (a daughter of Lord Crewe), with whom and
himself I had a good deal of talk. . . . Mr. Milnes told me
that he owns the land in Yorkshire, whence some of the
pilgrims of the Mayflower emigrated to Plymouth, and
that Elder Brewster was the Postmaster of the village.
He takes pride in this ownership. He also said that in the
next voyage of the Mayflower, after she carried the Pilgrims, she was employed in transporting a cargo of slaves
from Africa — to the West Indies, I suppose. This is a
queer fact, and would be nuts for the Southerners.

September 29

Mr. Monckton Milnes called on me at my office, day
before yesterday. He is pleasant and sensible; but
an intellectual and refined American is a higher man than
he — a higher and a finer one. Speaking of American
politicians, I remarked that they were seldom anything
but politicians, and had no literary nor other culture,
beyond their own calling. He said the case was the same
in England, and instanced Sir Robert Peel, who once
called on him for information when an appeal had been
made to him (Sir Robert) respecting two literary gentlemen. Sir Robert had *never heard* the names of either of

these gentlemen, and applied to Mr. Milnes, as being
somewhat conversant with the literary class, to know
whether they were distinguished, and what were their
claims. The names of the two literary men were James
Sheridan Knowles and Alfred Tennyson.

October 6

The people, for several days, have been in the utmost
anxiety, and latterly in the highest exultation about
Sebastopol — and all England, and Europe to boot, has
been fooled by the belief that it had fallen. This, however, now turns out to be incorrect; and the public
visage is somewhat grim, in consequence. I am glad of it.
In spite of his actual sympathies, it is impossible for a
true American to be otherwise than glad. Success makes
an Englishman intolerable; and, already, on the mistaken
idea that the way was open to a prosperous conclusion of
the war, The Times had begun to throw out menaces
against America. I shall never love England till she sues
us for help, and, in the mean time, the fewer triumphs
she obtains, the better for all parties. An Englishman in
adversity is a very respectable character; he does not
lose his dignity, but merely comes to a proper conceit of
himself, and is thereby a great deal less ridiculous than
he generally is. It is rather touching to a mere observer
like myself to see how much the universal heart is in this
matter — to see the merchants gathering round the tele-
graphic messages, posted on the pillars of the Exchange
news-room — the people in the streets, who cannot af-
ford to buy a paper, clustering round the windows of
the news-offices, where a copy is pinned up — the groups

of corporals and sergeants at the recruiting rendezvous, with a newspaper in the midst of them; — and all earnest and sombre, and feeling like one man together, whatever their rank. I seem to myself like a spy or a traitor, when I meet their eyes, and am conscious that I neither hope nor fear in sympathy with them, although (unless they detect me for an American by my aspect) they look at me in full confidence of sympathy. Their heart 'knoweth its own bitterness,' and as for me, being a stranger and an alien, I 'intermeddled not with their joy.' There is an account to settle between us and them for the contemptuous jealousy with which (since it has ceased to be unmitigated contempt) they regard us; and if they do not make us amends by coming humbly to ask our assistance, they must do it by fairly acknowledging us as their masters.

October 9

My ancestor left England in 1635. I return in 1853. I sometimes feel as if I myself had been absent these two hundred and eighteen years — leaving England just emerging from the feudal system, and finding it on the verge of republicanism. It brings the two far-separated points of time very closely together, to view the matter thus.

November 14

The other day, I saw an elderly gentleman walking along Dale Street, apparently in a state of mania; for as he limped along (being afflicted with lameness) he kept talking to himself, and sometimes breaking out into a threat against some casual passenger. He was a very respectable-looking man; and I remember to have seen him last summer, in the steamer, returning from the Isle of Man, where he had been staying at Castle Mona. What a strange and ugly fix it must be for a person of quiet and perfectly respectable habits to be suddenly smitten with lunacy at noonday in a crowded street, and to walk along through a dim maze of extravagancies — partly conscious of them, but unable to resist the impulse to commit them! A long repressed nature might be represented as bursting out in this way, for want of a safety-valve.

The English are a most intolerant people. Nobody is permitted, nowadays, to have any opinion but the prevalent one. There seems to be very little difference between their educated and ignorant classes in this respect; if any, it is to the credit of the latter, who do not show such tokens of intense interest in the war. It is agreeable, however, to observe how all Englishmen pull together — how each man comes forward with his little scheme for helping on the war — how they feel themselves members of one family, talking together about their common interest, as if they were gathered around one fireside. And then what a hearty meed of honor they award to their soldiers! It is worth facing death for. Whereas, in America, when our soldiers fought as good battles, in the Mexican War, with as great proportionate loss, and far more valuable triumphs, the country seemed rather ashamed than proud of them.

December 28

Commodore Perry called to see me this morning —
a brisk, gentlemanly, offhand, but not rough, unaffected
and sensible man, looking not so elderly as he ought, on
account of a very well made wig. He is now on his return
from his cruise in the East Indian seas, and goes home by
the Baltic, with a prospect of being very well received on
account of his treaty with Japan. I seldom meet with a
man who puts himself more immediately on conversable terms than the Commodore. He soon introduced
his particular business with me — it being to inquire
whether I could recommend some suitable person to pre-
pare his notes and materials for the publication of an account of his voyage. He was good enough to say that he
had fixed upon me, in his own mind, for this office, but
that my public duties would of course prevent me from
engaging in it. I spoke of Herman Melville, and one or
two others; but he seems to have some acquaintance with
the literature of the day, and did not grasp very cordially
at any name that I could think of; nor, indeed, could I
recommend any one with full confidence. It would be a
very desirable labor for a young literary man, or, for that
matter, an old one; for the world can scarcely have in
reserve a less hackneyed theme than Japan.

I think I have been happier this Christmas than ever
before — by my own fireside, and with my wife and
children about me. More content to enjoy what I had
— less anxious for anything beyond it in this life. My
early life was perhaps a good preparation for the declining
half of life; it having been such a blank that any possible

thereafter would compare favorably with it. For a long, long while, I have occasionally been visited with a singular dream; and I have an impression that I have dreamed it even since I have been in England. It is, that I am still at college — or, sometimes, even at school — and there is a sense that I have been there unconscionably long, and have quite failed to make such progress as my contemporaries have; and I seem to meet some of them with a feeling of shame and depression that broods over me when I think of it, even at this moment. This dream, recurring all through these twenty or thirty years, must be one of the effects of that heavy seclusion in which I shut myself up for twelve years after leaving college, when everybody moved onward and left me behind. How strange that it should come now, when I may call myself famous and prosperous! — when I am happy, too! — still that same dream of life hopelessly a failure!

January 3, 1855

The progress of the age is trampling over the aristocratic institutions of England, and they crumble beneath it. This war has given the country a vast impulse towards democracy. The nobility will never hereafter, I think, assume, or be permitted, to rule the nation in peace, or command armies in war, on any ground except the individual ability which may appertain to one of their number, as well as to a commoner. And yet the nobles were never positively more noble than now — never, perhaps, so chivalrous, so honorable, so highly cultivated; but, relatively to the rest of the world, they do not main-tain their old place. The pressure of the war has tested and proved this fact, at home and abroad. At this moment, it would be an absurdity in the nobles to pretend to the position which was quietly conceded to them, a year ago. This one year has done the work of fifty ordinary ones; or, more accurately, perhaps, it has made apparent what has long been preparing itself.

January 6

Mr. Buchanan called on me to-day and stayed a good while — an hour or two. He is now staying at Mr. William Browne's, at Richmond Hill, having come to this region to bring his niece, who is to be bride's-maid at the wedding of an American girl. I like Mr. Buchanan. He cannot exactly be called gentlemanly in his manners, there being a sort of rusticity about him; moreover, he has a habit of squinting one eye, and an awkward carriage of his head; but, withal, a dignity in his large white-headed person, and a consciousness of high position and importance, which gives him ease and freedom. Very simple and frank in his address; he may be as crafty as other diplomatists are said to be; but I see only good sense and plainness of speech — appreciative, too, and genial enough to make himself conversable. He talked very freely of himself and other public people, and American and English affairs. He returns to America, he says, next October, and then retires forever from public life, being sixty-four years of age, and having now no desire except to write memoirs of his times, and especially of the administration of Mr. Polk. I suggested a doubt whether the people would permit him to retire; and he immediately responded to my hint as regards his prospects for the Presidency. He said that his mind was fully made up, and that he would never be a candidate, and that he had expressed this intention to his friends in such a way as to put it out of his own power to change it. He acknowledged that he should have been glad of the nomination for the Presidency in 1852, but that it was now too late, and that he was too old — and, in short, he seemed to be quite sincere in his *nolo episcopari;* although, really, he is the only Democrat, at this moment, whom it would not be absurd to talk of for the office. As he talked, his face flushed, and he seemed to get inwardly excited. Doubtless, it was the high vision of half his lifetime which he here relinquished. I cannot question that he is sincere; but, of course, should the people insist upon having him for President, he is too good a patriot to disobey. I wonder whether he can have had any object in saying all this to me. He might see that it would be perfectly natural for me to tell it to General Pierce. But it is a very vulgar idea — this of seeing craft and subtlety, when there is a plain and honest aspect.

January 20

God himself cannot compensate us for being born, in any period short of eternity. All the misery we endure here constitutes a claim for another life; — and, still more, all the happiness, because all true happiness involves something more than the earth owns, and something more than a mortal capacity for the enjoyment of it.

After receiving an injury on the head, the person fancied, all the rest of his life, that he heard voices of people flouting, jeering, and upbraiding him.

February 19

After writing the foregoing account of a civic banquet, where I ate turtle-soup, salmon, woodcock, oyster patties, and I know not what else, and might have eaten twenty other things, I have been to the News-room and found the Exchange pavement densely thronged with people of all ages and of all manner of dirt and rags. They were waiting for soup-tickets, and waiting very patiently too, without outcry or disturbance, or even sour looks — only patience and meekness in their faces. Well, I don't know that they have a right to be impatient of starvation; but still there does seem to be an insolence of riches and prosperity, which one day or another will have a downfall. And this will be a pity, too.

February 21

I think that the feeling of an American, divided, as I am, by the ocean from his country, has a continual and immediate correspondence with the national feeling at home; and it seems to be independent of any external communication. My thermometer stands at the same point where theirs does. Thus, my ideas about the Russian war vary in accordance with the state of the public mind at home, so that I am conscious whereabouts public sympathy is.

April 7

I dined at Mr. J. P. Heywood's on Thursday; and met

there Mr. and Mrs. Ainsworth of Smithell's Hall. The Hall is an old edifice of some five hundred years or so; and Mrs. Ainsworth says there is a bloody footstep in the entrance hall, at the foot of a staircase. The tradition is that a certain martyr, in Bloody Mary's time, being examined before the then occupant of the Hall, and committed to prison, stamped his foot in earnest protest against the injustice with which he was treated. Blood issued from his foot, which slid along the stone pavement of the hall, leaving a long footmark printed in blood; and there it has remained ever since, in spite of the scrubbings of all after generations.[1] Mrs. Ainsworth spoke of it with much solemnity, real or affected; she says that they now cover the bloody impress with a carpet, being unable to remove it. In a History of Lancashire, which I looked at, last night, there is quite a different account — according to which, the footstep is not a bloody one, but is a slight cavity or inequality in the surface of the stone, somewhat in the shape of a man's foot with a peaked shoe. The martyr's name was George Marsh; he was a curate, and was afterwards burnt. Mrs. Ainsworth asked me to come and see the Hall and the footmark; and, as it is in Lancashire, and not a great way off, and a curious old place, perhaps I may.

April 12

In my Romance, the original emigrant to America may have carried away with him a family secret, whereby it was in his power, had he so chosen, to have brought about the ruin of the family. This secret he transmits to his

[1] 'The Ancestral Footstep'; 'Dr. Grimshawe's Secret.'

American progeny, by whom it is inherited throughout all the intervening generations. At last, the hero of the Romance comes to England, and finds, that, by means of this secret, he still has it in his power to procure the downfall of the family. It would be something similar to the story of Meleager, whose fate depended on the firebrand that his mother had snatched out of the flames.

June 2

The English women of the lower classes have a grace of their own (not seen in each individual, but nevertheless belonging to their order) which is not to be found in American women of the corresponding class. The other day, in the police court, a girl was put into the witness-box, whose native graces of this sort impressed me a good deal. She was coarse, and her dress was none of the cleanest, and nowise smart; she appeared to have been up all night, too, drinking at the Tranmere wake, and had since ridden in a cart, covered up with a rug. She described herself as a servant-girl out of place; and her charm lay in all her manifestations, her tones, her gestures, her look, her way of speaking and what she said, being so appropriate and natural in a girl of that class; nothing affected; no proper grace thrown away by attempting to appear lady-like — which an American girl *would* have attempted, and succeeded in, to a certain degree. If each class would but keep within itself, and show its respect for itself by aiming at nothing beyond, they would all be more respectable. But this kind of fitness is evidently not to be expected in the future; and something else must be substituted for it.

June 24 [Leamington]

It is rather wearisome, to an American, to think of a place where no change comes for centuries, and where a peasant does but step into his father's shoes, and lead just his father's life, going in and out over the old threshold, and finally being buried close by his father's grave, time without end; and yet it is rather pleasant to know that such things are.

July 1

We were now rather tired and sated (for old things, and old houses, and all sorts of antiquities, pall upon the taste, after a little while), and went to the railroad, intending to go home; but we got into the wrong train, and were carried by express, with hurricane speed, to Bradon, where we alighted, and waited a good while for the return train to Coventry. At Coventry again we had more than an hour to wait, and therefore wandered wearily up into the city, and took another look at its bustling streets, in which there seems to be a good emblem of what England itself really is — with a great deal of antiquity in it, and which is now chiefly a modification of the old. The new things are based and supported on the sturdy old things, and often limited and impeded by them; but this antiquity is so massive that there seems to be no means of getting rid of it without tearing the whole structure of society to pieces.

July 4 [Liverpool]

From Uttoxeter I rode in the first class to Crewe; thence in the second class through Chester to Liverpool,

arriving at just nine P.M. It is foolish ever to travel in
the first-class carriages, except with ladies in charge.
Nothing is to be seen or learnt there; nobody to be seen
but civil and silent gentlemen, sitting on their enshrined
dignities. In the second class, it is very different.

July 21 [Ambleside]

I question whether any part of the world looks so
beautiful as England — this part of England, at least [the
Lake Country] — on a fine summer morning. It makes
one think the more cheerfully of human life to see such
a bright universal verdure; such sweet, rural, peaceful,
flower-bordered cottages — not cottages of gentility, but
dwellings of the laboring poor; such nice villas along the
roadside, so tastefully contrived for comfort and beauty,
and adorned more and more, year after year, with the
care and after-thought of people who mean to live in
them a great while, and feel as if their children might
live in them also — and so they plant trees to overshadow
their walks, and train ivy and all beautiful vines up
against their walls, and thus live for the future in another
sense than we Americans do. And the climate helps them
out, and makes everything moist, and green, and full of
tender life, instead of dry and arid, as human life and
vegetable life is so apt to be with us. Certainly, England
can present a more attractive face than we can; even in
its humbler modes of life, to say nothing of the beautiful
lives that might be led, one would think, by the higher
classes, whose gateways, with broad, smooth gravelled
drives leading through them, you see every mile or two
along the road, winding into some proud seclusion. All

this is passing away, and society must assume new relations; but there is no harm in believing that there has
been something very good in English life — good for all
classes while the world was in a state out of which these
forms naturally grew.

July 21 [Ullswater]

As for Southey himself, my idea is, that few better or
more blameless men have ever lived; but he seems to
lack color, passion, warmth, or something that should
enable me to bring him into close relation with myself.

We rode down the valley, and gazed at the vast slope of
Helvellyn, and at Thirlmere beneath it, and at Eagle's
Crag and Raven's Crag, which beheld themselves in it,
and we cast many a look behind at Blencathra, and that
noble brotherhood of mountains out of the midst of which
we came. But, to say the truth, I was weary of fine scenery, and it seemed to me that I had eaten a score of mountains, and quaffed down as many lakes, all in the space of
two or three days — and the natural consequence was a
surfeit. There was scarcely a single place in all our tour
where I should not have been glad to spend a month; but,
by flitting so quickly from one point to another, I lost all
the more recondite beauties, and had come away without
retaining even the surface of much that I had seen. I am
slow to feel — slow, I suppose, to comprehend; and, like
the anaconda, I need to lubricate any object a great deal
before I can swallow it and actually make it my own. Yet
I shall always be glad of this tour, and shall wonder the
more at England, which comprehends so much, such a

rich variety, within its narrow bounds. If England were all the world, it still would have been worth while for the Creator to have made it, and mankind would have had no cause to find fault with their abode; except that there is not room enough for so many as might be happy here.

July 30 [*Liverpool*]

I have betaken myself [in the absence of Mrs. Hawthorne and the children] to the Rock Ferry Hotel, where I am as comfortable as I could be anywhere but at home; but it is rather comfortless to think of home as three years off, and three thousand miles away. With what a sense of utter weariness, not fully realized till then, we shall sink down on our own threshold, when we reach it. The moral effect of being without a settled abode is very wearisome.

August 12

For the last week or two I have passed my time between the hotel and the Consulate, and a weary life it is, and one that leaves little of profit behind it. I am sick to death of my office — brutal captains and brutal sailors; continual complaints of mutual wrong, which I have no power to set right, and which, indeed, seem to have no right on either side; calls of idleness or ceremony from my travelling countrymen, who seldom know what they are in search of at the commencement of their tour, and never have attained any desirable end at the close of it; beggars, cheats, simpletons, unfortunates, so mixed up that it is impossible to distinguish one from another, and so, in self-defence, the Consul distrusts them all. I see many specimens of mankind, but come to the conclusion that there is but little variety among them, after all.

Thackeray has a dread of servants, insomuch that he hates to address them, or to ask them for anything. His morbid sensibility, in this regard, has perhaps led him to study and muse upon them, so that he may be presumed to have a more intimate knowledge of this class than any other man.

Carlyle dresses so badly, and wears such a rough outside, that the flunkies are rude to him at gentlemen's doors.

September 13 [*London*]

Mr. Buchanan, the American Minister, called on me on Tuesday, and left his card; an intimation that I ought sooner to have paid my respects to him; so yesterday forenoon I set out to find his residence, 56 Harley Street. It is a street out of Cavendish Square, in a fashionable quarter, although fashion is said to be ebbing away from it. The ambassador seems to intend some little state in his arrangements; but, no doubt, the establishment compares shabbily enough with those of the legations of other great countries, and with the houses of the English aristocracy. A servant, not in livery, or in a very unrecognizable one, opened the door for me, and gave my card to a sort of upper attendant, who took it in to Mr. Buchanan. He had three gentlemen with him, so desired that I should be ushered into the office of the legation, until he should be able to receive me. Here I found a clerk or *attaché*, Mr. Moran, who has been two or three years on this side of the water; an intelligent person, who seems to be in correspondence with the New York Courier and Enquirer. By and by came in another American to get a passport for the Continent, and soon the three gentlemen took leave of the ambassador, and I was invited to his presence.

The tall, large figure of Mr. Buchanan has a certain air of state and dignity; he carries his head in a very awkward way (in consequence, as the old scandal says, of his having once attempted to cut his throat) but still looks like a man of long and high authority, and, with his white hair, is now quite venerable. There is certainly a lack of polish, a kind of rusticity, notwithstanding which you feel him to be a man of the world. I should think he might succeed very tolerably in English society, being heavy and sensible, cool, kindly, and good-humored, with a great deal of experience of life. We talked about various matters, politics among the rest; and he observed that if the President had taken the advice which he gave him in two long letters, before his inauguration, he would have had a perfectly quiet and successful term of office. The advice was, to form a perfectly homogeneous cabinet of Union men, and to satisfy the extremes of the party by a fair distribution of minor offices; whereas Pierce formed his cabinet of extreme men, on both sides, and gave the minor offices to moderate ones. But the antislavery people, surely, had no representative in the cabinet. Mr. Buchanan further observed, that he thought the President has a fair chance of re-nomination, for that the South could not, in honor, desert him; to which I replied

that the South had been guilty of such things heretofore.
Mr. Buchanan thinks that the next Presidential term will
be more important and critical, both as to our foreign
relations and internal affairs, than any preceding one —
which I should judge likely enough to be the case, although I heard the same prophecy often made respecting
the present term.

Mr. Buchanan was very kind in his inquiries about my
wife, with whom he is acquainted from having dined
with us at Rock Park a year or two ago. I always feel,
as if he were a man of heart, feeling, and simplicity,
and certainly it would be unjust to conclude otherwise,
merely from the fact (very suspicious, it is true) of his
having been a life-long politician.

September 14

At seven o'clock we (mamma, Una, and I) went to dine
with Mr. Russell Sturgis in Portland Place. . . . Mr.
Sturgis's house is a very fine one, and he gave us a very
quiet, elegant, and enjoyable dinner, in much better
taste and with less fuss than Liverpool dinners. Mr.
Sturgis is a friend of Thackeray, and, speaking of the last
number of The Newcomes — so touching that nobody
can read it aloud without breaking down — he mentioned
that Thackeray himself had read it to James Russell
Lowell and William Story in a cider-cellar! I read all the
preceding numbers of The Newcomes to my wife, but
happened not to have an opportunity to read this last,
and was glad of it — knowing that my eyes would fill,
and my voice quiver. Mr. Sturgis likes Thackeray, and
thinks him a good fellow. Mr. Sturgis has a — or I

don't know but I ought better to say *the* — beautiful full-length picture of Washington by Stuart, and I was proud to see that noblest face and figure here in England; the picture of a man beside whom, considered merely as a physical man, any English nobleman whom I have seen would look like common beef or clay.

Speaking of Thackeray, I cannot but wonder at his coolness in respect to his own pathos, and compare it with my emotions, when I read the last scene of The Scarlet Letter to my wife, just after writing it — tried to read it rather, for my voice swelled and heaved, as if I were tossed up and down on an ocean as it subsides after a storm. But I was in a very nervous state then, having gone through a great diversity and severity of emotion, for many months past. I think I have never overcome my own adamant in any other instance.

September 17 [Liverpool]

I saw in an American paper yesterday, that an opera (still unfinished) had been written on the story of the Scarlet Letter, and that several scenes of it had been performed successfully in New York. I should think it might possibly succeed as an opera, though it would certainly fail as a play.

September 24 [London]

In the evening I walked forth to Charing Cross, and thence along the Strand and Fleet Street, where I made no new discoveries, unless it were the Mitre Tavern. I mean to go into it some day. The streets were much thronged, and there seemed to be a good many young people — lovers, it is to be hoped — who had spent the day together, and were going innocently home. Perhaps so — perhaps not. At every street corner, too, under archways, and at other places of vantage, or loitering along, with some indescribable peculiarity that distinguished her, and perhaps turning to re-tread her footsteps, was a woman; or sometimes two walked arm in arm — hunting in couples — and separated when they saw a gentleman approaching. One feels a curious and reprehensible sympathy for these poor nymphs; it seems such a pity that they should not each and all of them find what they seek! — that any of them should tramp the pavement the whole night through, or should go hungry and forlorn to their beds. They are much more tolerable than in Liverpool, where it is impossible to go out, after nightfall, without having to decline the overtures of some girl of the town.

September 25

In the evening I strolled out, and walked as far as Saint Paul's — never getting enough of the bustle of London, which may weary, but can never satisfy me. By night London looks wild and dreamy, and fills me with a sort of pleasant dread. It was a clear evening, with a bright English moon — that is to say, what we Americans should call rather dim.

September 26

Yesterday, at eleven, I walked towards Westminster Abbey; and as I drew near, the Abbey-bells were clamorous for joy, chiming merrily, musically, and obstreperously — the most rejoicing sound that can be conceived;

and we ought to have a chime of bells in every American
town and village, were it only to keep alive the celebra-
tion of the Fourth of July. I conjectured that there might
have been another victory over the Russians — that perhaps the northern side of Sebastopol had surrendered; but
soon I saw the riddle that these merry bells were pro-
claiming. There were a great many private carriages,
and a large concourse of loungers and spectators, near the
door of the church that stands close under the eaves of
the Abbey. Gentlemen and ladies, gayly dressed, were
issuing forth; carriages driving away, and others drawing
up to the door, in their turn; and, in short, a marriage had
just been celebrated in the church, and this was the
wedding-party. The last time I was there, Westminster
was flinging out its great voice of joy for a national triumph; now, for the happy union of two lovers. What a
mighty sympathizer is this old Abbey!

September 28

A very great majority of the memorials [in Saint
Paul's] are to naval and military men, slain in Bonaparte's
wars; men in whom one feels little or no interest (except
Picton, Abercrombie, Moore, Nelson, of course, and a
few others really historic), they having done nothing
remarkable, save having been shot, nor shown any more
brains than the cannon-balls that killed them.

September 29

Yesterday we walked to the British Museum. . . .
It is a hopeless — and to me, generally, a depressing —
business to go through an immense multifarious show

like this (if there were any other like it) glancing at a
thousand things, and conscious of some little titillation
of mind from them, but really taking in nothing, and getting no good from anything. One need not go beyond the
limits of the British Museum to be profoundly accomplished in all branches of science, art, literature; only it
would take a lifetime to exhaust it in any one department; but, to see it as we did, and with no prospect of
ever seeing it more at leisure, only impressed me with the
old apothegm, 'Life is short, and Art is long.' The fact
is, the world is accumulating too many materials for
knowledge. We do not recognize for rubbish what is
really rubbish; and under this head might be reckoned
almost every thing one sees in the British Museum; and,
as each generation leaves its fragments and potsherds
behind it, such will finally be the desperate conclusion of
the learned.

October 3

There is a woman who has several times passed through
our street, stopping occasionally to sing songs under the
windows; and last evening, between nine and ten o'clock,
she came and sang 'Kathleen O'Moore' richly and
sweetly — a voice that rose up out of the dim, chill
street, and made our hearts throb in unison with it, here
in our comfortable drawing-room. I never heard a voice
that touched me more. Somebody told her to go away,
and she stopped like a nightingale suddenly shot; but,
finding that Sophia wished to know something about her,
Fanny and one of the maids ran after her, and brought
her into the hall. It seems she was brought up to sing at

the opera, and married an Italian opera-singer, who is
now dead; lodging at a model lodging-house at three-
pence a night, and being a penny short to-night, she tried
this method, in hope of getting that penny. She takes in
plain sewing when she can get any, and picks up a trifle
about the street by means of her voice, which, she says,
was once sweet, but has now been injured by the poorness
of her living. She is a pale woman, with black eyes,
Fanny says, and may have been pretty once, but is not so
now. It seems very strange, that, with such a gift of
Heaven, so cultivated, too, as her voice is, and making
even an unsusceptible heart vibrate like a harp-string,
she should not have had some sort of an engagement
among the hundred theatres and singing-rooms of London; that she should throw away her melody in the
streets for the mere chance of a penny, when sounds not
a hundredth part so sweet are worth purses of gold from
other lips.

October 5

When I reached home, at about half past two, I found
Sophia awaiting me anxiously; for Mrs. Sturgis had noti-
fied Leigh Hunt that we were coming to visit him at
Hammersmith, and she was to send her carriage for us at
three o'clock. Barry Cornwall had likewise written me a
note, and a note of introduction to Leigh Hunt. At three,
the carriage came; and though the sky looked very omi-
nous, we drove off, and reached Hammersmith in half an
hour, or little more — the latter part of the drive in a
real gush and pour of rain. Mr. Hunt met us at the door
of his little house; a very plain and shabby little house, in

a contiguous range of others like it, with no view but an
ugly village-street, and nothing beautiful inside or out.
But Leigh Hunt is a beautiful and venerable old man,
tall and slender, with a striking face, and the gentlest
and most naturally courteous manners. He ushered us
into his little study, or parlor, or both; a very mean room,
with poor paper-hangings and carpet, few books, and an
awful lack of upholstery; all which defects it is sad to see,
because Leigh Hunt would so much enjoy all beautiful
things, and would seem to be in his place among them;
nor has he the grim dignity that makes nakedness the
better robe.

He is a beautiful man. I never saw a finer face, either
as to the cut of the features, or the expression, or that
showed the play of feeling so well. At my first glimpse of
his face, when he met us in the entry, I saw that he was
old, his long hair being quite white, and his wrinkles
many; an aged visage, in short. But as he talked, and
became earnest in conversation, I ceased to see his age;
and sometimes a flash of youth came out of his eyes, and
illuminated his whole face. It was a really wonderful
effect. I have never met an Englishman whose manners
pleased me so well; with so little that was conventional,
and yet perfect good-breeding, it being the growth of a
kindly and sensitive nature, without any reference to
rule. His eyes are dark, and very fine, and his voice ac-
companies them like music; — a very pleasant voice. He
is exceedingly appreciative of what is passing among
those who surround him. I felt that no effect of what he
said — no flitting feeling in myself — escaped him; and,
indeed, it rather confused me to see always a ripple on his

face, responsive to any slightest breeze over my mind. His figure is very mobile; and as he talks, he folds his hands nervously, and betokens in many ways a nature delicate and immediately sensitive, quick to feel pleasure or pain. There is not an English trait in him, from head to foot, nor either intellectually or physically; no beef, no ale or stout; and this is the reason that the English have appreciated him no better, and that they leave this sweet and delicate poet poor, and with scanty laurels, in his old age. It is his American blood (his mother was a Pennsylvanian) that gives him whatever excellence he has — the fineness, subtlety, and grace that characterize him — and his person, too, is thoroughly American. I wonder that America has not appreciated him better, were it only for our own claims in him.

He loves dearly to be praised; that is, he loves sympathy as a flower likes sunshine; and in response to all that we said about his writings (and, for my part, I went quite to the extent of my conscience) his face shone, and he expressed great delight. He could not tell us, he said, the happiness that such appreciation gave him; it always took him by surprise, he remarked, for — perhaps because he cleaned his own boots, and performed other little ordinary offices for himself — he never was conscious of anything wonderful in his own person. And then he smiled. It is usually very difficult for me to praise a man to his face; but Mr. Hunt snuffs up the incense with such gracious satisfaction that it was comparatively easy to praise him; and then, too, we were the representatives of our country, and spoke for thousands. The rain poured, while we were talking, the lightning flashed, and the

thunder broke; but I fancy it was really a sunny hour for
Leigh Hunt. He, on his part, praised the Scarlet Letter;
but I really do not think that I like to be praised *viva
voce;* at least, I am glad when it is said and done with,
though I will not say that my heart does not expand a
little towards the man who rightly appreciates my books.
But I am of somewhat sterner stuff and tougher fibre than
Leigh Hunt; and the dark seclusion — the atmosphere
without any oxygen of sympathy — in which I spent all
the years of my youthful manhood — have enabled me
to do almost as well without as with it.

Leigh Hunt must have suffered keenly in his life, and
enjoyed keenly; keeping his feelings so much upon the
surface as he does, and convenient for everybody to play
upon. But happiness has greatly predominated, no
doubt. A light, mildly joyous nature, gentle, graceful,
yet perhaps without that deepest grace that results from
strength. I am inclined to imagine that he may be more
beautiful, now, both in person and character, than in his
earlier days; for the gravity of age sheds a venerable
grace about him, after all, and gives a dignity which he
may have lacked at first. I was glad to hear him say, that
he had most cheering views about a future life; and there
were many tokens of cheerfulness, resignation, enjoyment of whatever he had to enjoy, quiet relinquishment
of what was denied him, and piety, and hope, that made
me both like and respect him. I should delight to see him
in a beautiful house, with a delightful climate and everything elegant about him, and a succession of tender and
lovely women to praise him to his face, from morning till
night. He is better for women's companionship than

for men's, because they can better give him the tender
appreciation which he needs.

The sun shone out once, while we were talking, but
was soon over-clouded; and it rained briskly again when
we left his door. As we took leave he kissed Una's hand;
for she had accompanied us, and sat listening earnestly,
and looking very pretty, though saying not a word. He
shook and grasped warmly both my hands, at parting;
and seemed as much interested as if he had known us for
years; and all this was genuine feeling, a quick, luxuriant
growth out of his heart — a soil in which to sow flower-
seeds, not acorns — but a true heart, nevertheless. His
dress, by the by, was black, the coat buttoned up so high
that I saw no sign of a shirt. His housemaid (my wife and
Una say) was particularly slovenly in appearance. But
Leigh Hunt himself is a beautiful object.

November 16 [*Liverpool*]

I went to the North Hospital, yesterday, to take the
deposition of a dying man, as to his ill-treatment by the
second and third mates of the ship Assyria, on the voyage
from New Orleans. This hospital is a very gloomy place,
with its wide bleak entries and staircases, which may be
very good for summer weather, but which are most ungenial at this black November season. I found the physi-
cians of the house talking and laughing very cheerfully
with Mr. Wilding, who had preceded me. We went
forthwith, up two or three pairs of stairs, to the ward
where the sick man lay, and where there were six or eight
other beds, in almost each of which was a patient —
narrow beds, shabbily furnished. The man whom I came

to see was the only one who was not perfectly quiet; neither was he very restless. The doctor, informing him of my presence, intimated that his disease might be fatal, and that I was come to hear what he had to say as to the causes of his death. Afterwards, a Testament was sought for, in order to swear him; and I administered the oath, and made him kiss the book. He then (in response to Mr. Wilding's questions) told how he had been beaten and ill-treated, banged and thwacked, from the moment he came on board; to which usage he ascribed his death. Sometimes his senses seemed to sink away, so that I almost thought him dead; but, by-and-by, the questions would appear to reach him, and bring him back, and he went on with his evidence, interspersing it, however, with dying groans, and almost death rattles. In the midst of whatever he was saying, he often recurred to a sum of four dollars and a half, which he said he had put into the hands of the porter of the hospital, and which he wanted to get back. Several times, he expressed his wish to get back to America (of which he was not a native), and, on the whole, I do not think he had any real sense of his precarious condition, notwithstanding that he assented to the doctor's hint to that effect. He sank away so much, at one time, that they brought him wine in a tin cup, with a spout to drink out of; and he mustered strength to raise himself in his bed and drink; then hemmed, with a rather disappointed air, as if it did not stimulate and refresh him, as drink ought. When he had finished his evidence (which Mr. Wilding took down in writing, from his mouth), he marked his cross at the foot of the paper; and we ceased to torment him with further question. His deposition will probably do no good, so far as the punishment of the persons implicated is concerned; for he appears to have come on board in a sickly state, and never to have been well during the passage. On a pallet close by his bed lay another seaman of the same ship, who had likewise been abused by the same men, and bore more ostensible marks of ill usage than this man did, about the head and face. There is a most dreadful state of things aboard our ships. Hell itself can be no worse than some of them; and I do pray that some New-Englander, with the itch of reform in him, may turn his thoughts this way. The first step towards better things — the best practicable step for the present — would be, to legalize flogging on shipboard; thereby doing away with the miscellaneous assaults and batteries, kickings, fisticuffings, ropes'-endings, marline-spikings, which the inferior officers continually perpetrate, as the only mode of keeping up anything like discipline. As in many other instances, Philanthropy has overshot itself by the prohibition of flogging, causing the captain to avoid the responsibility of solemn punishment, and leave his mates to make devils of themselves by habitual (and hardly avoidable) ill-treatment of the seamen.

Before I left the dying sailor, his features seemed to contract and grow sharp. Some young medical students stood about the bed, watching death creep upon him, and anticipating, perhaps, that, in a day or two, they would have the poor fellow's body on the dissecting-table. Dead patients, I believe, undergo this fate, unless somebody chooses to pay their funeral expenses; but the captain of Assyria (who seems to be respectable and kind-hearted, though master of a floating-hell) tells me that he means to bury this man at his own cost. This morning, there is a note from the surgeon of the hospital, announcing his death, and likewise the dangerous state of his shipmate, whom I saw on the pallet beside him.

November 28

I have grown wofully aristocratic, in my tastes, I fear, since coming to England; at all events, I am conscious of a certain disgust at going to dine in a house with a small entrance-hall, and narrow staircase, parlor with chintz curtains, and all other arrangements on a similar scale. This is pitiable. However, I really do not think I should mind these things, were it not for the bustle, the affectation, the intensity, of the mistress of the house. It is certain, that a woman in England is either decidedly a lady, or decidedly not a lady. There seems to be no respectable medium. Bill of fare: broiled soles, half of a roast pig, a haricot of mutton, stewed oysters, a tart, pears, figs, with sherry and port wine, both good, and the port particularly so. I ate some pig, and could hardly resist the lady's importunities to eat more; though, to my fancy, it tasted of swill — had a flavor of the pigsty. On the parlor-table were some poor editions of popular books, Longfellow's poems, and others. The lady affects a literary taste, and bothered me about my own productions.

A beautiful subject for a romance, or for a sermon, would be the subsequent life of the young man whom Jesus bade to sell all he had, and give to the poor; and he went away sorrowful, and is not recorded to have done what he was bid.

January 1, 1856

To a cool observer, a country does not show to best advantage during a time of war. All its self-conceit is doubly visible, and, indeed, is sedulously kept uppermost by direct appeals to it. The country must be humbugged, in order to keep its courage up.

Sentiment seems to me more abundant in middle-aged ladies, in England, than in the United States. I don't know how it may be with young ladies.

January 16

I have suffered wofully from low spirits for some time past; and this has not often been the case, since I grew to be a man, even in the least auspicious periods of my life. My desolate, bachelor condition, I suppose, is the cause. Really, I have no pleasure in anything; and I feel my tread to be heavier, and my physical movement more sluggish, than in happier times; a weight is always upon me. My appetite is not good. I sleep ill, lying awake late at night, to think sad thoughts and to imagine sombre things, and awaking before light with the same thoughts and fancies still in my mind. My heart sinks always as I ascend the stairs to my office, from a dim augury of ill news that I may perhaps hear — of black-sealed letters — or some such horrors. Nothing gives me any joy. I have learned what the bitterness of exile is, in these days; and I never should have known it but for the absence of my wife. 'Remote, unfriended, melancholy, slow' — I can perfectly appreciate that line of Goldsmith; for it well expresses my own torpid, unenterprising, joyless state of mind and heart. I am like an uprooted plant, wilted and drooping. Life seems so purposeless as not to be worth the trouble of carrying it on any further.

February 28

Why did Christ curse the fig-tree? It was not in the least to blame; and it seems most unreasonable to have expected it to bear figs out of season. Instead of withering it away, it would have been as great a miracle, and far more beautiful — and, one would think, of more beneficent influence — to have made it suddenly rich with ripe fruit. Then, to be sure, it might have died joyfully, having answered so good a purpose. I have been reminded of this miracle by the story of a man in Heywood, a town in Lancashire, who used such horribly profane language that a plane-tree in front of his cottage is said to have withered away from that hour. I can draw no moral from the incident of the fig-tree, unless it be that all things perish from the instant when they cease to answer some divine purpose.

March 24 [London]

But what a noble palace, nobly enriched, this Hampton Court is! The English government does well to keep it up, and to admit the people freely into it, for it is impossible for even a Republican not to feel something like awe — at least a profound respect — for all this state, and for the institutions which are here represented, the sovereigns whose moral magnificence demands such a residence; and its permanence, too, enduring from age to age, and each royal generation adding new splendors to those accumulated by their predecessors. If one views the matter in another way, to be sure, we may feel indignant that such dolt-heads, scamps, rowdies, and every way mean people, as most of the English sovereigns have been, should inhabit these stately halls (which, by the by, they have not for a long time past), and contrast its splendors with their littleness; but, on the whole, I readily consented within myself to be impressed for a moment with the feeling that royalty has its glorious side. By no possibility can we ever have such a place in America.

March 25

I had the pleasure [at a dinner at Bennoch's] to be introduced to Mrs. Newton Crosland — a rather tall, thin, pale, and lady-like person, looking, I thought, of a sensitive character. She expressed in a low tone and quiet way great delight at seeing my distinguished self; for she is a vast admirer of The Scarlet Letter, and especially of the character of Hester; indeed, I remember seeing a most favorable criticism of the book from her pen, in one of the London magazines. I should gladly have responded by praising her own works, but, though she sent me one of them, three or four years ago, I had quite forgotten its subject, and so could not say anything greatly to the purpose. Neither would it have been easy, in any case, to respond in due measure, for Mrs. Crosland was awfully lavish in her admiration, preferring poor me to all the novelists of this age, or, I believe, any other; and she and Mr. Bennoch discussed, right across me, the uses to which I had better put my marvelous genius, as respects the mode of working up my English experiences. Oh Lord!

Dear me! I suppose this may be the tone of London literary society.

March 27

Yesterday, I went out at about twelve, and visited the British Museum; an exceedingly tiresome affair. It quite crushes a person to see so much at once; and I wandered from hall to hall with a weary and heavy heart, wishing (Heaven forgive me!) that the Elgin marbles and the frieze of the Parthenon were all burnt into lime, and that the granite Egyptian statues were hewn and squared into building-stones, and that the mummies had all turned to dust, two thousand years ago; and, in fine, that all the material relics of so many successive ages had disappeared with the generations that produced them. The present is burthened too much with the past. We have not time, in our earthly existence, to appreciate what is warm with life, and immediately around us; yet we heap up all these old shells, out of which human life has long emerged, casting them off forever. I do not see how future ages are to stagger onward under all this dead weight, with the additions that will be continually made to it.

April 7 [At Lord Mayor's Dinner in London]

My eyes were mostly drawn to a young lady,[1] who sat nearly opposite me, across the table. She was, I suppose, dark, and yet not dark, but rather seemed to be of pure white marble, yet not white; but the purest and finest complexion, without a shade of color in it, yet anything but sallow or sickly. Her hair was a wonderful deep raven-

[1] Miriam in 'The Marble Faun.'

black, black as night, black as death; *not* raven-black, for
that has a shiny gloss, and hers had not, but it was hair
never to be painted nor described — wonderful hair,
Jewish hair. Her nose had a beautiful outline, though I
could see that it was Jewish too; and that, and all her
features, were so fine that sculpture seemed a despicable
art beside her, and certainly my pen is good for nothing.
If any likeness could be given, however, it must be by
sculpture, not painting. She was slender and youthful,
and yet had a stately and cold, though soft and womanly
grace; and, looking at her, I saw what were the wives of
the old patriarchs in their maiden or early-married days
— what Rachel was, when Jacob wooed her for seven
years and seven more — what Judith was, for, womanly
as she looked, I doubt not that she could have slain a man
in a good cause — what Bathsheba was, only she seemed
to have no sin in her — perhaps what Eve was, though
one could hardly think her weak enough to eat the apple.
I should never have thought of touching her, nor desired
to touch her; for, whether owing to distinctness of race,
or my sense that she was a Jewess, or whatever else, I
felt a sort of repugnance, simultaneously with my perception that she was an admirable creature. . . .

April 8

From Downing Street we crossed over and entered
Westminster Hall, and passed through it, and up the
flight of steps at its farthest end, and along the avenue of
statues, into the vestibule of the House of Commons. It
was now somewhat past five, and we stood at the inner
entrance of the House, to see the members pass in, Ben-

noch pointing out to me the distinguished ones. I was not much impressed with the appearance of the members generally; they seemed to me rather shabbier than English gentlemen usually, and I saw or fancied in many of them a certain self-importance, as they passed into the interior, betokening them to be very full of their dignity. Some of them looked more American — more like American politicians — than most Englishmen do. There was now and then a gray-headed country gentleman, the very type of stupidity; and two or three city members came up and spoke to Bennoch, and showed themselves quite as dull, in their aldermanic way, as the country squires. . . . Bennoch pointed out Lord John Russell, a little, very short, elderly gentleman, in a brown coat, and so large a hat — not large of brim, but large like a peck-measure — that I saw really no face beneath it. By and by came a rather tall, slender person, in a black frock-coat, buttoned up, and black pantaloons, taking long steps, but I thought rather feebly or listlessly. His shoulders were round, or else he had a habitual stoop in them. He had a prominent nose, a thin face, and a sallow, very sallow complexion; and was a very unwholesome looking person; and had I seen him in America I should have taken him for a hard-working editor of a newspaper, weary and worn with night-labor and want of exercise — aged before his time. It was Disraeli, and I never saw any other Englishman look in the least like him; though, in America, his appearance would not attract notice as being unusual. I do not remember any other note-worthy person whom we saw enter; in fact, the House had already been some time in session, and most of the members were in their places. . . .

While we were drinking our wine, we again saw Disraeli, another adventurer, who has risen from the people by modes perhaps as quackish as those of Mr. Ingram. He came and stood near our table, looking at the bill of fare, and then sat down on the opposite side of the room with another gentleman, and ate his dinner. He don't look as if he had a healthy appetite. Bennoch says that he makes himself up with great care, and spends a long time plucking the white hairs from among his sable locks. He is said to be poor; and though he had property with his wife, it is all gone. The story of his marriage (which Bennoch told me, but which I do not remember well enough to record it) does him much credit; and indeed I am inclined to like Disraeli, as a man who has made his own place good among a hostile aristocracy, and leads instead of following them.

April 9

Mr. [Tom] Taylor is reckoned a brilliant conversationist; but I suppose he requires somebody to draw him out and assist him; for I could see nothing that I thought very remarkable on this occasion. He is not a kind of man whom I can talk with, or greatly help to talk; so, though I sat next to him, nothing came of it. He told me some stories of his life in the Temple — little funny incidents, that he afterwards wrought into his dramas; in short, a sensible, active-minded, clearly perceptive man, with a humorous way of showing up men and matters, but without originality, or much imagination, or dance of fancy. I wish I could know exactly what the English style good conversation. Probably it is something like plum-pudding — as heavy, but seldom so rich. . . .

I grew weary of so many people, especially of the ladies, who were rather superfluous in their oblations, quite stifling me, indeed, with the incense that they burnt under my nose. So far as I could judge, they had all been invited there to see me. It is ungracious, even hoggish, not to be gratified with the interest they expressed in me; but then it is really a bore, and one does not know what to do or say. I felt like a hippopotamus, or — to use a more modest illustration — like some strange insect imprisoned under a tumbler, with a dozen eyes watching whatever I did.

May 10 [*Glasgow*]

In truth, I doubt if anybody ever does really see a mountain, who goes for the set and sole purpose of seeing it. Nature will not let herself be seen, in such cases. You must patiently bide her time; and, by and by, at some unforeseen moment, she will quietly and suddenly unveil herself, and, for a brief space, let you look right into the heart of her mystery. But if you call out to her peremptorily, 'Nature! unveil yourself this very instant!' she only draws her veil the closer; and you may look with all your eyes, and imagine you see all that she can show, and yet see nothing. . . . I think that this fashion of the picturesque will pass away.

[*Abbotsford*]

Reaching Melrose, we drew up at the inn-door, and drank some ale, fortified with which and without alighting, we set off for Abbotsford, three miles off. The neighborhood of Melrose, leading to Abbotsford, has

many handsome residences of modern build and very
recent date — suburban villas, each with its little lawn
and garden ground, such as we see in the vicinity of
Liverpool. I noticed, too, one castellated house, of no
great size, but old, and looking as if its tower were built,
not for show, but for actual defence in the old border
warfare.

We were not long in reaching Abbotsford. The house,
which is more compact, and of considerably less extent
than I anticipated, stands in full view from the road, and
at only a short distance from it, lower down towards the
river. Its aspect disappointed me; but so does everything. It is but a villa, after all; no castle, nor even a
large manor-house, and very unsatisfactory when you
consider it in that light. Indeed, it impressed me, not
as a real house, intended for the home of human beings
— a house to die in or to be born in — but as a plaything — something in the same category as Horace Wal-
pole's Strawberry Hill. The present owner seems to have
found it insufficient for the actual purposes of life; for he
is adding a wing, which promises to be as extensive as the
original structure.

We rang at the front door (the family being now absent), and were speedily admitted by a middle-aged or
somewhat elderly man — the butler, I suppose, or some
upper servant — who at once acceded to our request to
be permitted to see the house. We stepped from the porch
immediately into the entrance-hall; and having the great
Hall of Battle Abbey, I believe, in my memory, and the
ideal of a baronial hall in my mind, I was quite taken
aback at the smallness and narrowness and lowness of

this; which, however, is a very fine one, on its own little
scale. In truth, it is not much more than a vestibule.
The ceiling is carved; and every inch of the walls is covered with claymores, targets, and other weapons and
armor, or old-time curiosities, tastefully arranged, many
of which, no doubt, have a history attached to them —
or had, in Sir Walter's own mind. Our attendant was
a very intelligent person, and pointed out much that was
interesting; but in such a multitudinous variety it was almost impossible to fix the eye upon any one thing. Probably the apartment looked smaller than it really was, on
account of being so wainscoted and festooned with curiosities. I remember nothing particularly, unless it be the
coal-grate in the fireplace, which was one formerly used
by Archbishop Sharpe, the prelate whom Balfour of Bur-
ley murdered. Either in this room or the next one, however, there was a glass case containing the suit of clothes
last worn by Scott — a short green coat, somewhat worn,
with silvered buttons, a pair of gray tartan trousers, and
a white hat. It was in the hall that we saw these things;
for there too, I recollect, were a good many walking-sticks
that had been used by Scott, and the hatchet with which
he was in the habit of lopping branches from his trees, as
he walked among them.

From the hall we passed into the study — a small
room, lined with the books which Sir Walter, no doubt,
was most frequently accustomed to refer to; and our
guide pointed out some volumes of the *Moniteur*, which
he used while writing the History of Napoleon. Probably
these were the driest and dullest volumes in his whole
library. About mid-height of the walls of the study there

is a gallery, with a short flight of steps for the convenience
of getting at the upper books. A study-table occupied the
centre of the room, and at one end of the table stands an
easy-chair, covered with morocco, and with ample space
to fling one's self back. The servant told me that I might
sit down in this chair, for that Sir Walter sat there while
writing his romances, 'and perhaps,' quoth the man, smiling, 'you may catch some inspiration!' What a bitter
word this would have been if he had known me to be a
romance-writer! 'No, I never shall be inspired to write
romances!' I answered, as if such an idea had never occurred to me. I sat down, however. This study quite
satisfied me, being planned on principles of common-
sense, and made to work in, and without any fantastic
adaptation of old forms to modern uses.

Next to the study is the library, an apartment of respectable size, and containing as many books as it can
hold, all protected by wire-work. I did not observe what
or whose works were here; but the attendant showed us
one whole compartment full of volumes having reference
to ghosts, witchcraft, and the supernatural generally. It
is remarkable that Scott should have felt interested in
such subjects, being such a worldly and earthly man as he
was; but then, indeed, almost all forms of popular super-
stition do clothe the ethereal with earthly attributes, and
so make it grossly perceptible.

The library, like the study, suited me well — merely
the fashion of the apartment, I mean — and I doubt not
it contains as many curious volumes as are anywhere to
be met with within a similar space. The drawing-room
adjoins it; and here we saw a beautiful ebony cabinet,

which was presented to Sir Walter by George IV; and
some pictures of much interest — one of Scott himself at
thirty-five, rather portly, with a heavy face, but shrewd
eyes, which seem to observe you closely. There is a full-
length of his eldest son, an officer of dragoons, leaning on
his charger; and a portrait of Lady Scott — a brunette,
with black hair and eyes, very pretty, warm, vivacious,
and un-English in her aspect. I am not quite sure whether
I saw all of these pictures in the drawing-room, or some
of them in the dining-room; but the one that struck me
most — and very much indeed — was the head of Mary,
Queen of Scots, literally the head cut off, and lying on a
dish. It is said to have been painted by an Italian or
French artist, two days after her death. The hair curls or
flows all about it; the face is of a death-like hue, but has an
expression of quiet, after much pain and trouble — very
beautiful, very sweet and sad; and it affected me strongly
with the horror and strangeness of such a head being
severed from its body. Methinks I should not like to
have it always in the room with me. I thought of the
lovely picture of Mary that I had seen at Edinburgh
Castle, and reflected what a symbol it would be — how
expressive of a human being having her destiny in her
own hands — if that beautiful young Queen were painted
as carrying this dish, containing her own woful head, and
perhaps casting a curious and pitiful glance down upon
it, as if it were not her own.

Also, in the drawing-room (if I mistake not), there was
a plaster cast of Sir Walter's face, taken after death; the
only one in existence, as our guide assured us. It is not
often that one sees a homelier set of features than this;

no elevation, no dignity, whether bestowed by nature or thrown over them by age or death; sunken cheeks, the bridge of the nose depressed, and the end turned up; the mouth puckered, and no chin whatever, or hardly any. The expression was not calm and happy; but rather as if he were in a perturbed slumber, perhaps nothing short of nightmare. I wonder that the family allow this cast to be shown — the last record that there is of Scott's personal reality, and conveying such a wretched and unworthy idea of it.

Adjoining the drawing-room is the dining-room, in one corner of which, between two windows, Scott died. It was now a quarter of a century since his death; but it seemed to me that we spoke with a sort of hush in our voices, as if he were still dying here, or had but just departed. I remember nothing else in this room. The next one is the armory, which is the smallest of all that we had passed through; but its walls gleam with the steel blades of swords, and the barrels of pistols, matchlocks, firelocks, and all manner of deadly weapons, whether European or Oriental; for there are many trophies here of East Indian warfare. I saw Rob Roy's gun, rifled and of very large bore; and a beautiful pistol, formerly Claverhouse's; and the sword of Montrose, given him by King Charles, the silver hilt of which I grasped. There was also a superb claymore, in an elaborately wrought silver sheath, made for Sir Walter Scott, and presented to him by the Highland Society, for his services in marshalling the clans when George IV came to Scotland. There were a thousand other things, which I knew must be most curious, yet did not ask nor care about them, because so many curiosities drive one crazy, and fret one's heart to death. On the whole, there is no simple and great impression left by Abbotsford; and I felt angry and dissatisfied with myself for not feeling something which I did not and could not feel. But it is just like going to a museum, if you look into particulars; and one learns from it, too, that Scott could not have been really a wise man, nor an earnest one, nor one that grasped the truth of life; he did but play, and the play grew very sad toward its close. In a certain way, however, I understand his romances the better for having seen his house; and his house the better for having read his romances. They throw light on one another.

We had now gone through all the show-rooms; and the next door admitted us again into the entrance-hall, where we recorded our names in the visitors' book. It contains more names of Americans, I should judge, from casting my eyes back over last year's record, than of all other people in the world, including Great Britain.

Bidding farewell to Abbotsford, I cannot but confess a sentiment of remorse for having visited the dwelling-place — as just before I visited the grave — of the mighty minstrel and romancer with so cold a heart and in so critical a mood — *his* dwelling-place and *his* grave whom I had so admired and loved, and who had done so much for my happiness when I was young. But I, and the world generally, now look at him from a different point of view; and, besides, these visits to the actual haunts of famous people, though long dead, have the effect of making us sensible, in some degree, of their human imperfections, as if we actually saw them alive. I felt this effect, to a certain extent, even with respect to Shakespeare, when I visited Stratford-on-Avon. As for Scott, I still cherish him in a warm place, and I do not know that I have any pleasanter anticipation, as regards books, than that of reading all his novels over again after we get back to the Wayside.

May 24 [Liverpool]

Dining at Mr. Rathbone's one evening last week (May 21st), it was mentioned that Borrow, author of the Bible in Spain, is suppósed to be of gypsy descent by the mother's side. Hereupon, Mr. Martineau mentioned that he had been a schoolfellow of Borrow; and though he had never heard of his gypsy blood, he thought it probable, from Borrow's traits of character. He said that Borrow had once run away from school, and carried with him a party of other boys, meaning to lead a wandering life. They were intercepted and sent back, however; and when Borrow was flogged for this offense, he was 'horsed' on Mr. Martineau's back. Mr. Martineau is of opinion that the accuracy of Borrow's statements on any subject is not to be depended on; not that he means to be untrue, but that his imagination misleads him.

June 17 [Salisbury]

Seven miles from Salisbury, we turned aside from the turnpike, and drove two miles or so across Salisbury Plain, which is an apparently boundless extent of unenclosed land, treeless, and houseless. It is not exactly a plain, but a green sea of long and gentle swells and subsidences, affording views of miles upon miles, to a very far horizon. We passed large flocks of sheep, with the shep-

herds watching them; but the dogs seemed to take most
of the care of the flocks upon their own shoulders, and
would scamper to turn the sheep, when they inclined to
stray whither they should not; and then arose a thousand-
fold bleating, not unpleasant to the ear, for it did not appear to indicate any fear or discomfort on the part of
the flock. The sheep and lambs are all black-faced, and
have a very funny expression.

As we drove over the plain (my seat was beside the
driver), I saw, at a distance, a cluster of large gray stones,
mostly standing upright, and some of them slightly inclined towards each other — very irregular, and, so far
off, forming no very picturesque or noteworthy spectacle.
Of course I knew at once that this was Stonehenge, and
also knew that the reality was going to dwindle wofully within my ideal, as almost everything else does.
When we reached the spot, we found a picnic-party just
finishing their dinner, on one of the overthrown stones
of the druidical temple; and within the sacred circle, an
artist was painting a wretched daub of the scene; and an
old shepherd (I suppose, the very Shepherd of Salisbury
Plain) sat erect in the centre of the ruin.

There never was a ruder thing than Stonehenge made
by mortal hands; it is so very rude, that it seems as if Nature and man had worked upon it with one consent, and
so it is all the stranger and more impressive from its rude-
ness. The spectator wonders to see art and contrivance,
and a regular and even somewhat intricate plan, beneath
all the uncouth simplicity of this arrangement of rough
stones; and, certainly, whatever was the intellectual and
scientific advancement of the people who built Stone-

henge, no succeeding architects will ever have a right to triumph over them; for nobody's work, in after times, is likely to endure till it becomes a mystery who built it, and how, and for what purpose. Apart from the moral considerations suggested by it, Stonehenge is not very well worth seeing. Materially, it is one of the poorest of spectacles; and when complete, it must have been even less picturesque than now — a few huge, rough stones, very imperfectly squared, standing on end, and each group of two supporting a third huge stone on their two tops; other stones, of the same pattern, overthrown, and tumbled one upon another; and the whole comprised within a circuit of about a hundred feet diameter; the short, sheep-cropped grass of Salisbury Plain growing among all these uncouth boulders. I am not sure that a misty, lowering day would not have better suited Stonehenge, as the dreary midpoint of the great, desolate, trackless plain; not literally trackless, however, for the London and Exeter Road passes within fifty yards of the ruins, and another road intersects it.

July 3 [*London*]

In the evening I went with Mr. and Mrs. Bennoch to a conversazione at Mrs. Newton Crosland's, who lives on Blackheath. I was quite weary of it, but I met with one person who interested me — Mr. Bailey, the author of Festus; and I was surprised to find myself already acquainted with him. It is the same Mr. Bailey whom I met a few months ago, when I first dined at Mr. Bennoch's — a dark, handsome, rather picturesque-looking man, with a gray beard, and dark hair, a little dimmed with gray.

He is of quiet and very agreeable deportment, and I liked him and believed in him. Bennoch says that he has a small property, but just enough to support him, and hinted that he is unhappily married, though himself a most irreproachable husband. There is sadness glooming out of him, but no unkindness nor asperity. Mrs. Crosland's conversazione was enriched with a supper, and terminated with a dance, in which Mr. Bennoch joined with heart and soul, but Mrs. Bennoch went to sleep in her chair, and I would gladly have followed her example if I could have found a chair to sit upon. In the course of the evening I had some talk with a pale, nervous young lady, who has been a noted spiritual medium.

July 9

(Our wedding-day.) — We were invited, yesterday evening, to Mrs. S. C. Hall's, where Jenny Lind was to be; so Bennoch, Sophia, and I left here at about eight o'clock in a brougham, and reached Ashley Place, as the dusk was gathering — that is to say, at past nine. The Halls have let Firfield, and now reside in a handsome set of apartments, arranged on the new system of flats, each story constituting a separate tenement, and the various families having an entrance-hall and some other conveniences in common. The plan is borrowed from the Continent, and seems rather alien to the traditionary habits of the English; though, no doubt, a good degree of seclusion is compatible with it. Mr. Hall received us with the greatest cordiality, before we entered the drawing-room. . . . Good, round Mrs. Hall, too, greeted us with most kindly warmth. . . . Jenny Lind had not yet arrived; but I found

Dr. Mackay there, and I was introduced to Miss Catherine Sinclair, who seems to be a literary lady, though
none of her works happen to be known to me. . . . Soon,
the servant announced Madam Goldschmidt [Jenny Lind];
and this famous lady made her appearance, looking quite
different from what I expected. Mrs. Hall established her
in the inner drawing-room, where was a piano and a harp;
and, shortly after, our hostess came to me, and announced
that Madam Goldschmidt wished to be introduced to me.
There was a kind of gentle peremptoriness in the sum-
mons, that made it something like being commanded into
the presence of a princess; a great favor, no doubt, but
yet a little humbling to the recipient. However, I ac-
quiesced with due gratitude, and was presented accordingly. She made room for me on the sofa, and I sat down,
and began to talk.

Jenny Lind is rather tall — quite tall, for a woman —
and not in the least plump; extremely light hair, a longish
nose, tending upward at the end — a face without any
color at all — pale, and a little scrawniness about the
neck; certainly no beauty, but with sense and self-reliance
in her aspect and manners. She was suffering under a
severe cold, and seemed worn down besides, so probably
I saw her under disadvantages. Her conversation is quite
simple, and I should have great faith in her sincerity; but
still there is about her the manner of a person who knows
the world, and has conquered it. She said something or
other about The Scarlet Letter; and, on my part, I paid
her such compliments as a man could pay who had never
heard her sing nor greatly cared to hear her. Her con-
versational voice is an agreeable one, rather deep, and not

particularly smooth. She talked about America, and about our unwholesome modes of life as to eating and exercise, and the ill-health especially of our women; but I opposed this view, as far as I could with any truth, insinuating my opinion that we are about as healthy as other people, and affirming for a certainty that we live longer. In good faith, so far as I have any knowledge of the matter, the women of England are as generally out of health as those of America; always, something has gone wrong with their clockwork; and as for Jenny Lind, she looks wan and worn enough to be an American herself. This charge of ill-health is almost universally brought forward against us, nowadays; and, taking the whole country together, I do not believe the statistics will bear it out.

On the whole, I was not very greatly interested in Madam Goldschmidt, nor sorry to take an early opportunity of resigning my seat to somebody else. The rooms, which were respectably filled when we arrived, were now getting quite full. I saw . . . Mr. Samuel Lover, a most good-natured, pleasant Irishman, with a shining and twinkling visage. . . .

Leaving out the illustrious Jenny Lind, I suspect that I was myself the greatest lion of the evening; for a good many persons sought the felicity of knowing me, and had little or nothing to say, when that honor and happiness was conferred on them. It is surely very wrong and ill-mannered in people to ask for an introduction, unless they are prepared to make talk; it throws too great an expense and trouble on the wretched lion, who is compelled, on the spur of the moment, to concoct a conversable substance out of thin air, perhaps for the twentieth time that evening. On the whole, I am sure I did not say — and I think I did not hear said — one rememberable word, in the course of this evening; though, nevertheless, it was rather an agreeable one.... After supper, Mr. Lover sang some Irish songs (his own, in music and words) with rich humorous effect, to which the comicality of his face contributed almost as much as his voice.

July 10

Speaking of Dickens last evening, Mr. Milnes mentioned his domestic tastes — how he preferred home enjoyments to all others, and did not willingly go much into society. Mrs. Bennoch, too, the other day told us how careful he was of his wife, taking on himself all possible trouble as regards his domestic affairs, making bargains at butchers and bakers, and doing, as far as he could, whatever pertains to an English wife. There is a great variety of testimony, various and variant, as to the character of Dickens. I must see him before I finally leave England.

July 13

On Friday morning (11th), at nine o'clock, I took the rail into town to breakfast with Mr. Milnes.... Mrs. Milnes greeted me very kindly, and Mr. Milnes came towards me with an elderly gentleman in a blue coat and gray pantaloons — with a long, rather thin, homely visage, exceedingly shaggy eyebrows, though no great weight of brow, and thin gray hair, and introduced me to the Marquis of Lansdowne. The Marquis had his right

hand wrapped up in a black-silk handkerchief; so he gave
me his left, and, from some awkwardness in meeting it,
when I expected the right, I gave him only three of my
fingers — a thing I never did before to any person, and it
is queer that I should have done it to a Marquis. He addressed me with great simplicity and natural kindness,
complimenting me on my works, and speaking about the
society of Liverpool in former days. Lord Lansdowne was
the friend of Moore, and has about him the fragrance communicated by the memories of many illustrious people,
with whom he has associated.

Mr. Ticknor, the Historian of Spanish Literature, now
greeted me. He looks greyer than when I saw him in
Boston, but in good preservation. Mr. Milnes introduced
me to Mrs. Browning, and assigned her to me to conduct
into the breakfast-room. She is a small, delicate woman,
with ringlets of black hair — I think they were ringlets and
am sure they were black — a pleasant, intelligent, and sensitive face, and a low, agreeable voice. She is more youthful and comely than I supposed, and is very gentle and
lady-like. And so we proceeded to the breakfast-room,
which is hung round with pictures; and in the middle
of it stood a large round table, worthy to have been
King Arthur's, and here we seated ourselves without
any question of precedence or ceremony. On one side
of me was an elderly lady, with a very fine countenance, and altogether more agreeable to look at than
most English dames of her age; and in the course of
breakfast I discovered her to be the mother of Florence
Nightingale. One of her daughters (not *the* daughter)
was likewise present. Mrs. Milnes, Mrs. Browning,

Mrs. Nightingale, and her daughter were the only
ladies at table; and I think there were as many as
eight or ten gentlemen, whose names — as I came so late
— I was left to find out for myself, or to leave unknown.

It was a pleasant and sociable meal, and, thanks to my
cold beef and coffee at home, I had no occasion to trouble
myself much about the fare; so I just ate some delicate
chicken, and a very small cutlet, and a slice of dry toast,
and thereupon surceased from my labors. Mrs. Browning
and I talked a good deal during breakfast, for she is of
that quickly appreciative and responsive order of women
with whom I can talk more freely than with any man;
and she has, besides, her own originality, wherewith to
help on conversation, though, I should say, not of a
loquacious tendency. She introduced the subject of
spiritualism, which, she says, interests her very much;
indeed, she seems to be a believer. Her husband, she
told me, utterly rejects the subject, and will not believe
even in the outward manifestations, of which there is such
overwhelming evidence. We also talked of Miss Bacon;
and I developed something of that lady's theory respecting Shakespeare, greatly to the horror of Mrs. Browning, and that of her next neighbor — a nobleman, whose
name I did not hear. On the whole, I like her the better
for loving the man Shakespeare with a personal love. We
talked, too, of Margaret Fuller, who spent her last night
in Italy with the Brownings; and of William Story, with
whom they have been intimate, and who, Mrs. Browning
says, is much stirred about spiritualism. Really, I cannot
help wondering that so fine a spirit as hers should not reject the matter, till, at least, it is forced upon her. But I

like her very much — a great deal better than her poetry, which I could hardly suppose to have been written by such a quiet little person as she.

Mrs. Nightingale had been talking at first with Lord Lansdowne, who sat next her, but by and by she turned to me, and began to speak of London smoke. . . . Then, there being a discussion about Lord Byron on the other side of the table, she spoke to me about Lady Byron, whom she knows intimately, characterizing her as a most excellent and exemplary person, high-principled, unself-ish, and now devoting herself to the care of her two grandchildren — their mother, Byron's daughter, being dead. Lady Byron, she says, writes beautiful verses. Somehow or other, all this praise, and more of the same kind, gave me an idea of an intolerably irreproachable person; and I asked Mrs. Nightingale if Lady Byron were warm-hearted. With some hesitation, or mental reservation — at all events, not quite outspokenly — she answered that she was.

I was too much engaged with these personal talks to attend much to what was going on elsewhere; but all through breakfast, I had been more and more impressed by the aspect of one of the guests, sitting next to Milnes. He was a man of large presence — a portly personage — gray-haired, but scarcely as yet aged; and his face had a remarkable intelligence, not vivid nor sparkling, but conjoined with great quietude; and if it gleamed or bright-ened, at one time more than another, it was like the sheen over a broad surface of sea. There was a somewhat care-less self-possession, large and broad enough to be called dignity; and the more I looked at him, the more I knew that he was somebody, and wondered who. He might have been a minister of state; only there is not one of them who has any right to such a face and presence. At last — I do not know how the conviction came — but I became aware that it was Macaulay, and began to see some slight resemblance to his portraits. But I have never seen any that is not wretchedly unworthy of the original. As soon as I knew him, I began to listen to his conversation; but he did not talk a great deal — contrary to his usual custom, for I am told he is apt to engross all the talk to himself. Probably he may have been restrained by the presence of Ticknor, and Mr. [J. G.] Palfrey, who were among his auditors and interlocutors; and as the conversation seemed to turn much on American subjects, he could not well have assumed to talk them down. Well, I am glad to have seen him — a face fit for a scholar, a man of the world, a cultivated intelligence.

After we left the table, and went into the library, Mr. Browning introduced himself to me — a younger man than I expected to see, handsome, with brown hair a very little frosted. He is very simple and agreeable in manner, gently impulsive, talking as if his heart were uppermost. He spoke of his pleasure in meeting me, and his appreciation of my books; and — which has not often happened to me — mentioned that The Blithedale Romance was the one he admired most. I wonder why. I hope I showed as much pleasure at his praise as he did at mine; for I was glad to see how pleasantly it moved him. After this, I talked with Ticknor and Milnes, and with Mr. Palfrey, to whom I had been introduced very long ago by George Hillard, and had never seen him since.

We looked at some autographs, of which Mr. Milnes has two or three large volumes. I recollect a leaf from Swift's Journal to Stella; a letter from Addison; one from Chatterton, in a most neat and legible hand; and a characteristic sentence or two and signature of Oliver Cromwell, written in a religious book. There were many curious volumes in the library, but I had not time to look at them.

I liked greatly the manners of almost all — yes, all as far as I observed — all the people at this breakfast, and it was doubtless owing to their being all people either of high rank or remarkable intellect, or both. An Englishman can hardly be a gentleman, unless he enjoy one or other of these advantages; and perhaps the surest way to give him good manners is to make a lord of him, or rather of his grandfather or great-grandfather. In the third generation, scarcely sooner, he will be polished into simplicity and elegance, and his deportment will be all the better for the homely material out of which it is wrought and refined. The Marquis of Lansdowne, for instance, would have been a very commonplace man in the common ranks of life; but it has done him good to be a nobleman. Not that his tact is quite perfect. In going up to breakfast, he made me precede him; in returning to the library, he did the same, although I drew back, till he impelled me up the first stair, with gentle persistence. By insisting upon it, he showed his sense of condescension much more than if, when he saw me unwilling to take precedence, he had passed forward, as if the point were not worth either asserting or yielding. Heaven knows, it was in no humility that I would have trodden behind him.

But he is a kind old man; and I am willing to believe of
the English aristocracy generally that they are kind, and
of beautiful deportment; for certainly there never can
have been mortals in a position more advantageous for
becoming so. If any, they must be Americans; and,
really, I hope there will come a time when we shall be so;
and I already know a few Americans, whose noble and
delicate manners may compare well with any I have seen.

September 9 [*Hampton Court*]

How beautifully the royal robe of a monarchy is
embroidered! Palaces, pictures, parks! They do enrich
life; and kings and aristocracies cannot keep these things
to themselves — they merely take care of them for others.
Even a king, with all the glory that can be shed around
him, is but the liveried and bedizened footman of his
people, and the toy of their delight. I am very glad that
I came to this country, while the English are still playing
with such a toy.

November 20 [*Southport*]

A week ago last Monday, Herman Melville came to see
me at the Consulate, looking much as he used to do (a
little paler, and perhaps a little sadder), in a rough outside coat, and with his characteristic gravity and reserve
of manner. He had crossed from New York to Glasgow
in a screw steamer, about a fortnight before, and had
since been seeing Edinburgh, and other interesting places.
I felt rather awkward at first, because this is the first
time I have met him since my ineffectual attempt to get
him a consular appointment from General Pierce. How-

ever, I failed only from real lack of power to serve him; so there was no reason to be ashamed, and we soon found ourselves on pretty much our former terms of sociability and confidence. Melville has not been well of late; he has been affected with neuralgic complaints in his head and his limbs, and no doubt has suffered from too constant literary occupation, pursued without much success latterly; and his writings, for a long while past, have indicated a morbid state of mind. So he left his place at Pittsfield, and has established his wife and family, I believe, with his father-in-law in Boston, and is thus far on his way to Constantinople. I do not wonder that he found it necessary to take an airing through the world, after so many years of toilsome pen-labor following after so wild and adventurous a youth as his was. I invited him to come and stay with us at Southport as long as he might remain in this vicinity; and, accordingly, he did come, on the next day, taking with him, by way of luggage, the least little bit of a bundle, which, he told me, contained a nightshirt and a toothbrush. He is a person of very gentlemanly instincts in every respect, save that he is a little heterodox in the matter of clean linen.

He stayed with us from Tuesday till Thursday; and, on the intervening day, we took a pretty long walk together, and sat down in a hollow among the sandhills (sheltering ourselves from the high, cool wind) and smoked a cigar. Melville, as he always does, began to reason of Providence and futurity, and of everything that lies beyond human ken, and informed me that he had 'pretty much made up his mind to be annihilated'; but still he does not seem to rest in that anticipation, and, I think, will never rest until he gets hold of a definite belief. It is strange how he persists — and has persisted ever since I knew him, and probably long before — in wandering to and fro over these deserts, as dismal and monotonous as the sandhills amid which we were sitting. He can neither believe, nor be comfortable in his unbelief; and he is too honest and courageous not to try to do one or the other. If he were a religious man, he would be one of the most truly religious and reverential; he has a very high and noble nature and is better worth immortality than most of us.

He went back with me to Liverpool on Thursday; and, the next day, Henry Bright met him at my office, and showed him whatever was worth seeing in town. On Saturday, Melville and I went to Chester together. I love to take every opportunity of going to Chester; it being the one only place, within easy reach of Liverpool, which possesses any old English interest. . . . We left Chester at about four o'clock; and I took the rail for Southport at half-past six, parting from Melville at a street-corner in Liverpool, in the rainy evening. I saw him again on Monday, however. He said that he already felt better than in America; but observed that he did not anticipate much pleasure in his rambles, for that the spirit of adventure is gone out of him. He certainly is much overshadowed since I saw him last; but I hope he will brighten as he goes onward. He sailed from Liverpool in a steamer on Tuesday, leaving his trunk behind him at my consulate, and taking only a carpet-bag to hold all his travelling-gear. This is the next best thing to going naked; and as he wears his beard and moustache, and so needs no dressing-case — nothing but a tooth-brush — I do not know a more independent personage. He learned his travelling-habits by drifting about, all over the South Sea, with no other clothes or equipage than a red flannel shirt and a pair of duck trousers. Yet we seldom see men of less criticizable manners than he.

December 31 [*Liverpool*]

On the mantel-piece in the coroner's court the other day, I saw corked and labelled phials, which, it may be presumed, contained samples of poisons that have brought some poor wretches to their deaths — either by murder or suicide. This court might be wrought into a very good and pregnant description, with its grimy gloom, illuminated by a conical skylight, constructed to throw daylight down on corpses; its greasy Testament, covered over with millions of perjured kisses; the Coroner himself, whose life is fed on all kinds of unnatural death; its subordinate officials, who go about scenting murder, and might be supposed to have caught the scent in their own garments; its stupid, brutish juries, settling round corpses like flies; its criminals, whose guilt is brought face to face with them here, in closer contact than at the subsequent trial.

April 12 [*Easter*], 1857 [*York Minster*]

It is not good to see musicians, for they are usually coarse and vulgar people, and so the auditor loses faith in any fine and spiritual tones that they may breathe forth.

The spirit of my Puritan ancestors was mighty in me,

and I did not wonder at their being out of patience with all this mummery, which seemed to me worse than papistry because it was a corruption of it. At last, a canon gave out the text, and preached a sermon of about twenty minutes long, the coldest, driest, most superficial rubbish; for this gorgeous setting of the magnificent cathedral, the elaborate music, and the rich ceremonial seem inevitably to take the life out of the sermon — which, to be anything, must be all. The Puritans showed their strength of mind and heart, by preferring a sermon of an hour and a half long, into which the preacher put his whole soul and spirit, and lopping away all these externals, into which religious life had first leafed and flowered, and then petrified.

April 19 [*Liverpool*]

From the scene of the corner-stone [of the Free Library], we went to St. George's Hall, where a drawing-room and dressing-room had been prepared for the principal guests. Before the banquet, I had some conversation with Sir James Kay-Shuttleworth, who had known Miss Brontë very intimately, and bore testimony to the wonderful fidelity of Mrs. Gaskell's life of her. He seemed to have had an affectionate regard for her, and said that her marriage promised to have been productive of great happiness; her husband being not a remarkable man, but with the merit of an exceeding love for her.

May 10

Yesterday we all of us except Rose went to Liverpool to see the performances of an American circus company.

I had previously been, a day or two before, with Julian, and had been happy to perceive that the fact of its being an American establishment really induced some slight swelling of the heart within me. It is ridiculous enough, to be sure, but I like to find myself not wholly destitute of this noble weakness, patriotism. As for the circus, I never was fond of that species of entertainment, nor do I find in this one the flash and glitter and whirl which I seem to remember in American exhibitions.

May 27 [Peterborough]

Of all the lovely churchyards that I ever beheld, that of Peterborough Cathedral seems to me the most delightful; so quiet it is, so solemnly and nobly cheerful, so verdant, so sweetly shadowed, and so presided over by the noble minster, and surrounded by quiet, ancient, and comely habitations of Christian men. The most delightful place, the most enviable as a residence, in all this world, seemed to me that of the Bishop's secretary, standing in the rear of the cathedral, and bordering on the churchyard; so that you seem to pass through hallowed precincts in order to come at it, and find it a sort of Paradise, the holier and sweeter for the dead men that sleep so near. We looked through the gateway into the lawn, which really looked as if it hardly belonged to this world, so bright and soft the sunshine was, so fresh the grass, so lovely the trees, so trimmed and refined, and softened down, was the whole nature of the spot; and so shut in and guarded from all intrusion. It is in vain to write about [it]; nowhere but in England can there be such a spot, nor anywhere but in the close of Peterborough Cathedral.

June 7 [Matlock]

The representative men of England are the showmen and the policemen; both very good people in their way.

Thus ended our tour, in which we had seen but a little bit of England, yet rich with variety and interest. What a wonderful land! It is our forefathers' land; our land, for I will not give up such a precious inheritance.

July 2 [Inverannan]

Morally, the Highlands must have been more completely sophisticated by the invention of railways and steamboats, than almost any other part of the world; but physically it can have wrought no great change. These mountains, in their general aspect, must be very much the same as they were a thousand years ago; for their sides never were capable of cultivation, nor even, with such a soil and so bleak an atmosphere, have been much more richly wooded than we see them now. They seem to me to be among the unchangeable things of Nature, like the sea and sky; but there is no saying what use human ingenuity may hereafter put them to. At all events, I have no doubt in the world that they will go out of fashion in due time; for the taste for mountains and wild scenery is, with most people, an acquired taste; and it was easy to see to-day that nine people in ten really care nothing about them. One group of gentlemen and ladies — men and women, at least — spent the whole time in listening to a trial for murder, which was read aloud by one of their number from a newspaper. I rather imagine that a taste for trim gardens is the most natural and universal taste, as regards landscape. But perhaps it is necessary for the health of the human mind and heart that there should be a possibility of taking refuge in what is wild, and uncontaminated by any culture; and so it has been ordained that science shall never alter the aspect of the sky, whether stern, angry, or beneficent, nor of the awful sea, either in calm or tempest, nor of these rude Highlands. But they will go out of general fashion, as I have said; and perhaps the next fashionable taste will be for Cloud Land — that is, looking skyward, and observing the wonderful variety of scenery, that now constantly passes unnoticed among the clouds.

July 5 [*The Trosachs*]

Scott evidently used as much freedom with his natural scenery as he did with his historic incidents; and he could have made nothing of either one or the other if he had been more scrupulous in his arrangement and adornment of them. In his description of the Trosachs, he has produced something very beautiful, and as true as possible, though certainly its beauty has a little of the scene-painter's gloss on it. Nature is better, no doubt; but Nature cannot be exactly reproduced on canvas or in print; and the artist's only resource is to substitute something that may stand in stead of and suggest the truth.

There are many scenes as good in America, needing only the poet.

July 7

It will be worth while to go back to America, were it only for the chance of finding a still virgin scene.

[Stirling Castle]

I forgot to tell the things that awakened rather more sympathy in us than any other objects in the castle armory. These were some rude weapons — pikes, very roughly made, and old rusty muskets, broken and otherwise out of order, and swords, by no means with Damascus blades — that had been taken from some poor weavers and other handicraft men, who rose against the government in 1820. I pitied the poor fellows much, seeing how wretched were their means of standing up against the cannon, bayonets, swords, shot, shell, and all manner of murderous facilities possessed by their oppressors. Afterwards, our guide showed, in a gloomy quadrangle of the castle, the low windows of the dungeons where two of the leaders of the insurrectionists had been confined, before their execution. I have not the least shadow of doubt that these men had a good cause to fight for; but what availed it with such weapons, and so few even of those.

July 9 *[Edinburgh]*

After tea I went down into the valley between the old town and the new, which is now laid out as an ornamental garden, with grass, shrubbery, flowers, gravelled walks, and frequent seats. Here the sun was setting, and gilded the Old Town with its parting rays, making it absolutely the most picturesque scene that I ever beheld. The mass of tall, ancient houses, heaped densely together, looked like a Gothic dream; for there seemed to be towers and all sorts of stately architecture, and spires ascended out of the mass; and above the whole was the Castle, with a crown of gold on its topmost turret. It wanted less than a quarter of nine when the last gleam faded from the windows of the old town, and left the mass of buildings dim and indistinguishable; to reappear on the morrow in squalor, lifting their meanness skyward, the home of layer upon layer of unfortunate humanity. The change symbolized the difference between a poet's imagination of life in the past — or in a state which he looks at through a colored and illuminated medium — and the sad reality.

July 11 [*Abbotsford*]

It was not a pleasant morning; but we started immediately after breakfast for Abbotsford, which is but about three miles distant. The country between Melrose and that place is not in the least beautiful, nor very noteworthy — one or two old, irregular villages; one tower, that looks principally domestic, yet partly warlike, and seems to be of some antiquity; and an undulation, or rounded hilly surface of the landscape, sometimes affording wide vistas between the slopes. These hills (I suppose they are, some of them, on the Abbotsford estate) are partly covered with woods, but of Scotch fir, or some tree of that species, which creates no softened undulation, but overspreads the hill like a tightly fitting wig. It is a cold, dreary, disheartening neighborhood, that of Abbotsford; at least, it has appeared so to me at both of my visits; one of which was on a bleak and windy May morning, and another on a chill, showery morning of midsummer.

The entrance-way to the house is somewhat altered

since my last visit; and we now, following the direction
of a painted finger on the wall, went round to a back-door
in the basement story, where we found an elderly man
waiting as if in expectation of visitors. He asked me to
write our names in a book, and told us that the desk, on
the leaf of which it lay, was the one in which Sir Walter
found the forgotten manuscript of Waverley, while looking for some fishing-tackle. There was another desk in
the room, which had belonged to the Colonel Gardiner
who appears in Waverley. The first apartment, into
which our guide showed us, was Sir Walter's study, where
I again saw his clothes, and remarked how the sleeve of
his old green coat was worn at the cuff — a minute circumstance that seemed to bring Sir Walter very near me.
Thence into the library; thence into the drawing-room;
whence, methinks, we should have entered the dining-
room, the most interesting of all, as being the room where
he died. But this room seems not to be shown now. We
saw the armory, with the gun of Rob Roy, into the muz-
zle of which I put my finger, and found the bore very
large; the beautifully wrought pistol of Claverhouse, and
a pair of pistols that belonged to Napoleon; the sword of
Montrose, which I grasped, and drew half out of the
scabbard; and Queen Mary's iron jewel-box, six or eight
inches long, and two or three high, with a lid rounded like
that of a trunk, and much corroded with rust. There is
no use in making a catalogue of these curiosities. The
feeling in visiting Abbotsford is not that of awe; it is little
more than going to a museum. I do abhor this mode of
making pilgrimages to the shrines of departed great men;
there is certainly something wrong in it, for it seldom or

never produces (in me, at least) the right feeling. It is a queer truth, too, that a house is forever after spoiled and ruined, as a home, by having been the abode of a great man. His spirit haunts it, as it were, with a malevolent effect, and takes hearth and hall away from the nominal possessors, giving all the world (because he had such intimate relations with all) the right to enter there.

[Durham]

I love to find the graves of men connected with literature. They interest me more, even though of no great eminence, than those of persons far more illustrious in other walks of life. I know not whether this is because I happen to be one of the literary kindred, or because all men feel themselves akin, and on terms of intimacy, with those whom they know, or might have known, in books. I rather believe that the latter is the case.

July 28 [*Manchester Arts' Exhibition*]

The only modern pictures that accomplish a higher end than that of pleasing the eye — the only ones that really take hold of the mind (and they do it with a kind of acerbity, like unripe fruit) — are the works of Hunt, and one or two other painters of the Pre-Raphaelite school. They seem wilfully to abjure all beauty, and to make their pictures disagreeable out of mere malice; but, at any rate, for the thought and feeling which are ground up with the paint, they will bear looking at, and disclose a deeper value the longer you look. Never was anything so stiff and unnatural as they appear; although every single thing represented seems to be taken directly out of life and reality, and, as it were, pasted down upon the canvas. They almost paint even separate hairs. Accomplishing so much, and so perfectly, it seems unaccountable that the picture does not live; but Nature has an art beyond these painters, and they leave out some medium — some enchantment that should intervene, and keep the object from pressing so baldly and harshly upon the spectator's eyeballs. With the most lifelike reproduction, there is no illusion. I think if a semi-obscurity were thrown over the picture, after finishing it to this nicety, it might bring it nearer to nature. I remember a heap of autumn leaves, every one of which seems to have been stiffened with gum and varnish, and then put carefully down into the stiffly disordered heap. Perhaps these artists may hereafter succeed in combining the truth of detail with a broader and higher truth. Coming from such a depth as their pictures do, and having really an idea as the seed of them, it is strange that they should look like the most made-up things imaginable. One picture of Hunt's, that greatly interested me, was of some sheep that had gone astray among heights and precipices; and I could have looked all day at these poor, lost muttons — so true was their meek alarm and hopeless bewilderment, their huddling together without the slightest confidence of mutual help; all that the courage and wisdom of the bravest and wisest of them could do, being to bleat, and only a few having spirits enough even for this.

July 30

After getting through the portrait-gallery, I went among the engravings and photographs, and then glanced along the old masters, but without seriously looking at anything. While I was among the Dutch painters, a gentleman accosted me. It was Mr. Ireland, whom I once met at dinner with Bennoch. He told me that 'the Poet Laureate' (and it was rather English that he should designate him by this fantastic dignity, instead of by his name) was in the Exhibition Rooms; and as I expressed great interest, Mr. Ireland was kind enough to go in quest of him. Not for the purpose of introduction, however, for he was not acquainted with Tennyson, and I was rather glad of it than otherwise. Soon Mr. Ireland returned to tell me that he had found the Poet Laureate — and, going into the saloon of the old masters, we saw him there, in company with Mr. Woolner, whose bust of him is now in the Exhibition.

Tennyson is the most picturesque figure, without affectation, that I ever saw; of middle-size, rather slouching, dressed entirely in black, and with nothing white about him except the collar of his shirt, which methought might have been cleaner the day before. He had on a black, wide-awake hat, with round crown and wide, irregular brim, beneath which came down his long, black hair, looking terribly tangled; he had a long, pointed beard, too, a little browner than the hair, and not so abundant as to encumber any of the expression of his face. His frock coat was buttoned across the breast, though the afternoon was warm. His face was very dark, and not exactly a smooth face, but worn, and expressing great sensitiveness, though not, at that moment, the pain and sorrow which is seen in his bust. His eyes were black; but I know little of them, as they did not rest on me, nor on anything but the

pictures. He seemed as if he did not see the crowd nor
think of them, but as if he defended himself from them
by ignoring them altogether; nor did anybody but myself
cast a glance at him. Mr. Woolner was as unlike Tennyson as could well be imagined; a small, smug man, in a
blue frock and brown pantaloons. They talked about the
pictures, and passed pretty rapidly from one to another,
Tennyson looking at them through a pair of spectacles
which he held in his hand, and then standing a minute before those that interested him, with his hands folded behind his back. There was an entire absence of stiffness in
his figure; no set-up in him at all; no nicety or trimness;
and if there had been, it would have spoilt his whole
aspect. Gazing at him with all my eyes, I liked him well,
and rejoiced more in him than in all the other wonders of
the exhibition.

Knowing that my wife would delight to see him, I
went in search of her, and found her and the rest of us
under the music-gallery; and we all, Fanny and Rosebud
included, went back to the saloon of the Old Masters.
So rapid was his glance at the pictures, that, in this little
interval, Tennyson had got half-way along the other side
of the saloon, and, as it happened, an acquaintance had
met him, an elderly gentleman and lady, and he was talking to them as we approached. I heard his voice; a bass
voice, but not of resounding depth; a voice rather broken
as it were, and ragged about the edges, but pleasant to the
ear. His manner, while conversing with these people, was
not in the least that of an awkward man, unaccustomed to
society; but he shook hands with them, evidently as soon
as he courteously could, and shuffled away quicker than

before. He betrayed his shy and secluded habits more in this, than in anything else that I observed; though, indeed, in his whole presence, I was indescribably sensible of a morbid painfulness in him, a something not to be meddled with. Very soon, he left the saloon, shuffling along the floor with short irregular steps, a very queer gait, as if he were walking in slippers too loose for him. I had observed that he seemed to turn his feet slightly inward, after the fashion of Indians. How strange that in these two or three pages I cannot get one single touch that may call him up hereafter!

I would most gladly have seen more of this one poet of our day, but forbore to follow him; for I must own that it seemed mean to be dogging him through the saloons, or even to look at him, since it was to be done stealthily, if at all. I should be glad to smoke a cigar with him. Mr. Ireland says that, having heard that he was to be at the Exhibition, and not finding him there, he conjectured that he must have gone into the continuous Botanical Gardens to smoke; and sure enough, he found him there. He told us an anecdote, which he received from Professor P——, about Tennyson while on a visit to Paris. He had a friend with him, who could not speak very good French, any more than the poet himself. They were sitting by the fireside in their parlor at the hotel; and the friend proposed a walk about the city, and finally departed, leaving Tennyson by the fireside, and saying to the waiter, 'Ne souffrez pas le faire sortir.' By and by Tennyson also rose to go out; but the waiter opposed him with might and main, and called another waiter to his assistance; and when Tennyson's friend returned, he found him really almost fit for a straitjacket. He might well enough pass for a madman at any time, there being a wildness in his aspect, which doubtless might readily pass from quietude to frenzy. He is exceedingly nervous, and altogether as un-English as possible; indeed an Englishman of genius usually lacks the national characteristics, and is great abnormally. Even the great sailor, Nelson, was unlike his countrymen in the qualities that constituted him a hero; he was not the perfection of an Englishman, but a creature of another kind — sensitive, nervous, excitable, and really more like a Frenchman.

Un-English as he was, and sallow, and unhealthy, Tennyson had not, however, an American look. I cannot well describe the difference; but there was something more mellow in him — softer, sweeter, broader, more simple than we are apt to be. Living apart from men as he does would hurt any one of us more than it does him. I may as well leave him here, for I cannot touch the central point.

August 9

Una and I spent an hour together, looking principally at the old Dutch masters, who seem to me the most wonderful set of men that ever handled a brush. Such lifelike representations of cabbages, onions, turnips, cauliflowers, and peas; such perfect realities of brass kettles, and kitchen crockery; such blankets, with the woollen fuzz upon them; such everything (except the human face, which moreover is fairly enough depicted) I never thought that the skill of man could produce! Even the photograph cannot equal their miracles. The

closer you look, the more minutely true the picture is
found to be; and I doubt if even the microscope could see
beyond the painter's touch. Gerard Dow seems to be the
master among these queer magicians. A straw mat, in
one of his pictures, is the most miraculous thing that
human art has yet accomplished; and there is a metal
vase, with a dent in it, that is absolutely more real than
reality. These painters accomplish all they aim at — a
praise, methinks, which can be given to no other men
since the world began. They must have laid down their
brushes with perfect satisfaction, knowing that each one
of their million touches had been necessary to the effect,
and that there was not one too little or too much. And it
is strange how spiritual and suggestive the common-
est household article — an earthen pitcher, for example —
becomes when represented with entire accuracy. These
Dutchmen get at the soul of common things, and so make
them types and interpreters of the spiritual world.

August 16

I went again to the Exhibition, day before yesterday,
and looked much at both the modern and ancient pictures, as also at the water-colors. I am making some
progress as a connoisseur, and have got so far as to be
able to distinguish the broader differences of style; as,
for example, between Rubens and Rembrandt. I should
hesitate to claim any more for myself, thus far. In fact,
however, I do begin to have a liking for good things, and
to be sure that they are good. Murillo seems to me about
the noblest and purest painter that ever lived, and his
'Good Shepherd' the loveliest picture I ever saw. It is a

hopeful symptom, moreover, of improving taste, that I see more merit in the crowd of painters than I was at first competent to acknowledge. I could see some of their defects from the very first; but that is the very earliest stage of connoisseurship, after a formal and ignorant admiration. Mounting a few steps higher, one sees beauties. But how much study, how many opportunities, are requisite to form and cultivate a taste! The Exhibition must be quite thrown away on the mass of spectators.

November 12 [*London*]

The morning began with such fog, that, at the window of my chamber, lighted only from a small court-yard enclosed by high, dingy walls, I could hardly see to dress. It kept alternately darkening, and then brightening a little, and darkening again, so much that we could but just see across the street; but, at eleven or thereabouts it grew so much lighter that we resolved to venture out. Our plan for the day was to go in the first place to Westminster Abbey, and to the National Gallery, if we should find time. . . . The fog darkened again as we went down Regent Street, and the Duke of York's Column was but barely discernible, looming vaguely before us; nor, from Pall Mall, was Nelson's Pillar much more distinct, though methought his statue stood aloft in a somewhat clearer atmosphere than ours. Passing Whitehall, however, we could scarcely see Inigo Jones's Banqueting-House, on the other side of the street; and the towers and turrets of the new Houses of Parliament were all but invisible, as was the Abbey itself; so that we really were in some doubt whither we were going. We found our way to Poets'

Corner, however (the name always reminds me of the poetical department in village-newspapers) and entered those holy precincts, which looked very dusky and grim in the smoky light. . . .

I am not aware that I had any new sensation, though I was strongly impressed with the perception that very commonplace people compose the great bulk of society in this home of the illustrious dead. It is wonderful how few names there are that one cares anything about, a hundred years after their departure; but perhaps each generation acts in good faith, in canonizing its own men. It is pleasant to think of Westminster Abbey as incrusted all over, in its interior, with marble immortalities; but, looking at them more closely, you find that the fame of the buried person does not make the marble live, but the marble keeps merely a cold and sad memory of a man who would else be forgotten. No man, who needs a monument, ever ought to have one.

November 19

It seems to me nobody else runs such risks as a man of business, because he risks everything. Every other man, into whatever depth of poverty he may sink, has still something left, be he author, scholar, handicraftman, or what not; the merchant has nothing.

December 6

All these days, since my last date, have been marked by nothing very well worthy of detail and description. I have walked the streets a great deal, in the dull November days, and always take a certain pleasure in being in the midst of

human life — as closely encompassed by it as it is possible
to be, anywhere in this world; and, in that way of viewing
it, there is a dull and sombre enjoyment always to be
had in Holborn, Fleet Street, Cheapside, and the other
thronged parts of London. It is human life; it is this
material world; it is a grim and heavy reality. I have
never had the same sense of being surrounded by material-
isms, and hemmed in with the grossness of this earthly
life, anywhere else; these broad, thronged streets are
so evidently the veins and arteries of an enormous city.
London is evidenced in every one of them, just as a
megatherium is in each of its separate bones, even if they
be small ones. Thus I never fail of a sort of self-congratu-
lation in finding myself, for instance, passing along Lud-
gate Hill; but, in spite of this, it is really an ungladdened
life to wander through these huge, thronged ways, over a
pavement foul with mud, ground into it by a million of
footsteps; jostling against people who do not seem to be
individuals, but all one mass, so homogeneous is the street-
walking aspect of them; the roar of vehicles pervading
me, wearisome cabs and omnibuses; everywhere, the dingy
brick edifices heaving themselves up, and shutting out all
but a strip of sullen cloud, that serves London for a sky;
— in short, a general impression of grime and sordidness;
and, at this season, always a fog scattered along the vista
of streets, sometimes so densely as almost to spiritualize
the materialism and make the scene resemble the other
world of worldly people, gross even in ghostliness. It is
strange how little splendor and brilliancy one sees in
London streets; in the city, almost none, though some in
the shops of Regent Street.

December 7

Lastly, I passed through the Ethnographical Rooms [in the British Museum]; but I care little for the varieties of the human race — all that is really important and interesting being found in our own variety. Perhaps equally in any other.

1858–1862

[EARLY in January, 1858, the Hawthornes left England for the continent, spending a week in Paris, and then traveling slowly, by way of Marseilles and Genoa, to Rome. Here they remained until June, spent the summer in and near Florence, visited the Storys in Siena on their way southward in the fall, and were again in Rome from October, 1858, to May, 1859. Most of June, 1859, was spent in France and Switzerland. Returning to England, Hawthorne settled down, first at Redcar in Yorkshire, then at Leamington in Warwickshire, to the writing of 'The Marble Faun,' which was published in the spring of 1860. The journal, during all this time, was suspended only during the illness of Hawthorne's daughter, in the winter of 1858–59, and during most of the time at Redcar and Leamington.

In June, 1860, Hawthorne returned to the United States, and settled again at the Wayside. Owing to increasing ill-health, to the low spirits induced in him by the Civil War, and doubtless also to the strain of attempting to write (against the grain) professionally, Hawthorne discontinued his journal entirely, save for a short period at West Gouldsborough, Maine, whither he went with his son for a little excursion in the summer of 1862. Less than two years later, on May 19, 1864, Hawthorne died, on a trip with Franklin Pierce undertaken for his health, at Plymouth, New Hampshire.]

January 3, 1858 [London]

On Thursday we had the pleasure of a call from Mr. Coventry Patmore, to whom Dr. Wilkinson gave me a letter of introduction, and on whom I had called twice at the British Museum without finding him. We had read his Betrothal and Angel in the House with unusual pleasure and sympathy, and therefore were very glad to make his personal acquaintance. He is a man of much more youthful aspect than I had expected, looking younger than his real age, which he told us is thirty-four; a slender person to be an Englishman, though not remarkably so had he been an American; with an intelligent, pleasant, and sensitive face — a man very evidently of refined feelings and cultivated mind; but, it seemed to me, not exhibiting altogether the air of an English born-and-bred gentleman. He is very simple and agreeable in his manners; a little shy, or rather awkward, yet perfectly frank, and easy to meet on real grounds. He said that his wife had purposed to come with him, and had indeed accompanied him to town, but was kept away by the naughty behavior of their boy, a little fellow of six years old, who refused to be of the party. We were very sorry for this, because Mr. Patmore seems to acknowledge her as the real 'Angel in the House,' although he says she herself ignores all connection with the poem. It is well for her to do so, and for her husband to feel that the character is her real portrait; and both, I suppose, are right. It is a most beautiful and original poem — a poem for happy married people to read together, and to understand by the light of their own past and present life; but I doubt whether the generality of English people are capable of appreciating it.

I told Mr. Patmore that I thought his popularity in
America would be greater than at home, and he said that
it was already so; and he appeared to estimate highly his
American fame, and also our general gift of quicker and
more subtle recognition of genius than the English
public. Mr. Patmore is not a man of flowing conversation
— at least, not when he meets three or four strangers for
the first time: — so that the conversation sometimes
dragged, during his short call, and was only set afloat by
the skill in starting new topics which I have acquired in
the reception of many dry visitors during my consular
experience. We mutually gratified each other by expressing high admiration of one another's works, and Mr. Patmore regretted that in the few days of our further stay
here we should not have more time to visit him at his
home. It would really give me pleasure. His situation in
the Museum occupies him from nine till two o'clock,
every day, and affords him four weeks of vacation, which
he may take at any time of the year, or in driblets. In
my new freedom, I could not help mentally pitying him
for being thus confined. I expressed a hope of seeing him
in Italy during our residence there, and he seemed to
think it possible, as his friend, and our countryman,
Thomas Buchanan Read, had asked him to come thither
and be his guest. He took his leave, shaking hands with
all of us, and making it (as it was pleasant to see) a
matter of conscience not to neglect any one; because
he saw that we were of his own people, recognizing him
as a true poet. He has since sent me the new edition of
his poems, with a kind note.

January 6 [Paris]

We might have dined at the *table d'hôte*, but preferred the restaurant connected with and within the hotel. All the dishes were very delicate, and a vast change from the simple English system, with its joints, shoulders, beef-steaks, and chops; but I doubt whether English cookery, for the very reason that it is so gross, is not better for men's moral and spiritual nature than French. In the former case, you know that you are gratifying your animal needs and propensities, and are duly ashamed of it; but, in dealing with these French delicacies, you delude yourself into the idea that you are cultivating your taste while filling your belly. This last, however, it requires a good deal of perseverance to accomplish.

January 9

This morning Miss [Maria] Mitchell, the celebrated astronomical lady, of Nantucket, called. She had brought a letter of introduction to me, while consul; and her business now was, to see if we could take her as one of our party to Rome, whither she likewise is bound. We readily consented, for she seems to be a simple, strong, healthy-humored woman, who will not fling herself as a burden on our shoulders; and my only wonder is, that a person evidently so able to take care of herself should care about having an escort.

January 10

In the same suite of apartments [in the Louvre], there is a collection of miniatures, some of them very exquisite, and absolutely lifelike, on their small scale. I observed two of Franklin, both good and picturesque; one of them especially so, with its cloud-like white hair. I do not think we have produced a man so interesting to contemplate, in many points of view, as he. Most of our great men are of a character that I find it impossible to warm into life by thought, or by lavishing any amount of sympathy upon them; not so Franklin, who had a great deal of common and uncommon human nature in him.

Among the relics of kings and princes [in the Louvre], I do not know that there was anything more interesting than a little brass cannon, two or three inches long, which had been a toy of the unfortunate Dauphin, son of Louis XVI. There was a map — a hemisphere of the world — which his father had drawn for this poor boy; very neatly done, too. The sword of Louis XVI, a magnificent rapier, with a beautifully damasked blade, and a jewelled scabbard, but without a hilt, is likewise preserved; as is the hilt of Henry IV's sword. But it is useless to begin a catalogue of these things. What a collection it is, including Charlemagne's sword and sceptre, and the last Dauphin's little toy cannon, and so much between the two!

January 12

Like the trees in the Champs Elysées, those, I presume, in the gardens of the Tuileries need renewing every few years. The same is true of the human race — families becoming extinct after a generation or two of residence in Paris. Nothing really thrives here; man and vegetables have but an artificial life, like flowers stuck in a little mould, but never taking root. I am quite tired of Paris, and never longed for a home so much.

January 17 [*The Mediterranean Sea*]

If I had remained at Marseilles, I might have found many peculiarities and characteristics of that Southern city to notice; but I fear that these will not be recorded, if I leave them till I touch the soil of Italy. Indeed, I doubt whether there be anything really worth recording in the little distinctions between one nation and another; at any rate, after the first novelty is over, new things seem equally commonplace with the old. There is but one little interval when the mind is in such a state that you can catch the fleeting aroma of a new scene. And it is always so much pleasanter to enjoy this delicious newness than to attempt arresting it, that it requires great force of will to insist with one's self upon sitting down to write. I can do nothing with Marseilles, especially here, on the Mediterranean, long after nightfall, and when the steamer is pitching in a pretty lively way.

January 24 [*Rome*]

I say nothing of the immense pictorial treasures which hung upon the walls of all the rooms [in the Balbi Palace, Genoa] through which we passed; for I soon grew so weary of admirable things, that I could neither enjoy nor understand them. My receptive faculty is very limited, and when the utmost of its small capacity is full, I become perfectly miserable, and the more so the better worth seeing are the things I am forced to reject. I do not know a greater misery; to see sights, after such repletion, is

to the mind what it would be to the body to have dainties forced down the throat, long after the appetite was
satiated.

February 7

Whatever beauty there may be in a Roman ruin is the
remnant of what was beautiful originally; whereas an
English ruin is more beautiful often in its decay than
ever it was in its primal strength. If we ever build such
noble structures as these Roman ones, we can have just
as good ruins, after two thousand years, in the United
States; but we never can have a Furness Abbey or a
Kenilworth. . . .

I have not yet fairly begun the sight-seeing of Rome.
I have been three or four times to St. Peter's, and always
with pleasure, because there is such a delightful, summer-
like warmth the moment we pass beneath the heavy,
padded leather curtains that protect the entrances. It is
almost impossible not to believe that this genial tempera-
ture is the result of furnace-heat, but, really, it is the
warmth of last summer, which will be included within
those massive walls, and in that vast immensity of space,
till, six months hence, this winter's chill will just have
made its way thither. It would be an excellent plan for a
valetudinarian to lodge during the winter in St. Peter's,
perhaps establishing his household in one of the papal
tombs. I become, I think, more sensible of the size of St.
Peter's, but am as yet far from being overwhelmed by it.
It is not, as one expects, so big as all out o' doors, nor is its
dome so immense as that of the firmament. It looked
queer, however, the other day, to see a little ragged boy,

the very least of human things, going round and kneeling
at shrine after shrine, and a group of children standing on
tiptoe to reach the vase of holy water.

St. Peter's offers itself as a place of worship and religious
comfort for the whole human race; and in one of the tran-
septs, I found a range of confessionals where the penitent
might tell his sins in the tongue of his own country,
whether French, German, Polish, English, or what not.[1]
If I had a murder on my conscience, or any other great
sin, I think I should have been inclined to kneel down
there, and pour it into the safe secrecy of the confessional.
What an institution that is! Man needs it so, that it
seems as if God must have ordained it. This popish religion certainly does apply itself most closely and comfortably to human occasions; and I cannot but think that
a great many people find their spiritual advantage in it,
who would find none at all in our formless mode of worship. You cannot think it all a farce, when you see peasant, citizen, and soldier, coming into the church, each on
his own hook, and kneeling for moments or for hours, di-
recting his silent devotions to some particular shrine; too
humble to approach his God directly, and therefore asking
the mediation of some saint who stands beside his infinite
Presence. In the church of San Carlos, yesterday, I saw a
young man standing before a shrine, writhing and wringing his hands in an agony of grief and contrition. If he
had been a Protestant, I think he would have shut all
this up within his heart, and let it burn there till it seared
him.

[1] 'The Marble Faun,' Vol. II, Chap. XIV.

February 9

I go out but little — yesterday only as far as Paken-ham's and Hooker's bank in the Piazza di Spagna, where I read *Galignani* and the American papers. At last, after seeing more of my fellow-citizens during four years than ever before, I really am disjoined from my country.

February 14

The most interesting thing that we saw in this church [St. John Lateran] (and, admitting its authenticity, there can scarcely be a more interesting relic anywhere) was the table on which the Last Supper was eaten. It is preserved in a corridor, on one side of the tribune, or chancel, and is shown by torchlight, suspended upon the wall, beneath a covering of glass. Only the top of the table is shown, presenting a broad, flat surface of wood, evidently very old, and showing traces of dry-rot in one or two places. There are nails in it; and the attendant said that it had formerly been covered with bronze. As well as I can re-member, it may be five or six feet square, and I suppose would accommodate twelve persons, though not if they reclined in the Roman fashion, nor if they sat as they do in Corregio's [sic] picture. It would be very delightful to believe in this table. . . .

In reference to the interior splendor of Roman churches, I must say that I think it a pity that painted windows are exclusively a Gothic ornament; for the elaborate orna-mentation of these interiors puts the ordinary daylight out of countenance; so that a window, with only the white sunshine coming through it, or even with a glimpse of the blue Italian sky, looks like a portion left unfinished, and

therefore a blotch in the rich wall. It is like the one spot
in Aladdin's palace which he left for the king, his father-
in-law, to finish, after his fairy architects had exhausted
their magnificence on the rest; and the sun, like the king,
fails in the effort.

February 15

This is a strange fascination that Rome exercises upon
artists; there is clay elsewhere, and marble enough, and
heads to model; and ideas may be made sensible objects
at home as well as here. I think it is the peculiar mode of
life, and its freedom from the enthralments of society,
more than the artistic advantages which Rome offers;
and then, no doubt, though the artists care little about
one another's works, yet they keep each other warm by
the presence of so many of them.

February 19

Perhaps there is something in the mind of the people of
these countries that enables them quite to dissever small
ugliness from great sublimity and beauty. They spit on
the glorious pavement of St. Peter's, and wherever else
they like; they place mean-looking wooden confessionals
beneath its sublime arches, and ornament them with
cheap little colored prints of the crucifixion; they hang tin
hearts and other tinsel and trumpery at the gorgeous
shrines of the saints, in chapels that are encrusted with
gems, or marbles almost as precious; they put pasteboard
statues of saints beneath the dome of the Pantheon; in
short, they let the sublime and the ridiculous come close
together, and are not in the least troubled by the prox-

imity. It must be that their sense of the beautiful is
stronger than in the Anglo-Saxon mind, and that it
observes only what is fit to gratify it.

February 20

This morning, after breakfast, I walked across the city,
making a pretty straight course to the Pantheon, and
thence to the bridge of St. Angelo, and to St. Peter's. . . .
Passing near the confessional for foreigners to-day, I saw
a Spaniard, who had just come out of the one devoted
to his native tongue, taking leave of his confessor, with
an affectionate reverence, which — as well as the benign
dignity of the good father — it was good to behold. The
relation between the confessor and his penitent might,
and ought to be, one of great tenderness and beauty; and
the more I see of the Catholic church, the more I wonder
at the exuberance with which it responds to the demands
of human infirmity. If its ministers were themselves a
little more than human, they might fulfil their office, and
supply all that men need.

I returned home early, in order to go with my wife to
the Barberini Palace at two o'clock. . . . But we passed
hastily by this [picture], and almost all others, being eager
to see the two which chiefly make the collection famous —
Raphael's Fornarina, and Guido's portrait of Beatrice
Cenci. These were found in the last of the three rooms,
and as regards Beatrice Cenci, I might as well not try to
say anything; for its spell is indefinable, and the painter
has wrought it in a way more like magic than anything
else I have known. It is a very youthful, girlish, perfectly
beautiful face, with white drapery all around it, and quite

enveloping the form. One or two locks of auburn hair
stray out. The eyes are large and brown, and meet those
of the spectator; and there is, I think, a little red about
the eyelids, but it is very slightly indicated. The whole
face is perfectly quiet; no distortion nor disturbance of
any single feature; nor can I see why it should not be
cheerful, nor why an imperceptible touch of the painter's
brush should not suffice to brighten it into joyousness.
Yet it is the very saddest picture that ever was painted,
or conceived; there is an unfathomable depth and sorrow
in the eyes; the sense of it comes to you by a sort of intuition. It is a sorrow that removes her out of the sphere of
humanity; and yet she looks so innocent, that you feel as
if it were only this sorrow, with its weight and darkness,
that keeps her down upon the earth and brings her within
our reach at all. She is like a fallen angel, fallen, without
sin. It is infinitely pitiful to meet her eyes, and feel that
nothing can be done to help or comfort her; not that she
appeals to you for help and comfort, but is more conscious
than we can be that there is none in reserve for her. It is
the most profoundly wrought picture in the world; no
artist did it, nor could do it again. Guido may have held
the brush, but he painted better than he knew. I wish,
however, it were possible for some spectator, of deep
sensibility, to see the picture without knowing anything
of its subject or history; for, no doubt, we bring all our
knowledge of the Cenci tragedy to the interpretation
of it.

February 21

Arriving at St. Peter's shortly after two, we walked

round the whole church, looking at all the pictures and most of the monuments, . . . and paused longest before Guido's 'Archangel Michael overcoming Lucifer.' This is surely one of the most beautiful things in the world, one of the human conceptions that are imbued most largely with the celestial. These old painters were wonderful men, and have done great things for the Church of Rome — great things, we may say, for the Church of Christ and the cause of good; for the moral of this picture (the immortal youth and loveliness of virtue, and its irresistible might against evil) is as much directed to a Puritan as to a Catholic.

February 23

In the next room [of the Capitol] there were better statues than we had yet seen; but neither do I retain any vivid recollection of these, nor yet of those in the succeeding apartment; but in the last room of the range we found the 'Dying Gladiator,' of which I had already caught a glimpse, in passing by the open door. It had made all the other treasures of the gallery tedious, in my eagerness to come to that. . . . I do not believe that so much pathos is wrought into any other block of stone. Like all other works of the highest excellence, however, it makes great demands upon the spectator; he must make a generous gift of his sympathies to the sculptor, and help out his skill with all his heart, or else he will see little more than a skilfully wrought surface. It suggests far more than it shows. I looked long at this statue, and little at anything else, though, among other famous works, a statue of Antinoüs was in the same room.

February 24

All the successive ages since Rome began to decay, have done their best to ruin the very ruins by taking away the marble and the hewn stone for their own structures, and leaving only the inner filling up of brickwork, which the ancient architects never designed to be seen. The consequence of all this is, that, except for the lofty and poetical associations connected with it — and except, too, for the immense difference in magnitude — a Roman ruin may be in itself not more picturesque than I have seen an old cellar, with a shattered brick chimney half crumbling down into it, in New England.

March 1

A picture by Marie Subleyras [in the Colonna Palace] — a miniature copy from one by her husband, of the woman anointing the feet of Christ — is most delicately and beautifully finished, and would be an ornament to a drawing-room; a thing that could not truly be said of one in a hundred of these grim masterpieces. When they were painted life was not what it is now, and the artists had not the same ends in view. There is something forced, if not feigned, in our tastes for pictures of the old Italian school. It depresses the spirits to go from picture to picture, leaving a portion of your vital sympathy at every one, so that you come, with a kind of half-torpid desperation, to the end. On our way down the staircase we saw several noteworthy bas-reliefs, and among them a very ancient one of Curtius plunging on horseback into the chasm in the Forum. It seems to me, however, that old sculpture affects the spirits even more dolefully than old painting; it strikes colder to the heart, and lies heavier upon it, being marble, than if it were merely canvas. . . .

The Catholics have taken a peculiar pleasure in planting themselves in the very citadels of paganism, whether temples or palaces. There has been a good deal of enjoyment in the destruction of old Rome. I often think so when I see the elaborate pains that have been taken to smash and demolish some beautiful column, for no purpose on earth, except the mere delight of annihilating a noble piece of work. There is something in the impulse with which one sympathizes; though I am afraid the destroyers were not sufficiently aware of the mischief they did to enjoy it fully. Probably, too, the early Christians were impelled by religious zeal to destroy the pagan temples, before the happy thought occurred to them of converting them into churches.

March 10

I am of opinion that good painters are quite as rare as good poets; and I do not see why we should pique ourselves on admiring any but the very best. One in a thousand, perhaps, ought to live in the applause of men, from generation to generation, till his colors fade or blacken out of sight, and his canvases rot away; the rest should be put in garrets, or painted over by newer artists, just as tolerable poets are shelved when their little day is over.

March 11

I do not think there is a better painter than Mr. [C. G.] Thompson living — among Americans at least; not one so earnest, faithful, and religious in his worship of art. I had

rather look at his pictures than at any except the very
finest of the old masters, and, taking into consideration
only the comparative pleasure to be derived, I would not
except more than one or two of those. In painting, as in
literature, I suspect there is something in the productions
of the day that takes the fancy more than the works of any
past age — not greater merit, nor nearly so great, but
better suited to this very present time.

March 14

The difference between the pre-Raphaelites and himself [the sculptor Gibson] is deep and genuine, they being
literalists and realists, in a certain sense, and he a pagan
idealist. Methinks they have hold of the best end of the
matter.

March 25

On Tuesday we went to breakfast at William Story's in
the Palazzo Barberini. We had a very pleasant time. He
is one of the most agreeable men I know in society. He
showed us a note from Thackeray, an invitation to dinner,
written in hieroglyphics, with great fun and pictorial
merit. He spoke of an expansion of the story of Blue
Beard, which he himself had either written or thought of
writing, in which the contents of the several chambers
which Fatima opened, before arriving at the fatal one,
were to be described. This idea has haunted my mind
ever since, and if it had but been my own I am pretty sure
that it would develop itself into something very rich. I
mean to press William Story to work it out. The chamber
of Blue Beard, too (and this was a part of his suggestion),

might be so handled as to become powerfully interesting.
Were I to take up the story I would create an interest
by suggesting a secret in the first chamber, which would
develop itself more and more in every successive hall of
the great palace, and lead the wife irresistibly to the
chamber of horrors.

March 26

One of the most striking objects in the first casino [in
the Villa Ludovisi] was a group by Bernini — Pluto, an
outrageously masculine and strenuous figure, heavily
bearded, ravishing away a little, tender Proserpine, whom
he holds aloft, while his forcible gripe impresses itself into
her soft virgin flesh. It is very disagreeable, but it makes
one feel that Bernini was a man of great ability. There
are some works in literature that bear an analogy to his
works in sculpture, when great power is lavished a little
outside of nature, and therefore proves to be only a fashion, and not permanently adapted to the tastes of mankind.

March 27

Yesterday forenoon my wife and I went to St. Peter's
to see the pope pray at the chapel of the Holy Sacrament.
We found a good many people in the church, but not an
inconvenient number; indeed, not so many as to make any
remarkable show in the great nave, nor even in front of
the chapel. A detachment of the Swiss Guard, in their
strange, picturesque, harlequin-like costume, were on
duty before the chapel, in which the wax tapers were all
lighted, and a *prie-dieu* was arranged near the shrine, and

covered with scarlet velvet. On each side, along the breadth of the side aisle, were placed seats, covered with rich tapestry or carpeting; and some gentlemen and ladies — English, probably, or American — had comfortably deposited themselves here, but were compelled to move by the guards before the pope's entrance. His Holiness should have appeared precisely at twelve, but we waited nearly half an hour beyond that time; and it seemed to me particularly ill-mannered in the pope, who owes the courtesy of being punctual to the people, if not to St. Peter. By and by, however, there was a stir; the guard motioned to us to stand away from the benches, against the backs of which we had been leaning; the spectators in the nave looked towards the door, as if they beheld something approaching; and first, there appeared some cardinals, in scarlet skull-caps and purple robes, intermixed with some of the Noble Guard and other attendants. It was not a very formal and stately procession, but rather straggled onward, with ragged edges, the spectators standing aside to let it pass, and merely bowing, or perhaps slightly bending the knee, as good Catholics are accustomed to do when passing before the shrines of saints. Then, in the midst of the purple cardinals, all of whom were gray-haired men, appeared a stout old man, with a white skull-cap, a scarlet, gold-embroidered cape falling over his shoulders, and a white silk robe, the train of which was borne up by an attendant. He walked slowly, with a sort of dignified movement, stepping out broadly, and planting his feet (on which were red shoes) flat upon the pavement, as if he were not much accustomed to locomotion, and perhaps had known a twinge of the gout. His face was kindly and venerable, but not particularly impressive. Arriving at the scarlet-covered *prie-dieu*, he kneeled down and took off his white skull-cap; the cardinals also kneeled behind and on either side of him, taking off their scarlet skull-caps; while the Noble Guard remained standing, six on one side of his Holiness and six on the other. The pope bent his head upon the *prie-dieu*, and seemed to spend three or four minutes in prayer; then rose, and all the purple cardinals, and bishops, and priests, of whatever degree, rose behind and beside him. Next, he went to kiss St. Peter's toe; at least I believe he kissed it, but I was not near enough to be certain; and lastly, he knelt down, and directed his devotions towards the high altar. This completed the ceremonies, and his Holiness left the church by a side door, making a short passage into the Vatican.

I am very glad I have seen the pope, because now he may be crossed out of the list of sights to be seen. His proximity impressed me kindly and favorably towards him, and I did not see one face among all his cardinals (in whose number, doubtless, is his successor) which I would so soon trust as that of Pio Nono.

Undated

Mr. Mozier knew Margaret well, she having been an inmate of his during a part of his residence in Italy. . . . He says that the Ossoli family, though technically noble, is really of no rank whatever; the elder brother, with the title of Marquis, being at this very time a working bricklayer, and the sisters walking the streets without bonnets — that is, being in the station of peasant-girls. Ossoli himself,[1] to the best of his belief, was ——'s servant, or had something to do with the care of ——'s apartments. He was the handsomest man that Mr. Mozier ever saw, but entirely ignorant, even of his own language; scarcely able to read at all; destitute of manners — in short, half an idiot, and without any pretension to be a gentleman. At Margaret's request, Mr. Mozier had taken him into his studio, with a view to ascertain whether he were capable of instruction in sculpture; but after four months' labor, Ossoli produced a thing intended to be a copy of a human foot, but the great toe was on the wrong side. He could not possibly have had the least appreciation of Margaret; and the wonder is, what attraction she found in this boor, this man without the intellectual spark — she that had always shown such a cruel and bitter scorn of intellectual deficiency. As from her towards him, I do not understand what feeling there could have been; . . . as from him towards her I can understand as little, for she had not the charm of womanhood. But she was a person anxious to try all things, and fill up her experience in all directions; she had a strong and coarse nature, which she had done her utmost to refine, with infinite pains; but of course it could only be superficially changed. The solution of the riddle lies in this direction; nor does one's conscience revolt at the idea of thus solving it; for (at least, this is my own experience) Margaret has not left in the hearts and minds of those who knew her any deep witness of her

---

[1] This extremely disparaging account of the Marquis d'Ossoli, based by Hawthorne on Mozier's testimony, should be compared with the very different accounts by Mrs. William Wetmore Story used by T. W. Higginson in his life of Margaret Fuller Ossoli (American Men of Letters Series, Boston, 1884).

integrity and purity. She was a great humbug — of course, with much talent and much moral reality, or else she could never have been so great a humbug. But she had stuck herself full of borrowed qualities, which she chose to provide herself with, but which had no root in her.

Mr. Mozier added that Margaret had quite lost all power of literary production before she left Rome, though occasionally the charm and power of her conversation would reappear. To his certain knowledge, she had no important manuscripts with her when she sailed (she having shown him all she had, with a view to his procuring their publication in America), and the 'History of the Roman Revolution,' about which there was so much lamentation, in the belief that it had been lost with her, never had existence. Thus there appears to have been a total collapse in poor Margaret, morally and intellectually; and, tragic as her catastrophe was, Providence was, after all, kind in putting her and her clownish husband and their child on board that fated ship. There never was such a tragedy as her whole story — the sadder and sterner, because so much of the ridiculous was mixed up with it, and because she could bear anything better than to be ridiculous. It was such an awful joke, that she should have resolved — in all sincerity, no doubt — to make herself the greatest, wisest, best woman of the age. And to that end she set to work on her strong, heavy, unpliable, and, in many respects, defective and evil nature, and adorned it with a mosaic of admirable qualities, such as she chose to possess; putting in here a splendid talent and there a moral excellence, and polishing each separate

piece, and the whole together, till it seemed to shine afar
and dazzle all who saw it. She took credit to herself for
having been her own Redeemer, if not her own Creator;
and, indeed, she was far more a work of art than any of
Mozier's statues. But she was not working on an inani-
mate substance, like marble or clay; there was something
within her that she could not possibly come at, to re-
create or refine it; and, by and by, this rude old potency
bestirred itself, and undid all her labor in the twinkling of
an eye. On the whole, I do not know but I like her the
better for it; because she proved herself a very woman
after all, and fell as the weakest of her sisters might.

April 10

On Thursday I paid another visit to the Capitol, where
I was particularly struck with a bust of Cato the Censor,
who must have been the most disagreeable, stubborn,
ugly-tempered, pig-headed, narrow-minded, strong-willed
old Roman that ever lived. The collection of busts here
and at the Vatican are most interesting, many of the individual heads being full of character, and commending
themselves by intrinsic evidence as faithful portraits of
the originals. These stone people have stood face to face
with Cæsar, and all the other emperors, and with states-
men, soldiers, philosophers, and poets of the antique world,
and have been to them like their reflections in a mirror.
It is the next thing to seeing the men themselves.

April 12

I wonder whether other people are more fortunate than
myself, and can invariably find their way to the inner soul

of a work of art. I doubt it; they look at these things for just a minute, and pass on, without any pang of remorse, such as I feel, for quitting them so soon and so willingly. I am partly sensible that some unwritten rules of taste are making their way into my mind; that all this Greek beauty has done something towards refining me, though I am still, however, a very sturdy Goth.

April 16

The statue of Moses [in San Pietro in Vincoli] occupies a niche in one of the side aisles on the right, not far from the high altar. I found it grand and sublime, with a beard flowing down like a cataract; a truly majestic figure, but not so benign as it were desirable that such strength should be. The horns, about which so much has been said, are not a very prominent feature of the statue, being merely two diminutive tips rising straight up over his forehead, neither adding to the grandeur of the head, nor detracting sensibly from it. The whole force of this statue is not to be felt in one brief visit, but I agree with an English gentleman, who, with a large party, entered the church while we were there, in thinking that Moses has 'very fine features' — a compliment for which the colossal Hebrew ought to have made the Englishman a bow.

April 22

We have been recently to the studio of Mr. [G. L.] Brown, the American landscape-painter, and were altogether surprised and delighted with his pictures. He is a plain, homely Yankee, quite unpolished by his many years' residence in Italy; he talks ungrammatically, and in Yankee idioms; walks with a strange, awkward gait and stooping shoulders; is altogether unpicturesque; but wins one's confidence by his very lack of grace. It is not often that we see an artist so entirely free from affectation in his aspect and deportment. His pictures were views of Swiss and Italian scenery, and were most beautiful and true. One of them, a moonlight picture, was really magical — the moon shining so brightly that it seemed to throw a light even beyond the limits of the picture — and yet his sunrises and sunsets, and noontides too, were nowise inferior to this, although their excellence required somewhat longer study, to be fully appreciated. I seemed to receive more pleasure from Mr. Brown's pictures than from any of the landscapes by the old masters; and the fact serves to strengthen me in the belief that the most delicate if not the highest charm of a picture is evanescent, and that we continue to admire pictures prescriptively and by tradition, after the qualities that first won them their fame have vanished. I suppose Claude was a greater landscape-painter than Brown; but for my own pleasure I would prefer one of the latter artist's pictures — those of the former being quite changed from what he intended them to be by the effect of time on his pigments. Mr. Brown showed us some drawings from nature, done with incredible care and minuteness of detail, as studies for his paintings. We complimented him on his patience; but he said, 'O, it's not patience — it's love!' In fact, it was a patient and most successful wooing of a beloved object, which at last rewarded him by yielding itself wholly.

We afterwards went into the sculpture-gallery [at the

Capitol] where I looked at the Faun of Praxiteles, and was sensible of a peculiar charm in it; a sylvan beauty and homeliness, friendly and wild at once. The lengthened, but not preposterous ears, and the little tail, which we infer, have an exquisite effect, and make the spectator smile in his very heart. This race of fauns was the most delightful of all that antiquity imagined. It seems to me that a story, with all sorts of fun and pathos in it, might be contrived on the idea of their species having become intermingled with the human race; a family with the faun blood in them, having prolonged itself from the classic era till our own days. The tail might have disappeared, by dint of constant intermarriages with ordinary mortals; but the pretty hairy ears should occasionally reappear in members of the family; and the moral instincts and intellectual characteristics of the faun might be most picturesquely brought out, without detriment to the human interest of the story. Fancy this combination in the person of a young lady!

April 27

Now, here are three artists, Mr. Brown, Mr. Wilde, and this Mr. Müller, who have smitten me with vast admiration, within these few days past, while I am continually turning away disappointed from the landscapes of the most famous among the old masters, unable to find any charm or illusion in them. Yet I suppose Claude, Poussin, and Salvator Rosa must have won their renown by real achievements. But the glory of a picture fades like that of a flower.

April 30

I went yesterday to the sculpture-gallery of the Capitol, and looked pretty thoroughly through the busts of the illustrious men, and less particularly at those of the emperors and their relatives. I likewise took particular note of the Faun of Praxiteles, because the idea keeps recurring to me of writing a little romance about it, and for that reason I shall endeavor to set down a somewhat minutely itemized detail of the statue and its surroundings. The faun is the image of a young man, leaning with one arm upon the trunk or stump of a tree; he has a pipe, or some such instrument of music, in the hand which rests upon the tree, and the other, I think, hangs carelessly by his side. His only garment falls half way down his back, but leaves the whole front, and all the rest of his person, exposed, displaying a very beautiful form, but clad in more flesh, with more full and rounded outlines, and less development of muscle, than the old sculptors were wont to assign to masculine beauty. The figure is not fat, but neither has it the attribute of slender grace. The face has a character corresponding with that of the form; beautiful and most agreeable features, but rounded, especially about the throat and chin; a nose almost straight, yet very slightly curving inward, a voluptuous mouth that seems almost (not quite) to smile outright; — in short, the whole person conveys the idea of an amiable and sensual nature, easy, mirthful, apt for jollity, yet not incapable of being touched by pathos. The faun has no principle, nor could comprehend it, yet is true and honest by virtue of his simplicity; very capable, too, of affection. He might be refined through his feelings, so that the coarser, animal part of his nature would be thrown into the background, though liable to assert itself at any time. Praxiteles has only expressed this animal nature by one (or rather two) definite signs — the two ears, which go up in a little peak, not likely to be discovered on slight inspection, and, I suppose, are covered with fine, downy fur. A tail is probably hidden under his garment. Only a sculptor of the finest imagination, most delicate taste, and sweetest feeling, could have dreamed of representing a Faun in this guise; and if you brood over it long enough, all the pleasantness of sylvan life, and all the genial and happy characteristics of the brute creation, seem to be mixed in him with humanity — trees, grass, flowers, cattle, deer, and unsophisticated men.

May 1

This morning, I wandered for the thousandth time through some of the narrow intricacies of Rome, stepping here and there into a church. . . . To good Catholics, it must be a blessed convenience — this facility of finding a cool, quiet, silent, beautiful place of worship in even the hottest and most bustling street, into which they may step, leaving the fret and trouble of the world at the threshold, purifying themselves with a touch of holy water as they enter, and kneeling down to hold communion with some saint, their awful friend; or perhaps confessing all their sins to a priest, laying the whole dark burden at the foot of the cross, and coming forth in the freshness and elasticity of innocence. It is for Protestants to inquire whether some of these inestimable advantages are not compatible with a purified faith, and do not indeed belong to Christianity, making part of the blessings it was meant to bring. It would be a good time to suggest and institute some of them, now that the American public seems to be stirred by a revival, hitherto unexampled in extent. Protestantism needs a new apostle to convert it into something positive.

The effect of light and shade in a church where the windows are open and darkened with curtains that are occasionally lifted by a breeze, letting in the sunshine, which whitens a carved tombstone on the pavement of the church, disclosing, perhaps, the letters of the name and inscription, a death's-head, a crosier, or other emblem; then the curtain falls and the bright spot vanishes.

May 8

This morning my wife and I went to breakfast with Mrs. William Story at the Barberini Palace, expecting to meet Mrs. Jameson, who has been in Rome for a month or two. We had a very pleasant breakfast, but Mrs. Jameson was not present on account of indisposition, and the only other guests were Mrs. Apthorp and Miss Hunter, two sensible American ladies. Mrs. Story, however, received a note from Mrs. Jameson, asking her to bring us to see her at her lodgings; so in the course of the afternoon she called for us, and took us thither in her carriage. Mrs. Jameson lives on the first piano of an old palazzo on the Via di Ripetta, nearly opposite the ferry-way across the Tiber, and affording a pleasant view of the yellow river and the green bank and fields on the other side. I had ex-

pected to see an elderly lady, but not quite so venerable
a one as Mrs. Jameson proved to be; a rather short, round,
and massive personage, of benign and agreeable aspect,
with a sort of black skullcap on her head, beneath which
appeared her hair, which seemed once to have been fair,
and was now almost white. I should take her to be about
seventy years old. She began to talk to us with affectionate familiarity, and was particularly kind in her manifestations towards myself, who, on my part, was equally
gracious towards her. In truth, I have found great pleasure and profit in her works, and was glad to hear her say
that she liked mine. We talked about art, and she showed
us a picture standing up against the wall of the room; a
quaint old Byzantine painting, with a gilded background,
and two stiff figures (our Saviour and St. Catherine)
standing shyly at a sacred distance from one another, and
going through the marriage ceremony. There was a great
deal of expression in their faces and figures; and the
spectator feels, moreover, that the artist must have been
a devout man — an impression which we seldom receive
from modern pictures, however awfully holy the subject,
or however consecrated the place they hang in. Mrs.
Jameson seems to be familiar with Italy, its people and
life, as well as with its picture-galleries. She is said to be
rather irascible in her temper; but nothing could be
sweeter than her voice, her look, and all her manifestations to-day. When we were coming away she clasped
my hand in both of hers, and again expressed her pleasure
at having seen me, and her gratitude to me for calling on
her; nor did I refrain from responding anew to these ef-
fusions. Were we to meet often, I should be a little bit

afraid of her embracing me outright — a thing to be grateful for, but by no means to be glad of.

The Italians have a terrible dread of corpses, and never meddle with those of their nearest and dearest relatives. They have a horror of death, too, especially of sudden death, and most particularly of apoplexy; and no wonder, as it gives no time for the last rites of the Church, and so exposes them to a fearful risk of perdition forever. On the whole, the ancient practice was perhaps the preferable one; but Nature has made it very difficult for us to do anything pleasant and satisfactory with a dead body. God knows best; but I wish he had so ordered it that our mortal bodies, when we have done with them, might vanish out of sight and sense, like bubbles. A person of delicacy hates to think of leaving such a burthen as his decaying mortality, to be disposed of by his friends; but, I say again, how delightful it would be, and how helpful towards our faith in a blessed futurity, if the dying could disappear like vanishing bubbles, leaving perhaps a sweet fragrance, diffused for a minute or two throughout the death-chamber. This would be the odor of sanctity! And if sometimes the evaporation of a sinful soul should leave a smell not so delightful, a breeze through the open windows would soon waft it quite away.

Apropos of the various methods of disposing of dead bodies, William Story recalled a newspaper paragraph respecting a ring, with a stone of a new species in it, which a widower was observed to wear upon his finger. Being questioned as to what the gem was, he answered, 'It is my wife.' He had procured her body to be chemically resolved into this stone. I think I could make a story on this idea; the ring should be one of the widower's bridal gifts to a second wife; and, of course, it should have wondrous and terrible qualities, symbolizing all that disturbs the quiet of a second marriage — on the husband's part, remorse for his inconstancy, and the constant comparison between the dead wife of his youth, now idealized, and this grosser reality which he had now adopted into his bed and hers; while, on the new wife's finger, it should give pressures, shooting pangs into her heart, jealousies of the past, and all such miserable emotions.

May 9

She [Mrs. Jameson] is a very sensible old lady, and sees a great deal of truth; a good woman, too, taking elevated views of matters; but I doubt whether she has the highest and finest perceptions in the world. At any rate, she pronounced a good judgment on the American sculptors now in Rome, condemning them in the mass as men with no high aims, no worthy conception of the purposes of their art, and desecrating marble by the things they wrought in it. William Story, I presume, is not to be included in this censure, as she had spoken highly of his sculpturesque faculty in our previous conversation. On my part, I suggested that the English sculptors were little or nothing better than our own, to which she acceded generally, but said that Gibson had produced works equal to the antique — which I did not dispute, but still questioned whether the world needed Gibson, or was any the better for him. We had a great dispute about the propriety of adopting the costume of the day in modern sculpture, and I con-

tended that either the art ought to be given up (which
possibly would be the best course), or else should be used
for idealizing the man of the day to himself; and that, as
Nature makes us sensible of the fact when men and
women are graceful, beautiful, and noble, through whatever costume they wear, so it ought to be the test of the
sculptor's genius that he should do the same. Mrs.
Jameson decidedly objected to buttons, breeches, and all
other items of modern costume; and, indeed, they do degrade the marble, and make high sculpture utterly impossible. Then let the art perish as one that the world has
done with, as it has done with many other beautiful
things that belonged to an earlier time.

May 15

In the afternoon Mr. Thompson took me into the Via
Portoghese, and showed me an old palace, above which
rose — not a very customary feature of the architecture
of Rome — a tall, battlemented tower.[1] At one angle of
the tower we saw a shrine of the Virgin, with a lamp, and
all the appendages of those numerous shrines which we
see at the street-corners, and in hundreds of places about
Rome. Three or four hundred years ago this palace was
inhabited by a nobleman who had an only son and a large
pet monkey; and one day the monkey caught the infant
up in his arms and clambered with him to this lofty turret, and sat there with him in his arms, grinning and chat-
tering like the Devil himself. The father was in despair,
but was afraid to pursue the monkey lest he should fling
down the child from the height of the tower and make

[1] Hilda's Tower in 'The Marble Faun.'

his escape. At last, he vowed that if the boy were safely restored to him he would build a shrine at the summit of the tower, and cause it to be kept as a sacred place forever. By and by, the monkey came down and deposited the child on the ground; the father fulfilled his vow, built the shrine, and made it obligatory on all future possessors of the palace to keep the lamp burning before it. Centuries have passed; the property has changed hands; but still there is the shrine on the giddy top of the tower, far aloft over the street, on the very spot where the monkey sat; and there burns the lamp in memory of the father's vow. This being the tenure by which the estate is held, the extinguishment of that flame might yet turn the present owner out of the palace.

May 22

Yesterday, while we were at dinner, Mr. Bryant called. I never saw him but once before, and that was at the door of our little red cottage in Lenox; he sitting in a wagon with one or two of the Sedgwicks, merely exchanging a greeting with me from under the brim of his straw hat, and driving on. He presented himself now with a long white beard, such as a palmer might have worn as the growth of his long pilgrimages, a brow almost entirely bald, and what hair he has quite hoary; a forehead impending, yet not massive; dark, bushy eyebrows and keen eyes, without much softness in them; a dark and sallow complexion; a slender figure, bent a little with age; but at once alert and infirm. It surprised me to see him so venerable; for, as poets are Apollo's kinsmen, we are inclined to attribute to them his enviable quality of never growing old. There

was a weary look in Bryant's face, as if he were tired
of seeing things and doing things, though with activity
enough still to see and do, if need were. My family gathered about him, and he conversed with great readiness
and simplicity about his travels, and whatever other subject came up; telling us that he had been abroad five
times, and was now getting a little home-sick, and had no
more eagerness for sights, though his 'gals' (as he called
his daughter and another young lady) dragged him out to
see the sights of Rome again. His manners and whole
aspect are very particularly plain, though not affectedly
so; but it seems as if in the decline of life, and the security
of his position, he had put off whatever artificial polish he
may have heretofore had, and resumed the simpler habits
and deportment of his early New England breeding. Not
but what you discern, nevertheless, that he is a man of
refinement, who has seen the world, and is well aware of
his own place in it. He spoke with great pleasure of his recent visit to Spain. I introduced the subject of Kansas,
and methought his visage forthwith assumed something of
the bitter keenness of the editor of a political newspaper,
while speaking of the triumph of the administration over
the Free-Soil opposition. I inquired whether he had seen
Sumner recently, and he gave a very sad account of him
as he appeared at their last meeting, which was in Paris.
Sumner, he thought, had suffered terribly, and would
never again be the man he was; he was getting fat; he
talked continually of himself, and trifles concerning himself, and seemed to have no interest for other matters;
and Mr. Bryant feared that the shock upon his nerves
had extended to his intellect, and was irremediable. He

said that Sumner ought to retire from public life, but had
no friend true enough to tell him so. This is about as sad
as anything can be. I hate to have Sumner undergo the
fate of a martyr, because he was not naturally of the stuff
that martyrs are made of, and it is altogether by mistake
that he has thrust himself into the position of one. He was
merely, though with excellent abilities, one of the best fellows in the world, and ought to have lived and died in
good fellowship with all the world.

Bryant was not in the least degree excited about this or
any other subject. He uttered neither passion nor poetry,
but excellent good sense, and accurate information on
whatever subject came up; a very pleasant man to associate with, but rather cold, I should imagine, if one
should seek to touch his heart with one's own. He shook
hands kindly all round, but not with any warmth of gripe;
although the ease of his deportment had put us all on
sociable terms with him.

This afternoon we called on Mr. and Mrs. Bryant at
the Hôtel d'Europe, but found only the former at home.
We had a pleasant visit, but I made no observations of
his character save such as I have already sufficiently recorded; and when we had been with him a little while,
Mrs. Chapman, the artist's wife, Mr. Terry, the painter,
and my friend, Mr. Thompson, came in. Bryant received
them all with the same good degree of cordiality that he
did ourselves, not cold, not very warm, not bothered, not
ecstatically delighted; a man, I should suppose, not likely
to have warm individual preferences, though perhaps
capable of stern individual dislikes. But I take him, at

all events, to be a very upright man, and pursuing a narrow track of integrity; he is a man whom I would never forgive (as I might a thousand other men) for the slightest moral delinquency. I would not be bound to say, however, that he has not the little sin of a fretful and peevish habit; and yet perhaps I am a sinner myself for thinking so.

May 23

This morning I breakfasted at William Story's, and met there Mr. Bryant, Mr. T—— (an English gentleman), Mr. and Mrs. Apthorp, Miss Hosmer, and one or two other ladies. Bryant was very quiet, and made no conversation audible to the general table. . . . We had a very pleasant breakfast, and certainly a breakfast is much preferable to a dinner, not merely in the enjoyment while it is passing, but afterwards. . . . Apart, with William Story, he and I talked of the unluckiness of Friday, and both acknowledged that this nonsense has a certain degree of influence with us. We spoke also, and more seriously, of the idea (which has been realized in my own experience) that a piece of good fortune is apt to be attended by an equivalent misfortune, as its shadow or black twin. There seems to be a vein of melancholy in William Story, which I was not aware of in my very slight previous acquaintance with him, before meeting him now in Rome. He acknowledged that, for three years past, he has lived in dread that some sorrow would come to counterbalance the prosperity of his present life. I hope not; for I like him particularly well; and indeed it is very hard if we cannot enjoy a little sunshine in this short

and hard life, without a deadly shadow gliding close behind. Old age, and death in its due time, will surely come;
let those suffice. The notion, however, is a comfortable
one or otherwise, according to your point of view. If the
misfortune comes first, it is consolatory to think of the
good that is soon to follow; in the other category, it is
exceedingly disagreeable.

When the sun went down, we descended into the Piazza
del Popolo, and thence into the Via di Ripetta, and
emerged through a gate to the shore of the Tiber, along
which there is a pleasant walk beneath a grove of trees.
We traversed it once, and back again, looking at the rapid
river, which still kept its mud-puddly aspect even in the
clear twilight and beneath the brightening moon. The
great bell of St. Peter's tolled with a deep boom, a grand
and solemn sound; the moon gleamed through the
branches of the trees above us; and Una spoke with somewhat alarming fervor of her love for Rome and regret at
leaving it. We shall have done the poor child no good
office in bringing her here, if the rest of her life is to be
a dream of this 'city of the soul,' and an unsatisfied yearning to come back to it. On the other hand, nothing elevat-
ing and refining can be really injurious; and so I hope
she will always be the better for Rome, even if her life
should be spent where there are no pictures, no statues,
nothing but the dryness and meagreness of a New England village.

May 24 [Civita Castellana]

On the whole, I was not sorry to see the Gauls [French

troops] still pouring into Rome; but after all I begin to find that I have a strange affection for it, and so did we all — the rest of the family in a greater degree than myself. It is very singular, the sad embrace with which Rome takes possession of the soul. Though we intend to return in a few months, and for a longer residence than this has been, yet we felt the city pulling at our heartstrings far more than London did, where we shall probably never spend much time again. It may be because the intellect finds a home there more than in any other spot in the world, and wins the heart to stay with it, in spite of a good many things strewn all about to disgust us.

May 28 [*Assisi*]

Nothing is more strange than to think that this now dead city — dead, as regards the purposes for which men live nowadays — was, centuries ago, the seat and birthplace almost of art, the only art in which the beautiful part of the human mind then developed itself. How came that flower to grow among these wild mountains? I do not conceive, however, that the people of Assisi were ever much more enlightened or cultivated on the side of art than they are at present. The ecclesiastics were then the only patrons; and the flower grew here because there was a great ecclesiastical garden in which it was sheltered and fostered. But it is very curious to think of Assisi, a school of art within, and mountain and wilderness without.

May 30 [*Arezzo*]

Both last night and to-day, I found myself stirred more

sensibly than I expected by the influences of this scene [Lake Thrasymene]. The old battle-field is still fertile in thoughts and emotions, though it is so many ages since the blood spilt there has ceased to make the grass and flowers grow more luxuriantly. I doubt whether I should feel so much on the field of Saratoga or Monmouth; but these old classic battle-fields belong to the whole world, and each man feels as if his own forefathers fought them. Mine, by the by, if they fought them at all, must have been on the side of Hannibal; for, certainly, I sympathized with him, and exulted in the defeat of the Romans on their own soil. They excite much the same emotion of general hostility that the English do. Byron has written some very fine stanzas on the battle-field — not so good as others that he has written on classical scenes and subjects, yet wonderfully impressing his own perception of the subject on the reader. Whenever he has to deal with a statue, a ruin, a battle-field, he pounces upon the topic like a vulture, and tears out its heart in a twinkling, so that there is nothing more to be said.

There is no familiar object connected with daily life so interesting as a well; and this well of old Arezzo, whence Petrarch had drunk, around which he had played in his boyhood, and which Boccaccio has made famous, really interested me more than the cathedral. It lies right under the pavement of the street, under the sunshine, without any shade of trees about it, or any grass, except a little that grows in the crevices of its stones; but the shape of its stone-work would make it a pretty object in an engraving. As I lingered round it I thought of my own town-pump in old Salem,[1] and wondered whether my townspeople would ever point it out to strangers, and whether the stranger would gaze at it with any degree of such interest as I felt in Boccaccio's well. O, certainly not; but yet I made that humble town-pump the most celebrated structure in the good town. A thousand and a thousand people had pumped there, merely to water oxen or fill their teakettles; but when once I grasped the handle, a rill gushed forth that meandered as far as England, as far as India, besides tasting pleasantly in every town and village of our own country. I like to think of this, so long after I did it, and so far from home, and am not without hopes of some kindly local remembrance on this score.

June 4 [Florence]

His [Hiram Powers'] long absence from our country has made him think worse of us than we deserve; and it is an effect of which I myself am sensible, in my shorter exile: the most piercing shriek, the wildest yell, and all the ugly sounds of popular turmoil, inseparable from the life of a republic, being a million times more audible than the peaceful hum of prosperity and content which is going on all the while.

He talks of going home, but says that he has been talking of it every year since he first came to Italy; and between his pleasant life of congenial labor, and his idea of moral deterioration in America, I think it doubtful whether he ever crosses the sea again. Like most exiles of twenty years, he has lost his native country without

[1] 'A Rill from the Town Pump.'

finding another; but then it is as well to recognize the truth — that an individual country is by no means essential to one's comfort.

To me has been assigned the pleasantest room [in the Casa del Bello] for my study; and when I like I can overflow into the summerhouse or an arbor, and sit there dreaming of a story. The weather is delightful, too warm to walk, but perfectly fit to do nothing in, in the coolness of these great rooms. Every day I shall write a little, perhaps — and probably take a brief nap somewhere between breakfast and tea — but go to see pictures and statues occasionally, and so assuage and mollify myself a little after that uncongenial life of the consulate, and before going back to my own hard and dusty New England.

June 5

Florence at first struck me as having the aspect of a very new city in comparison with Rome; but, on closer acquaintance, I find that many of the buildings are antique and massive, though still the clear atmosphere, the bright sunshine, the light, cheerful hues of the stucco, and — as much as anything else, perhaps — the vivacious character of the human life in the streets, take away the sense of its being an ancient city. The streets are delightful to walk in after so many penitential pilgrimages as I have made over those little square, uneven blocks of the Roman pavement, which wear out the boots and torment the soul. I absolutely walk on the smooth flags of Florence for the mere pleasure of walking, and live in its atmosphere for the mere pleasure of living; and, warm as the weather is getting to be, I never feel that inclination to sink down in a heap and never stir again, which was my dull torment and misery as long as I stayed in Rome. I hardly think there can be a place in the world where life is more delicious for its own simple sake than here.

It is a pity that we cannot take as much interest in the history of these Italian Republics as in that of England, for the former is much the more picturesque and fuller of curious incident. The sobriety of the Anglo-Saxon race — in connection, too, with their moral sense — keeps them from doing a great many things that would enliven the page of history; and their events seem to come in great masses, shoved along by the agency of many persons, rather than to result from individual will and character. A hundred plots for a tragedy might be found in Florentine history for one in English.

June 8

I wish some competent person would undertake to analyze and develop his [Nero's] character, and how and by what necessity — with all his elegant tastes, his love of the beautiful, his artist nature — he grew to be such a monster. Nero has never yet had justice done him, nor have any of the wicked emperors; not that I suppose them to have been any less monstrous than history represents them; but there must surely have been something in their position and circumstances to render the terrible moral disease which seized upon them so generally almost inevitable. A wise and profound man, tender and reverent of the human soul, and capable of appreciating it in its height and depth, has a great field here for the exercise of his powers. It has struck me, in reading the history of the Italian republics, that many of the tyrants, who sprung up after the destruction of their liberties, resembled the worst of the Roman emperors. The subject of Nero and his brethren has often perplexed me with vain desires to come at the truth.

I could not quite believe that I was not to find the Venus de' Medici [in the Uffizi]; and still, as I passed from one room to another, my breath rose and fell a little, with the half-hope, half-fear, that she might stand before me. Really, I did not know that I cared so much about Venus, or any possible woman of marble. At last, when I had come from among the Dutchmen, I believe, and was looking at some works of Italian artists, chiefly Florentines, I caught a glimpse of her through the door of the next room. It is the best room of the series, octagonal in shape, and hung with red damask, and the light comes down from a row of windows, passing quite round, beneath an octagonal dome. The Venus stands somewhat aside from the centre of the room, and is surrounded by an iron railing, a pace or two from her pedestal in front, and less behind. I think she might safely be left to the reverence her womanhood would win, without any other protection. She is very beautiful, very satisfactory; and has a fresh and new charm about her unreached by any cast or copy. The hue of the marble is just so much mellowed by time, as to do for her all that Gibson tries,

or ought to try to do for his statues by color, softening
her, warming her almost imperceptibly, making her an
inmate of the heart, as well as a spiritual existence. I felt
a kind of tenderness for her; an affection, not as if she
were one woman, but all womanhood in one. Her modest
attitude, which before I saw her I had not liked, deeming
that it might be an artificial shame, is partly what un-
makes her as the heathen goddess, and softens her into
woman. There is a slight degree of alarm, too, in her
face; not that she really thinks anybody is looking at her,
yet the idea has flitted through her mind, and startled her
a little. Her face is so beautiful and intellectual, that it is
not dazzled out of sight by her form. Methinks this was a
triumph for the sculptor to achieve. I may as well stop
here. It is of no use to throw heaps of words upon her;
for they all fall away, and leave her standing in chaste and
naked grace, as untouched as when I began.

As we were at dinner to-day, at half past three, there
was a ring at the door, and a minute after our servant
brought a card. It was Mr. Robert Browning's, and on it
was written in pencil an invitation for us to go to see them
this evening. He had left the card and gone away; but
very soon the bell rang again, and he had come back,
having forgotten to give his address. This time he came
in; and he shook hands with all of us, children and grown
people, and was very vivacious and agreeable. He looked
younger and even handsomer than when I saw him in
London, two years ago, and his gray hairs seemed fewer
than those that had then strayed into his youthful head.
He talked a wonderful quantity in a little time, and told

us — among other things that we should never have dreamed of — that Italian people will not cheat you, if you construe them generously, and put them upon their honor.

Mr. Browning was very kind and warm in his expressions of pleasure at seeing us; and, on our part, we were all very glad to meet him. He must be an exceedingly likable man. . . . They are to leave Florence very soon, and are going to Normandy, I think he said, for the rest of the summer.

June 9

We went last evening, at eight o'clock, to see the Brownings; and, after some search and inquiry, we found the Casa Guidi, which is a palace in a street not very far from our own. It being dusk, I could not see the exterior, which, if I remember, Browning has celebrated in song; at all events, Mrs. Browning has called one of her poems 'Casa Guidi Windows.'

The street is a narrow one; but on entering the palace, we found a spacious staircase and ample accommodations of vestibule and hall, the latter opening on a balcony, where we could hear the chanting of priests in a church close by. Browning told us that this was the first church where an oratorio had ever been performed. He came into the anteroom to greet us, as did his little boy, Robert, whom they call Pennini for fondness. The latter cognomen is a diminutive of Apennino, which was bestowed upon him at his first advent into the world because he was so very small, there being a statue in Florence of colossal size called Apennino. I never saw such a boy as

this before; so slender, fragile, and spirit-like — not as if
he were actually in ill health, but as if he had little or
nothing to do with human flesh and blood. His face is very
pretty and most intelligent, and exceedingly like his mother's. He is nine years old, and seems at once less childlike
and less manly than would befit that age. I should not quite
like to be the father of such a boy, and should fear to stake
so much interest and affection on him as he cannot fail to
inspire. I wonder what is to become of him — whether he
will ever grow to be a man — whether it is desirable that
he should. His parents ought to turn their whole attention
to making him robust and earthly, and to giving him a
thicker scabbard to sheathe his spirit in. He was born in
Florence, and prides himself on being a Florentine, and is
indeed as un-English a production as if he were native of
another planet.

Mrs. Browning met us at the door of the drawing-room,
and greeted us most kindly — a pale, small person,
scarcely embodied at all; at any rate, only substantial
enough to put forth her slender fingers to be grasped, and
to speak with a shrill, yet sweet, tenuity of voice. Really,
I do not see how Mr. Browning can suppose that he has
an earthly wife any more than an earthly child; both are
of the elfin race, and will flit away from him some day
when he least thinks of it. She is a good and kind fairy,
however, and sweetly disposed towards the human race,
although only remotely akin to it. It is wonderful to see
how small she is, how pale her cheek, how bright and dark
her eyes. There is not such another figure in the world;
and her black ringlets cluster down into her neck, and
make her face look the whiter by their sable profusion.

I could not form any judgment about her age; it may range anywhere within the limits of human life or elfin life. When I met her in London at Lord Houghton's breakfast-table, she did not impress me so singularly; for the morning light is more prosaic than the dim illumination of their great tapestried drawing-room; and besides, sitting next to her, she did not have occasion to raise her voice in speaking, and I was not sensible what a slender voice she has. It is marvellous to me how so extraordinary, so acute, so sensitive a creature can impress us, as she does, with the certainty of her benevolence. It seems to me there were a million chances to one that she would have been a miracle of acidity and bitterness.

We were not the only guests. Mr. and Mrs. E——, Americans, recently from the East, and on intimate terms with the Brownings, arrived after us; also Miss F. H——, an English literary lady, whom I have met several times in Liverpool; and lastly came the white head and palmer-like beard of Mr. Bryant, with his daughter. Mr. Browning was very efficient in keeping up conversation with everybody, and seemed to be in all parts of the room and in every group at the same moment; a most vivid and quick-thoughted person, logical and common-sensible, as, I presume, poets generally are in their daily talk. Mr. Bryant, as usual, was homely and plain of manner, with an old-fashioned dignity, nevertheless, and a remarkable deference and gentleness of tone in addressing Mrs. Browning. I doubt, however, whether he has any high appreciation either of her poetry or her husband's, and it is my impression that they care as little about his.

We had some tea and some strawberries, and passed

a pleasant evening. There was no very noteworthy conversation; the most interesting topic being that disagreeable and now wearisome one of spiritual communications, as regards which Mrs. Browning is a believer, and her husband an infidel. Mr. Bryant appeared not to have made up his mind on the matter, but told a story of a successful communication between Cooper the novelist and his sister, who had been dead fifty years. Browning and his wife had both been present at a spiritual session held by Mr. Home, and had seen and felt the unearthly hands, one of which had placed a laurel wreath on Mrs. Browning's head. Browning, however, avowed his belief that these hands were affixed to the feet of Mr. Home, who lay extended in his chair, with his legs stretched far under the table. The marvellousness of the fact, as I have read of it, and heard it from other eye-witnesses, melted strangely away in his hearty gripe, and at the sharp touch of his logic; while his wife, ever and anon, put in a little gentle word of expostulation.

I am rather surprised that Browning's conversation should be so clear, and so much to the purpose at the moment, since his poetry can seldom proceed far without running into the high grass of latent meanings and obscure allusions.

Mrs. Browning's health does not permit late hours, so we began to take leave at about ten o'clock. I heard her ask Mr. Bryant if he did not mean to revisit Europe, and heard him answer, not uncheerfully, taking hold of his white hair, 'It is getting rather too late in the evening now.' If any old age can be cheerful, I should think his might be; so good a man, so cool, so calm, so bright, too, we may say. His life has been like the days that end in pleasant sunsets. He has a great loss, however, or what ought to be a great loss — soon to be encountered in the death of his wife, who, I think, can hardly live to reach America. He is not eminently an affectionate man. I take him to be one who cannot get closely home to his sorrow, nor feel it so sensibly as he gladly would; and, in consequence of that deficiency, the world lacks substance to him. It is partly the result, perhaps, of his not having sufficiently cultivated his emotional nature. His poetry shows it, and his personal intercourse, though kindly, does not stir one's blood in the least.

Little Pennini, during the evening, sometimes helped the guests to cake and strawberries; joined in the conversation, when he had anything to say, or sat down upon a couch to enjoy his own meditations. He has long curling hair, and has not yet emerged from his frock and short hose. It is funny to think of putting him into trousers. His likeness to his mother is strange to behold.

June 10

The most beautiful picture in the world, I am convinced, is Raphael's 'Madonna della Seggiola.' I was familiar with it in a hundred engravings and copies, and therefore it shone upon me as with a familiar beauty, though infinitely more divine than I had ever seen it before. An artist was copying it, and producing certainly something very like a fac-simile, yet leaving out, as a matter of course, that mysterious something that renders the picture a miracle. It is my present opinion that the pictorial art is capable of something more like magic, more wonderful and inscrutable in its methods, than poetry or any other mode of developing the beautiful. But how does this accord with what I have been saying only a minute ago? How then can the decayed picture of a great master ever be restored by the touches of an inferior hand? Doubtless it never can be restored; but let some devoted worshipper do his utmost, and the whole inherent spirit of the divine picture may pervade his restorations likewise.

June 13

The weather is very hot now — hotter in the sunshine, I think, than a midsummer day usually is in America, but with rather a greater possibility of being comfortable in the shade. The nights, too, are warm, and the bats fly forth at dusk, and the fireflies quite light up the green depths of our little garden. The atmosphere, or something else, causes a sort of alacrity in my mind and an affluence of ideas, such as they are; but it does not thereby make me the happier. I feel an impulse to be at work, but am kept idle by the sense of being unsettled with removals to be gone through, over and over again, before I can shut myself into a quiet room of my own, and turn the key. I need monotony too, an eventless exterior life, before I can live in the world within.

June 15

Until we learn to appreciate the cherubs and angels that Raphael scatters through the blessed air, in a picture of the 'Nativity,' it is not amiss to look at a Dutch fly settling on a peach, or a humblebee burying himself in a flower.

June 16

Talking of a taste for painting and sculpture, Powers observed that it was something very different and quite apart from the moral sense, and that it was often, perhaps generally, possessed by unprincipled men of ability and cultivation. I have had this perception myself. A genuine love of painting and sculpture, and perhaps of music, seems often to have distinguished men capable of every social crime, and to have formed a fine and hard enamel over their characters. Perhaps it is because such tastes are artificial, the product of cultivation, and, when highly developed, imply a great remove from natural simplicity.

June 17

Fra Angelico is a man much admired by those who have a taste for Pre-Raphaelite painters; and, though I take little or no pleasure in his works, I can see that there is great delicacy of execution in his heads, and that generally he produces such a Christ, and such a Virgin, and such saints, as he could not have foreseen, except in a pure and holy imagination, nor have wrought out without saying a prayer between every two touches of his brush. I might come to like him, in time, if I thought it worth while; but it is enough to have an outside perception of his kind and degree of merit, and so to let him pass into the garret of oblivion, where many things as good, or better, are piled away, that our own age may not stumble over them.

June 21

For my part, in this foreign country, I have no objection to policemen or any other minister of authority; though I remember, in America, I had an innate antipathy to constables, and always sided with the mob against law. This was very wrong and foolish, considering that I was one of the sovereigns; but a sovereign, or any number of sovereigns, or the twenty-millionth part of a sovereign, does not love to find himself, as an American must, included within the delegated authority of his own servants.

June 27

Last evening, we went to pass the evening with Miss [Isa] Blagden, who inhabits a villa at Bellosguardo, about a mile outside of the walls. The situation is very lofty, and there are good views from every window of the house, and an especially fine one of Florence and the hills beyond, from the balcony of the drawing-room. By and by came Mr. Browning, Mr. [Thomas A.] Trollope, Mr. Boott and his young daughter, and two or three other gentlemen. . . .

Browning was very genial and full of life, as usual, but his conversation has the effervescent aroma which you cannot catch, even if you get the very words that seem to be imbued with it. He spoke most rapturously of a portrait of Mrs. Browning, which an Italian artist is painting for the wife of an American gentleman, as a present from her husband. The success was already perfect, although there had been only two sittings as yet, and both on the same day; and in this relation, Mr. Browning remarked that P——, the American artist, had had no less than seventy-three sittings of him for a portrait. In the result, every hair and speck of him was represented; yet, as I inferred from what he did not say, this accumulation of minute truths did not, after all, amount to the true whole.

I do not remember much else that Browning said, except a playful abuse of a little King Charles spaniel, named Frolic, Miss Blagden's lap-dog, whose venerable age (he is eleven years old) ought to have pleaded in his behalf. Browning's nonsense is of very genuine and excellent quality, the true babble and effervescence of a bright and powerful mind; and he lets it play among his friends with the faith and simplicity of a child. He must be an amiable man. I should like him much, and should make him like me, if opportunities were favorable.

I conversed principally with Mr. Trollope, the son, I believe, of the Mrs. Trollope to whom America owes more for her shrewd criticisms than we are ever likely to repay. Mr. Trollope is a very sensible and cultivated man, and, I suspect, an author: at least, there is a literary man of repute of this name, though I have never read his works. He has resided in Italy eighteen years. It seems a pity to do this. It needs the native air to give life a reality; a truth which I do not fail to take home regretfully to myself, though without feeling much inclination to go back to the realities of my own.

June 28

In several chapels [of Santa Croce], moreover, there were some of those distressing frescos, by Giotto, Cimabue, or their compeers, which, whenever I see them — poor, faded relics, looking as if the Devil had been rub-

bing and scrubbing them for centuries, in spite against
the saints — my heart sinks and my stomach sickens.
There is no other despondency like this; it is a new shade
of human misery, akin to the physical disease that comes
from dry-rot in a wall. These frescos are to a church what
dreary, old remembrances are to a mind; the drearier because they were once bright: Hope fading into Disappointment, Joy into Grief, and festal splendor passing
into funereal duskiness, and saddening you all the more
by the grim identity that you find to exist between gay
things and sorrowful ones. Only wait long enough, and
they turn out to be the very same.

July 27

I seldom go out nowadays, having already seen Florence tolerably well, and the streets being very hot, and
myself having been engaged in sketching out a romance[1]
— which whether it will ever come to anything, is a point
yet to be decided. At any rate, it leaves me little heart
for journalizing and describing new things; and six
months of uninterrupted monotony would be more valuable to me just now, than the most brilliant succession
of novelties.

July 28

Last evening my wife, Una, and I went to the Powerses';
and sat with them on the terrace, at the top of the house,
till nearly ten o'clock. . . . We talked, furthermore, about
instinct and reason, and whether the brute creation have

[1] 'The Marble Faun.'

souls, and, if they have none, how justice is to be done them for their sufferings here; and came finally to the conclusion (at least, Mr. Powers did) that brutes suffer only in appearance, and that God enjoys for them all that they seem to enjoy, and that man is the only intelligent and sentient being, except his Creator. We reasoned high about other states of being; and I suggested the possibility that there might be beings inhabiting this earth, contemporaneously with us, and close beside us, but of whose existence and whereabout we could have no perception, nor they of ours, because we are endowed with different sets of senses; for certainly it was within God's power to create beings who should communicate with nature by innumerable other senses than those few which we possess. Mr. Powers gave hospitable reception to this idea, and said that it had occurred to himself; and he has evidently thought much and earnestly about such matters; but is rather too apt in my opinion to let his idea crystallize into a theory, before he can have sufficient data for it. He is a Swedenborgian in faith.

The moon had risen behind the trees, while we were talking; and Powers intimated his idea that beings analogous to men — men in everything except the modifications necessary to adapt them to their physical circumstances — inhabited the planets, and peopled them with beautiful shapes. Each planet, however, must have its own standard of the beautiful, I suppose; and probably his sculptor's eye would not see much to admire in the proportions of an inhabitant of Saturn.

The atmosphere of Florence (at least when we ascend a little way into it) seems to suggest planetary speculations. Galileo found it so, and Mr. Powers and I pervaded the whole universe; but finally crept down his garret-stairs, and parted, with a friendly pressure of the hand.

August 12

Mr. Kirkup is an intimate friend of Trelawny, author of 'Adventures of a Younger Son'; and, long ago, the latter promised him that, if he ever came into possession of the family estate, he would divide it with him. Trelawny (I know not how long since) did really succeed to the estate, and lost no time in forwarding to his friend the legal documents, entitling him to half of the property. But Mr. Kirkup declined the gift, as he himself was not destitute, and Trelawny had a brother. There were two pictures of Trelawny in the saloons, one a slight sketch on the wall, the other a half-length portrait in a Turkish dress; both handsome, but indicating no very amiable character. It is not easy to forgive Trelawny for uncovering dead Byron's legs, and telling that terrible story about them — equally disgraceful to himself, be it truth or a lie.

September 1

Powers seems to put full faith in the verity of spiritual communications, while acknowledging the difficulty of identifying spirits as being what they pretend. He is a Swedenborgian, and so far prepared to put faith in many of these phenomena. As for Home, Powers gives a decided opinion that he is a knave, but thinks him so organized, nevertheless, as to be a particularly good medium for spiritual communications. Spirits, I suppose, like earthly people, are obliged to use such instruments as will answer their purposes; but rather than receive a message from a dead friend through the organism of a rogue and a charlatan, methinks I would choose to wait till we meet. But what most astonishes me is, the indifference with which I listen to these marvels. They throw old ghost-stories quite into the shade; they bring the whole world of spirits down amongst us, visibly and audibly; they are absolutely proved to be sober facts by evidence that would satisfy us of any other alleged realities; and yet I cannot force my mind to interest itself in them. They are facts to my understanding (which, it might have been anticipated, would have been the last to acknowledge them), but they seem not to be facts to my intuitions and deeper perceptions. My inner soul does not in the least admit them. There is a mistake somewhere. So idle and empty do I feel these stories to be, that I hesitated long whether or no to give up a few pages of this not very important journal, to the record of them. . . .

The whole matter seems to me a sort of dreaming awake. It resembles a dream, in that the whole material is, from the first, in the dreamer's mind, though concealed at various depths below the surface; the dead appear alive, as they always do in dreams; unexpected combinations occur, as continually in dreams; the mind speaks through the various persons of the drama, and sometimes astonishes itself with its own wit, wisdom, and eloquence, as often in dreams; but, in both cases, the intellectual manifestations are really of a very flimsy texture. . . . I should be glad to believe in the genuineness

of these spirits, if I could; but the above is the conclusion
to which my soberest thoughts tend. There remains, of
course, a great deal for which I cannot account, and I
cannot sufficiently wonder at the pigheadedness both of
metaphysicians and physiologists, in not accepting the
phenomena, so far as to make them the subject of investi-
gation.

September 3

We looked at few other things in the gallery [the
Uffizi]; and, indeed, it was not one of the days when
works of art find me impressible. We stopped a little
while in the Tribune; but the Venus de' Medici seemed to
me little more than any other piece of yellowish white
marble. How strange that a goddess should stand before
us absolutely unrecognized, even when we know by previous revelations that she is nothing short of divine! It
is queer, too, that, unless when one feels the ideal charm
of a statue, it becomes one of the most tedious and irk-
some things in the world; either it must be a celestial
thing or an old lump of stone, dusty and time-soiled, and
tiring out your patience with eternally looking just the
same. Once in a while, you penetrate through the crust of
the old sameness, and see the statue forever new and
immortally young. . . .

We stood at the base of the Campanile, and looked at
the bas-reliefs which wreathe it around in two rows; and,
above them, a row of statues; and from bottom to top a
marvellous minuteness of inlaid marbles, filling up the
vast and beautiful design of this heaven-aspiring tower.
Looking upward to its lofty summit (where angels might

alight, lapsing downward from heaven, and gaze curiously at the bustle of men below) I could not but feel that there is a moral charm in this faithful minuteness of Gothic architecture, filling up its outline with a million of beauties that perhaps may never be studied out by a single spectator. It is the very process of nature, and, no doubt, produces an effect that we know not of. Classic architecture is nothing but an outline, and affords no little points, no interstices, where human feelings may cling and overgrow it like ivy. The charm, as I said, seems to me moral rather than intellectual; for, in the gem-room of the Uffizi, you may see fifty designs, elaborated on a small scale, that have just as much merit as the design of the Campanile. If it were only five inches long, it might be a tooth-pick case; being two hundred feet high, its prettiness develops into grandeur as well as beauty, and it becomes really one of the wonders of the world. The design of the Pantheon, on the contrary, would retain its sublimity on whatever scale it might be represented.

September 10

It was one of the days when my mind misgives me whether the pictorial art be not a humbug, and when the minute accuracy of a fly in a Dutch picture of fruit and flowers seems to me something more reliable than the master-touches of Raphael.

September 21

We went into the Uffizi gallery, and found it much thronged with the middle and lower classes of Italians; and the English, too, seemed more numerous than I have lately seen them. Perhaps the tourists have just arrived here, starting at the close of the London season. We were amused with a pair of Englishmen who went through the gallery; one of them criticising the pictures and statues audibly, for the benefit of his companion. The critic I should take to be a country-squire, not wholly untravelled; a tall, well-built, rather rough, but gentle-manly man enough; his friend, a small personage, ex-quisitely neat in dress, and of artificial deportment, every attitude and gesture appearing to have been practised before a glass. Being but a small pattern of a man, physi-cally and intellectually, he had thought it worth while to finish himself off with the elaborateness of a Florentine mosaic; and the result was something like a dancing-master, though without the exuberant embroidery of such characters. Indeed, he was a very quiet little man, and, though so thoroughly made up, there was something particularly green, fresh, and simple in him. Both these Englishmen were elderly, and the smaller one had per-fectly white hair, glossy and silken. It did not make him in the least venerable, however, but took his own char-acter of neatness and prettiness. He carried his well-brushed and glossy hat in his hand, in such a way as not to ruffle its surface; and I wish I could put into one word, or one sentence, the pettiness, the minikin, finical effect of this little man; his self-consciousness so lifelong, that, in some sort, he forgot himself even in the midst of it; his propriety, his cleanliness and unruffledness; his prettiness and nicety of manifestation, like a bird hopping daintily about.

His companion, as I said, was of a completely different

type; a tall, gray-haired man, with the rough English face, a little tinted with port wine; careless, natural manners, betokening a man of position in his own neigh-borhood; a loud voice, not vulgar, nor outraging the rules of society, but betraying a character incapable of much refinement. He talked continually in his progress through the gallery, and audibly enough for us to catch almost everything he said, at many yards' distance. His remarks and criticisms, addressed to his small friend, were so entertaining, that we strolled behind him for the sake of being benefited by them; and I think he soon became aware of this, and addressed himself to us as well as to his more immediate friend. Nobody but an Englishman, it seems to me, has just this kind of vanity; a feeling mixed up with scorn and good-nature; self-complacency on his own merits, and as an Englishman; pride at being in foreign parts; contempt of everybody around him; a rough kindliness towards people in general. I liked the man, and should be glad to know him better. As for his criticism, I am sorry to remember only one; it was upon the picture of the Nativity, by Correggio, in the Tribune, where the mother is kneeling before the Child, and ador-ing it in an awful rapture, because she sees the eternal God in its baby face and figure. The Englishman was highly delighted with this picture, and began to gesticu-late, as if dandling a baby, and to make a chirruping sound; it was to him merely a representation of a mother fondling her child. He then said, 'If I could have my choice of the pictures and statues in the Tribune, I would take this picture, and that one yonder' (it was a good enough Enthronement of the Virgin, by Andrea del

Sarto) 'and the Dancing Faun, and let the rest go.' A
delightful man! I love that wholesome coarseness of
mind and heart, which no education nor opportunity can
polish out of the genuine Englishman; a coarseness without vulgarity. When a Yankee is coarse (which is not the
case half so often as with an Englishman), he is pretty
sure to be vulgar too.

The two critics seemed to be considering whether it
were practicable to go from the Uffizi to the Pitti gallery;
but 'It confuses one,' remarked the little man, 'to see
more than one gallery in a day.' I should think so — the
Pitti Palace tumbling into his small receptacle, on the top
of the Uffizi.

September 25

Una and I walked to town, yesterday morning, and
went to the Uffizi gallery. It is not a pleasant thought
that we are so soon to give up this gallery, with little
prospect (none, or hardly any, on my part) of ever seeing
it again. It interests me and all of us far more than the
gallery of the Pitti Palace; wherefore, I know not, for the
latter is the richest of the two in admirable pictures.
Perhaps it is the picturesque variety of the Uffizi — the
combination of painting, sculpture, gems, and bronzes —
that makes the charm. The Tribune, too, is the richest
room in all the world; a heart, that draws all hearts to it.
The Dutch pictures, moreover, give a homely, human
interest to the Uffizi; and I really think that the frequency
of Andrea del Sarto's productions at the Pitti Palace —
looking so very like masterpieces, yet lacking the soul of
art and nature — have much to do with the weariness

that comes from better acquaintance with the latter gallery. The splendor of the gilded and frescoed saloons is perhaps another bore; but, after all, my memory will often tread there, as long as I live. What shall we do in America!

September 28

The nights are wonderfully beautiful now. When the moon was at the full, a few nights ago, its light was an absolute glory, such as I seem only to have dreamed of, heretofore, and that only in my younger days. At its rising, I have fancied that the orb of the moon has a kind of purple brightness, and that this tinge is communicated to its radiance, until it has climbed high aloft, and sheds a flood of white over hill and valley. Now that the moon is on the wane, there is a gentler lustre, but still bright; and it makes the Val d' Arno, with its surrounding hills, and its soft mist in the distance, as beautiful a scene as exists anywhere out of heaven. And the morning is quite as beautiful in its own way. This mist, which I have so often spoken of, sets it beyond the limits of actual sense, and makes it ideal; it is as if you were dreaming about the valley — as if the valley itself were dreaming, and met you half-way in your own dream. If the mist were to be withdrawn, I believe the whole beauty of the valley would go with it.

Until pretty late in the morning, we have the comet streaming through the sky, and dragging its interminable tail among the stars. It keeps brightening, from night to night; and, I should think, must blaze fiercely enough to cast a shadow, by and by. I know not whether it is

the vicinity of Galileo's tower, and in the influence of his
spirit; but I have hardly ever watched the stars and the
heavenly host with such interest as now.

September 29

I wish our great Republic had the spirit to do as much,
according to its vast means, as Florence did for sculpture
and architecture, when it was a republic; but we have the
meanest government and the shabbiest — and, if truly
represented by it, we are the meanest and shabbiest
people known in history. And yet, the less we attempt to
do for art the better, if our future attempts are to have no
better result than such brazen troopers as the equestrian
statue of General Jackson, or even such naked respecta-
bilities as Greenough's Washington. There is something
false and affected in our highest taste for art; and I suppose, furthermore, we are the only people who seek to
decorate their public institutions, not by the highest
taste among them, but by the average, at best.

This evening I have been on the tower-top [at the Villa
Montaüto] star-gazing, and looking at the comet, which
waves along the sky like an immense feather of flame.
Over Florence there was an illuminated atmosphere,
caused by the lights of the city gleaming upward into the
mists which sleep and dream above that portion of the
valley, as well as the rest of it. I saw dimly, or fancied I
saw, the hill of Fiesole on the other side of Florence, and
remembered how ghostly lights were seen passing thence
to the Duomo on the night when Lorenzo the Magnificent
died. From time to time the sweet bells of Florence rang

out, and I was loath to come down into the lower world, knowing that I shall never again look heavenward from an old tower-top in such a soft calm evening as this. Yet I am not loath to go away; impatient rather; for, taking no root, I soon weary of any soil in which I may be temporarily deposited. The same impatience I sometimes feel or conceive of as regards this earthly life; since it is to come to an end, I do not try to be contented, but weary of it while it lasts.

October 2

Mr. Powers and his two daughters called to take leave of us, and at parting I expressed a hope of seeing him in America. He said that it would make him very unhappy to believe that he should never return thither; but it seems to me that he has no such definite purpose of return as would be certain to bring itself to pass. It makes a very unsatisfactory life, thus to spend all the bulk of it in exile. In such a case we are always deferring the reality of life till a future moment, and, by and by, we have deferred it till there are no future moments; or, if we do go back, we find that life has shifted whatever of reality it had to the country where we deemed ourselves only living temporarily; and so between two stools we come to the ground, and make ourselves a part of one or the other country only by laying our bones in its soil. It is particularly a pity in Powers's case, because he is so very American in character, and also because, it appears to me, he profits little or nothing by the works of art around him, and, indeed, has never studied them to any great extent. The only convenience for him of his Italian residence is, that here he can supply himself with marble, and with workmen skilled to chisel it according to his designs.

October 3 [Siena]

The interest of the old town would soon be exhausted for the passing traveller; but I can conceive that a thoughtful and shy man might settle down here, with the view of making the place a home, and spend many years in a sombre kind of happiness. I should prefer it to Florence as a residence; but it would be terrible without an independent life in one's own mind.

October 4

[With the Storys in Siena.] We spent a very pleasant day, turning over books or talking on the lawn, whence we could behold scenes picturesque afar, and rich vineyard glimpses near at hand. Mr. Story is the most variously accomplished and brilliant person, the fullest of social life and fire, whom I ever met; and without seeming to make an effort, he kept us amused and entertained the whole day long; not wearisomely entertained neither, as we should have been if he had not let his fountain play naturally. Still, though he bubbled and brimmed over with fun, he left the impression on me that he is not a happy man; there must be some morbid sensibility, a pain and care, bred, it may be, out of the very richness of his gifts and abundance of his outward prosperity. Rich, in the prime of life, with a wife whom he loves, and children budding and blossoming around him as fairly as his heart could wish, with sparkling talents — so many, that if he chose to neglect or fling away one, or two, or three, he

would still have enough left to shine with — who should
be happy, if not he? It may be that he feels his strength,
in any one direction, not quite adequate to his perception,
his purpose, and his longing desire; he would rather have
one great diamond, than a larger bulk and weight divided
among many brilliants. The great difficulty with him, I
think, is a too facile power; he would do better things if it
were more difficult for him to do merely good ones. Then,
too, his sensibility is too quick; being easily touched by his
own thoughts, he cannot estimate what it requires to
touch a colder and duller person, and so stops short of the
adequate expression.

October 7

Yesterday morning, in the cathedral, I watched a
woman at confession, being curious to see how long it
would take her to tell her sins, the growth of a week or
two perhaps. I know not how long she had been at it
when I first observed her, but I believe nearly an hour
passed before the priest came suddenly out of the confessional, looking weary and moist with perspiration, and
took his way out of the cathedral. The woman was left
on her knees. This morning I watched another woman,
and she too was very long about it, and I could see the
face of the priest behind the curtain of the confessional,
scarcely inclining his ear to the perforated tin through
which the penitent communicated her outpourings. It
must be very tedious to listen, day after day, to the
minute and commonplace iniquities of the multitude of
penitents, and it cannot be often that these are redeemed
by the treasure-trove of a great sin. When her confession

was over the woman came and sat down on the same
bench with me, where her broad-brimmed straw hat was
lying. She seemed to be a country woman, with a simple,
matronly face, which was solemnized and softened with
the comfort that she had obtained by disburdening herself of the soil of worldly frailties and receiving absolu-
tion. An old woman, who haunts the cathedral, whis-
pered to her, and she went and knelt down where a procession of priests were to pass, and then the old lady
begged a cruzia of me, and got a half-paul.

October 11

It is a fine old town, with every promise of health and
vigor in its atmosphere, and really, if I could take root
anywhere, I know not but it could as well be here as in
another place. It would only be a kind of despair, however, that would ever make me dream of finding a home
in Italy; a sense that I had lost my country through absence or incongruity, and that earth, at any rate, is not
an abiding-place. I wonder that we Americans love our
country at all, it having no limits and no oneness; and
when you try to make it a matter of the heart, everything falls away except one's native State; neither can
you seize hold of that unless you tear it out of the Union,
bleeding and quivering. Yet unquestionably, we do
stand by our national flag as stoutly as any people in
the world, and I myself have felt the heart-throb at sight
of it as sensibly as other men. I think the singularity of
our form of government contributes to give us a kind of
patriotism, by separating us from other nations more
entirely. If other nations had similar institutions — if

England, especially, were a democracy — we should as readily make ourselves at home in another country as now in a new state.

October 15 [*Rome*]

They are a lovable people, these Italians, as I find from almost all with whom we come in contact; they have great and little faults, and no great virtues that I know of; but still are sweet (except to the sense of smell), amiable, pleasant to encounter, save when they beg, or when you have to bargain with them.

October 17

We left Viterbo on the 15th, and proceeded, through Monterosi, to Sette Vene.... The next day we drove along the Cassian Way towards Rome. It was a most delightful morning, a genial atmosphere; the more so, I suppose, because this was the Campagna, the region of pestilence and death. I had a quiet, gentle, comfortable pleasure, as if, after many wanderings, I was drawing near Rome, for, now that I have known it once, Rome certainly does draw into itself my heart, as I think even London, or even little Concord itself, or old sleepy Salem, never did and never will.

March 11, 1859

While we were at dinner, a gentleman called and was shown into the parlor, whither Una went to receive him. We supposed it to be Mr. May; but soon his voice grew familiar, and my wife declared it to be General Pierce, so I left the table, and found it to be really he. I was re-

joiced to see him, though a little saddened to see the
marks of care and coming age, in many a whitening hair,
and many a furrow, and, still more, in something that
seemed to have passed away out of him, without leaving
any trace. His voice, sometimes, sounded strange and
old, though generally it was what it used to be. He was
evidently glad to see me, glad to see my wife, glad to see
the children, though there was something melancholy in
his voice, when he remarked what a stout boy Julian had
grown. Poor fellow! he has neither son nor daughter to
keep his heart warm. This morning I have been with him
to St. Peter's, and elsewhere about the city, and find him
less changed than he seemed to be last night; not at all
changed in heart and affections. We talked freely about
all matters that came up; among the rest, about the pro-
ject — recognizable by many tokens — for bringing him
again forward as a candidate for the Presidency next
year. He appears to be firmly resolved not again to present himself to the country; and is content to let his one
administration stand, and to be judged by the public
and posterity on the merits of that. No doubt he is perfectly sincere; no doubt, too, he would again be a candidate, if a pretty unanimous voice of the party should
demand it. I retain all my faith in his administrative
faculty, and should be glad, for his sake, to have it fully
recognized; but the probabilities, as far as I can see, do
not indicate for him another Presidential term.

March 23

I am wearing away listlessly these last precious days
of my abode in Rome. Una's illness is disheartening, and

by confining my wife, it takes away the energy and enterprise that were the spring of all our enterprises. I am
weary of Rome, without having seen and known it as I
ought, and I shall be glad to get away from it, though no
doubt there will be many yearnings to return hereafter,
and many regrets that I did not make better use of the
opportunities within my grasp. Still, I have been in
Rome long enough to be imbued with its atmosphere, and
this is the essential condition of knowing a place; for such
knowledge does not consist in having seen every particular
object it contains. In the state of mind in which I now
stand towards Rome, there is very little advantage to be
gained by staying here longer. . . .

I believe I go to the Bank oftener than anywhere else,
and read *Galignani* and the American newspapers; thence
I stroll to the Pincian or to the Medici Gardens; I see a good
deal of General Pierce, and we talk over his Presidential
life, which, I now really think, he has no latent desire nor
purpose to renew. Yet he seems to have enjoyed it while
it lasted, and certainly he was in his element as an administrative man; not far-seeing, not possessed of vast
stores of political wisdom in advance of his occasions, but
endowed with a miraculous intuition of what ought to
be done just at the time for action. His judgment of
things about him is wonderful, and his Cabinet seems to
have recognized it as such; for though they were men of
great ability, he was evidently the master-mind among
them. None of them were particularly his personal friends
when he selected them; they all loved him when they
parted; and he showed me a letter, signed by all, in which
they expressed their feelings of respect and attachment at

the close of his administration. There appears to have
been a noble frankness on his part, that kept the atmosphere always clear among them, and in reference to this
characteristic Governor Marcy told him that the years
during which he had been connected with Pierce's Cabinet
had been the happiest of his life. Speaking of Caleb
Cushing, he told me that the unreliability, the fickleness,
which is usually attributed to him, is an actual characteristic, but that it is intellectual, not moral. He has such
comprehensiveness, such mental variety and activity,
that, if left to himself, he cannot keep fast hold of one
view of things, and so cannot, without external help, be a
consistent man. He needs the influence of a more single
and stable judgment to keep him from divergency, and,
on this condition, he is a most able and inestimable coad-
jutor. As regards learning and ability, he has no superior.

Pierce spoke the other day of the idea among some of
his friends (and some who had had good opportunities of
knowing him) that his life had been planned, from a very
early period, with a view to the station which he ultimately reached. He smiled at the notion, said that it was
inconsistent with his natural character, and that it im-
plied foresight and dexterity beyond what any mortal is
endowed with. I think so too; but nevertheless, I was
long and long ago aware that he cherished a very high
ambition, and that, though he might not anticipate the
highest things, he cared very little about inferior objects.
Then as to plans, I do not think that he had any definite
ones; but there was in him a subtle faculty, a real instinct,
that taught him what was good for him — that is to say,
promotive of his political success — and made him in-

evitably do it. He had a magic touch, that arranged matters with a delicate potency, which he himself hardly
recognized; and he wrought through other minds so that
neither he nor they always knew when and how far they
were under his influence. Before his nomination for the
Presidency I had a sense that it was coming, and it never
seemed to me an accident. He is a most singular character; so frank, so true, so immediate, so subtle, so simple,
so complicated.

April 19

General Pierce leaves Rome this morning for Venice,
by way of Ancona, and taking the steamer thence to
Trieste. I had hoped to make the journey along with him;
but Una's terrible illness has made it necessary for us to
continue here another month, and we are thankful that
this seems now to be the extent of our misfortune. Never
having had any trouble before that pierced into my very
vitals, I did not know what comfort there might be in the
manly sympathy of a friend; but Pierce has undergone so
great a sorrow of his own, and has so large and kindly a
heart, and is so tender and so strong, that he really did me
good, and I shall always love him the better for the recollection of these dark days. Thank God, the thing we
dreaded did not come to pass.

Pierce is wonderfully little changed. Indeed, now that
he has won and enjoyed — if there were any enjoyment in
it — the highest success that public life could give him, he
seems more like what he was in his early youth than at
any subsequent period. He is evidently happier than I
have ever known him since our college days; satisfied with

what he has been, and with the position in the country that remains to him, after filling such an office. Amid all his former successes — early as they came, and great as they were — I always perceived that something gnawed within him, and kept him forever restless and miserable. Nothing that he won was worth the winning, except as a step gained towards the summit. I cannot tell how early he began to look towards the Presidency; but I believe he would have died a miserable man without it. And yet what infinite chances there seemed to be against his attaining it! When I look at it in one way, it strikes me as absolutely miraculous; in another, it came like an event that I had all along expected. It was due to his wonderful tact, which is of so subtle a character that he himself is but partially sensible of it.

Well, I have found in him, here in Rome, the whole of my early friend, and even better than I used to know him; a heart as true and affectionate, a mind much widened and deepened by his experience of life. We hold just the same relation to one another as of yore, and we have passed all the turning-off places, and may hope to go on together still the same dear friends as long as we live. I do not love him one whit the less for having been President, nor for having done me the greatest good in his power; a fact that speaks eloquently in his favor, and perhaps says a little for myself. If he had been merely a benefactor, perhaps I might not have borne it so well; but each did his best for the other as friend for friend.

May 29 [Marseilles]

Wednesday was the day fixed for our departure from

Rome, and after breakfast I walked to the Pincian, and saw the garden and the city, and the Borghese grounds, and St. Peter's, in an earlier sunlight than ever before. Methought they never looked so beautiful; nor the sky so bright and blue. I saw Soracte on the horizon, and I looked at everything as if for the last time; nor do I wish ever to see any of these objects again, though no place ever took so strong a hold of my being, as Rome, nor ever seemed so close to me, and so strangely familiar. I seem to know it better than my birthplace, and to have known it longer; and though I have been very miserable there, and languid with the effects of the atmosphere, and disgusted with a thousand things in daily life, still I cannot say I hate it — perhaps might fairly own a love for it. But (life being too short for such questionable and troublesome enjoyments) I desire never to set eyes on it again.

June 1 [*Avignon*]

No end of historical romances might be made out of this castle of the popes; and there ought to be a ghost in every room, and droves of them in some of the rooms; for there have been murders here in the gross and in detail, as well hundreds of years ago, as no longer back than the French Revolution, when there was a great massacre in one of the courts.

June 12 [*Switzerland*]

Farther onward, we saw a white, ancient-looking group of towers, beneath a mountain, which was so high, and rushed so precipitately down upon this pile of building

as quite to dwarf it; besides which its dingy whiteness
had not a very picturesque effect. Nevertheless, this
was the Castle of Chillon. It appears to sit right upon
the water, and does not rise very loftily above it. I was
disappointed in its aspect, having imagined this famous
castle as situated upon a rock, a hundred, or, for aught
I know, a thousand feet above the surface of the lake;
but it is quite as impressive a fact (supposing it to be
true) that the water is eight hundred feet deep at its base.
By this time, the mountains had taken the beautiful lake
into their deepest heart; they girdled it quite round with
their grandeur and beauty, and, being able to do no more
for it, they here held it from extending any farther; and
here our voyage came to an end. I have never beheld any
scene so exquisite as this; nor do I ask of heaven to show
me any lovelier or nobler one, but only to give me such
depth and breadth of sympathy with nature, that I may
worthily enjoy this. It is beauty more than enough for
poor, perishable mortals; unless I am to live forever, it
was not worth while to tantalize me so. If this be earth,
what must heaven be!

June 14 [*Geneva*]

Some of these mountains [about Lake Leman], that
looked at no such mighty distance, were at least forty or
fifty miles off, and appeared as if they were near neighbors and friends of other mountains, from which they
were really still farther removed. The relations into which
distant points are brought, in a view of mountain scenery,
symbolize the truth that we can never judge, within our
partial scope of view, of the relations which we bear to

our fellow-creatures and human circumstances. These mighty mountains thought that they had nothing to do with one another; each deems itself its own centre, and existing for itself alone; and yet, to an eye that can take them all in, they are evidently portions of one grand and beautiful idea, which could not be consummated without the lowest and the loftiest of them. I do not express this satisfactorily, but have a genuine meaning in it, nevertheless.

To-day, I wrote to Mr. Wilding, requesting him to secure passages for us, from Liverpool, on the 15th of next month, or 1st of August. It makes my heart thrill, half pleasantly, half otherwise; so much nearer does this step seem to bring that home whence I have now been absent six years, and which, when I see it again, may turn out not to be my home any longer. I likewise wrote to Bennoch, though I know not his present address; but I should deeply grieve to leave England without seeing him. He and Henry Bright are the only two men in England to whom I shall be much grieved to bid farewell; but to the island itself I cannot bear to say that word, as a finality. I shall dreamily hope to come back again at some indefinite time; — rather foolishly, perhaps, for it will tend to take the substance out of my life in my own land. But this, I suspect, is apt to be the penalty of those who stay abroad, and stay too long.

February 15, 1860 [*Coventry*]

On our way to Mr. Bill's house, we looked into the quadrangle of a charity-school and old men's hospital,

and afterwards stepped into a large Roman Catholic
church, erected within these few years past, and closely
imitating the mediæval architecture and arrangement.
It is strange what a plaything, a trifle, an unserious affair,
this imitative spirit makes of a huge, ponderous edifice,
which if it had really been built five hundred years ago
would have been worthy of all respect. I think the time
must soon come when this sort of thing will be held in
utmost scorn, until the lapse of time shall give it a sort of
claim to respect. But, methinks, we had better strike
out any sort of architecture, so it be our own, however
wretched, than thus tread back upon the past. . . .

We found three or four people to meet us at dinner; a
Mr. Draper, a connection of Mr. Bill, and himself a manu-
facturer; and a Mr. [Charles] Bray, a retired manufac-
turer, and now editor of a newspaper in Coventry. He is
an author, too, having written a book called 'The Philosophy of Necessity,' and is acquainted with Emerson,
who spent two or three days at his house when last in
England. He was very kindly appreciative of my own
productions, as was also his wife, next to whom I sat at
dinner. She talked to me about the author of 'Adam
Bede,' whom she has known intimately all her life. Her
intimations were somewhat mysterious; but I inferred
from them that the lady in question had really been the
mistress of Mr. Lewes, though it seems that they are
now married. Miss Evans (the name of the Adam Bede
lady) was the daughter of a steward, and gained her ex-
act knowledge of English rural life by the connection
into which this origin brought her with the farmers. She
was entirely self-educated, and has made herself an ad-

mirable scholar, classical, as well as in modern languages. Those who knew her had always recognized her wonderful endowments, and only watched to see in what way they would develop themselves. She is a person of the simplest manners and character, amiable and unpretending, and Mrs. Bray seemed to speak of her with great affection and respect, notwithstanding all that may have been amiss or awry in the conduct of her life. By the by, she is no longer young.

Mr. Bill, our host, is an extremely sensible man; and it is remarkable how many sensible men there are in England — men who have read and thought, and can develop very good ideas, not exactly original, yet so much the product of their own minds that they can fairly call them their own.

May 16 [*London*]

I came hither from Bath on the 14th, and am staying with my friends, Mr. and Mrs. Motley. I would gladly journalize some of my proceedings, and describe things and people; but I find the same coldness and stiffness in my pen as always since our return to England. I dined with the Motleys at Lord Dufferin's, on Monday evening, and there met, among a few other notable people, the Honorable Mrs. Norton, a dark, comely woman, who doubtless was once most charming, and still has charms, at above fifty years of age. In fact, I should not have taken her to be greatly above thirty, though she seems to use no art to make herself look younger, and talks about her time of life, without any squeamishness. Her voice is very agreeable, having a sort of muffled quality, which is excellent in woman. She is of a very cheerful temperament, and so has borne a great many troubles without being destroyed by them. But I can get no color into my sketch, so shall leave it here.

Imagine a ghost just passed into the other state of being, looking back into this mortal world, and shocked by many things that were delightful just before — more shocked than the living one at the ghostly world.

A pretty young girl, so small and lustrous that you would like to set her in a brooch and wear her in your bosom.

August 15, 1862 [*West Gouldsborough, Maine*]

It is a week ago, Saturday, since Julian and I reached this place, . . . Mr. Barney S. Hill's.

At Hallowell, and subsequently all along our route, the country was astir with volunteers, and the war is all that seems to be alive — and even that doubtfully so. Nevertheless, the country certainly shows a good spirit, the towns offering everywhere most liberal bounties, and every able-bodied man feels an immense pull and pressure upon him to go to the wars. I doubt whether any people were ever actuated by a more genuine and disinterested public spirit; though, of course, it is not unalloyed with baser motives and tendencies. We met a train of cars with a regiment or two just starting for the war, and apparently in high spirits. Everywhere, some insignia of soldiership were to be seen — buttons, a red stripe down the trousers, a military cap; and sometimes, a round-

shouldered bumpkin in the entire uniform. They require
a great deal to give them the aspect of soldiers; indeed,
it seems as if they needed to have a good deal taken away
and added, like the rough clay of a sculptor as it grows to
be a model. The whole talk of the bar-rooms and every
other place of intercourse was about enlisting and the
war — this being the very crisis of trial, when the voluntary system is drawing to an end, and the draft almost
immediately to commence.

INDEX